CASS SERIES: STUDIES IN INTELLIGENCE
(Series Editors: Christopher Andrew and Richard J. Aldrich
ISSN: 1368-9916)

SECRET INTELLIGENCE IN THE TWENTIETH CENTURY

Also in the Intelligence Series

SECRET INTELLIGENCE
in the
TWENTIETH CENTURY

Editors

Heike Bungert

Jan G. Heitmann

Michael Wala

Foreword by

NIGEL WEST

FRANK CASS

LONDON • PORTLAND, OR

First published in 2003 in Great Britain by
FRANK CASS & CO. LTD
Crown House, 47 Chase Side
Southgate, London N14 5BP

and in the United States of America by
FRANK CASS
c/o ISBS, 5824 N. E. Hassalo Street
Portland, Oregon, 97213-3644

British Library Cataloguing in Publication Data

Secret intelligence in the twentieth century. – (Cass
series. Studies in intelligence)
1. Intelligence service – History – 20th century
I. Bungert, Heike   II. Heitmann, Jan G.   III. Wala, Michael
327.1′2′0904

ISBN 0-7146-5395-0 (cloth)
ISBN 0-7146-8331-0 (paper)

Library of Congress Cataloguing-in-Publication Data:

Secret intelligence in the twentieth century / editors, Heike Bungert, Jan G. Heitmann,
Michael Wala; with a foreword by Nigel West.
    p. cm. – (Cass series – studies in intelligence, ISSN 1368-9916)
  Includes bibliographical references and index.
  ISBN 0-7146-5395-0 (cloth) – ISBN 0-7146-8331-0 (pbk.)
    1. Intelligence service – History – 20th century. 2. Intelligence service – United
States – History – 20th century. 3. Intelligence service – Germany – History –
20th century. I. Bungert, Heike. II. Heitmann, Jan, 1960– III. Wala, Michael.
IV. Series.

JF1525.i6s43 2003
327.12′09′04 – DC21
                                                            2002041495

Typeset in 10.5/12pt Sabon by Frank Cass Publishers
Printed in Great Britain by Bookcraft Ltd, Midsomer Norton, Somerset

In memory of Jürgen Heideking
scholar, teacher, friend

Contents

List of Contributors

Horst Boog was Senior Director of Research and headed the Department of World War II Research of the Federal German Office of Military History in Freiburg until his retirement in 1993. From 1951 to 1964 he was a military analyst with NATO Intelligence. He is the author of a voluminous study of the Luftwaffe Command and Leadership 1935–45 (*Die deutsche Luftwaffenführung*, 1982) and of numerous articles on air operations and logistics, intelligence, military technology and sociology, the editor of *The Conduct of the Air War in the Second World War: An International Comparison*, 1992, and co-authored volumes 4, 6, and 7 of Germany and the Second World War (*Das Deutsche Reich und der Zweite Weltkrieg*). He is presently completing its final and 10th volume.

Heike Bungert is Assistant Professor at the Institute of Anglo-American History, University of Cologne, Germany. She has published a book on the Western reaction to German Communist emigrés and Soviet policies in founding the National Committee for a Free Germany in 1943, *Das Nationalkomitee und der Westen: Das NKFD und die Freien Deutschen Bewegungen aus der Sicht der Westalliierten, 1943–48* (Stuttgart: Steiner, 1997). She has also written several articles on the Office of Strategic Services and its Research and Analysis Branch as well as its infiltration of agents into Nazi Germany. At the moment, she is working on a monograph on the formation of a German–American identity via festivals in nineteenth-century America.

Frank Cain is at the University of New South Wales in Canberra, Australia where he teaches courses on twentieth-century Australian History, Intelligence History, and Defence and Foreign Policy History. His publishing and research interests are in intelligence history (*ASIO: An Unofficial History*, 1994), labour history (*The Wobblies at War: A History of the IWW and the Great War in*

Australia, 1993), and at present he is working on a history of the Great Depression in Australia and on several aspects of the Cold War in Europe and Asia.

James Critchfield, a World War II combat officer in Europe, remained in Germany for eight years, first as a US Army officer and then with the Central Intelligence Agency. He was the officer in charge of overseeing the development of the Gehlen Organization prior to its becoming the official German intelligence service, the BND. He went on to head the CIA's Middle East operations and prior to retirement served as the National Intelligence officer for energy. He was awarded the Officer's Cross of the Order of Merit of the Federal Republic of Germany in 2001. Currently, he serves on the Historical Advisory Panel to the US Inter-agency Working Group established to respond to the Nazi War Crimes Disclosure Act of 1998. His book *Germany: From Enemy to Ally: 1948–1956* is scheduled for publication in 2003.

Mario Del Pero teaches International History at the Faculty of Political Science of Forlì, University of Bologna. He received his Ph.D. from the University of Milan. In 2001/2002 he was Mellon Fellow at the International Center for Advanced Studies of New York University. He worked on US–Italian relations and psychological warfare. His most recent publications include a monograph on US–Italian relations in the early Cold War, a short introductory book on the history of the CIA and the article 'The United States and Psychological Warfare in Italy, 1948–1955' published by the *Journal of American History* in March 2001. Currently he is doing new research on the US reaction to the 1974 revolution in Portugal.

Jan G. Heitmann received his Ph.D. in Modern History in 1996 from Hamburg University. Since 1998 and after a number of years of university teaching and employment as a journalist, he is working in his own company as a consultant for museums and television productions. As a reserve officer holding the rank of Commander, he frequently serves as commanding officer of a marine battalion.

Sergei A. Kondrachev is a retired KGB lieutenant general and former head of its German Department. He spent time in Karlshorst and Vienna, and became a leading KGB disinformation activist. With

David E. Murphy and George Bailey he wrote *Battleground Berlin: CIA Vs. KGB in the Cold War* (New Haven, CT: Yale University Press, 1997).

Petra Marquardt-Bigman is the author of several articles and a book on American intelligence during World War II, *Amerikanische Geheimdienstanalysen über Deutschland 1942–1949* (Munich: Oldenbourg 1995)). She received her Ph.D. from Tübingen University, Germany, and was a research fellow at the Wiener Library, Tel Aviv, Israel, and at the German Historical Institute in Washington, DC.

Christian Ostermann is the director of the Woodrow Wilson Center's Cold War International History Project (CWIHP) and editor of the CWIHP Bulletin. Before joining CWIHP in January 1997 as associate director, he worked as a research fellow at the National Security Archive. He won the DAAD Article Award of the German Studies Association for 'Best Article in German Studies (History), 1994–1996', as well as a Society of Historians of American Foreign Relations Stuart L. Bernath grant and the W. Stull Holt Fellowship. Most recently he spent five months as a fellow at the Norwegian Nobel Institute in Oslo. He has taught courses on American diplomacy and German history at George Washington University and Georgetown University. Major publications include 'Keeping the Pot Simmering: "The United States and the East German Uprising of 1953"' and he edited *Uprising in East Germany, 1953: The Cold War, the German Question and the First Major Upheaval behind the Iron Curtain* (Budapest/New York: Central European University Press, 2001).

David E. Murphy is a former National Intelligence Officer and Soviet specialist with the Central Intelligence Agency. He served in Berlin from 1954 to 1961 and from 1963 to 1968 headed the Soviet Bloc Division. He has contributed to *Studies in Intelligence*, *The Journal of Soviet Military Studies*, *Low Intensity Conflict and Law Enforcement*, and *Intelligence and National Security*. He is co-author of *Battleground Berlin: CIA and KGB in the Cold War* (New Haven, CT: Yale University Press 1997).

Ludwig Richter is Privatdozent at the University of Cologne. He has published a number of works in the field of Weimar Republic and constitutional history. He is currently CEO of a software company.

Monika Tantzscher worked as a reader and editor of Russian *belles-lettres* in East Berlin publishing houses. In 1992, she began working for the Department for Education and Research for the Federal Commissioner for the Records of the State Security Service of the former German Democratic Republic (BStU), where she published two studies on the role the East German State Security had played in suppressing the reform movements in Czechoslovakia in 1968/69 and in Poland in 1980/81 ('Maßnahme Donau and Einsatz Genesung' and 'Was in Polen geschieht, ist for die DDR eine Lebensfrage!'). A number of additional papers on the co-operation of Eastern European secret services, e.g. on the data network of the Eastern Bloc alliance 'SOUND' (co-author Bodo Wegmann) followed.

Michael Wala currently teaches at the Amerika Institut of the Ludwig-Maximilians University, Munich. He edited Allen W. Dulles' book *The Marshall Plan* (Oxford: Berg Publishers, 1993) and is the author of a number of scholarly articles and books on American and German History, including *The Council on Foreign Relations and American Foreign Policy in the Early Cold War* (New York/Oxford: Berghahn Books, 1994) and most recently *Weimar und Amerika. Botschafter Friedrich von Prittwitz und Gaffron und die deutsch-amerikanischen Beziehungen von 1927 bis 1933* (Stuttgart: Steiner Verlag, 2001). He is the editor of the *Journal of Intelligence History*.

Wesley K. Wark is an Associate Professor of History at the University of Toronto. He has numerous publications dealing with intelligence studies and is the author of a forthcoming official history of the Canadian intelligence community in the Cold War. He is currently at work preparing the *Oxford University Press Companion to Modern Espionage*.

Gerhard L. Weinberg is Professor Emeritus of History of the University of North Carolina at Chapel Hill. He is the author of numerous books dealing with the origins and course of World War II, has been involved in issues pertaining to the German archives seized in World War II for over fifty years, and has served as Vice-President for Research of the American Historical Association and President of the German Studies Association.

Cornelia Wilhelm is currently a fellow of the Deutsche Forschungsgemeinschaft at Ludwig-Maximilians University in Munich, Germany. She is author of several publications on Nazi propaganda in America, on German–American relations and on nineteenth century American Jewish history, including *Bewegung oder Verein? Nationalsozialistische Volkstumspolitik in den USA*, 1998. She is a member of the Academic Council of the American Jewish Historical Society in New York City and worked from 1997–2002 as a visiting research fellow at Hebrew Union College, Cincinnati, on a nineteenth-century history of the Independent Order B'nai B'rith.

List of Abbreviations

AISW	Air Intelligence Service Wing (USA)
A-2	Army Air Force intelligence organization (USA)
B-Dienst	*Beobachtungsdienst* – German Naval Intelligence Service
BfV	*Bundesamt für Verfassungsschutz* – Federal Office for the Protection of the Constitution, the German counter-intelligence service
BND	*Bundesnachrichtendienst* – Federal Intelligence Service
BOB	Berlin Operations Base (USA)
BSSO	British Intelligence Organization
CDU	*Christlich Demokratische Union* – Christian Democratic Union (Germany)
CENTO	Central Treaty Organization
CFM	Council of Foreign Ministers
CHINCOM	China Committee Co-Ordinating Committee for the Control of East–West Trade
CI	Committee of Information
CIA	Central Intelligence Agency (USA)
CIC	Counter-Intelligence Corps (USA)
CIG	Central Intelligence Group (USA)
CJIC	Canadian Joint Intelligence Committee
COCOM	Co-Ordinating Committee for the Control of East–West Trade
COI	Coordinator of Information (USA)
COMINT	communications intelligence (USA)
COS	Chiefs of Staff [Canada]
CPSU	Communist Party of the Soviet Union
CSE	Communications Security Establishment (Canada)
CSIS	Canadian Security Intelligence Service
DAI	*Deutsche Ausland Institut* – German Foreign Institute
DC	*Democracia Christiana* – Christian Democratic Party [Italy]
DCI	Director of Central Intelligence (USA)
ECA	European Cooperation Administration
EE	Eastern European
EAM/ELAS	Greek National Popular Liberation Army (Greece)
FBI	Federal Bureau of Investigation (USA)
FDP	*Freie Demokratische Partei* – Free Democratic Party (West Germany)

FO	Foreign Organization (Germany)
GA	German Academy
GDR	German Democratic Republic
GRÜ	Main Intelligence Administration of the Soviet Red Army
G-2	Military Intelligence Division
HICOG	US High Commission in Germany
HNV	*Heeresnachrichtenwesen* – German Army Intelligence
HUMINT	human intelligence
HVA	*Hauptverwaltung Aufklärung* – Main Administration Intelligence (East Germany)
ICBM	intercontinental ballistic missile
IRA	Irish Republican Army
JCS	Joint Chiefs of Staff (USA)
K-5	*Kommissariate 5* – Political Police (East Germany)
KGB	Committee for State Security (USSR)
LDPD	*Liberaldemokratische Partei Deutschlands* – Liberal Democrats (Germany)
MfS	*Ministerium für Staatssicherheit* – Ministry for State Security (East Germany)
MGB	Soviet Ministry for State Security
MVD	Soviet Ministry of Internal Affairs
NATO	North Atlantic Treaty Organization
NIE	National Intelligence Estimates (USA)
NKVD	Soviet People's Commissariat of Internal Affairs
NSA	National Security Agency (USA)
NSC	National Security Council (USA)
NSDAP	*Nationalsozialistische Deutsche Arbeiterpartei* – National Socialist German Workers Party (Germany)
OKW	*Oberkommando der Wehrmacht* – German High Command of the Armed Forces
OKW/CHI	*Oberkommando der Wehrmacht/Chiffrierungsabteilung* – German High Command of the Armed Forces, Cipher Department
OMGUS	Office Military Government for Germany, United States
ONE	Office of National Estimates (USA)
OPC	Office of Policy Coordination (USA)
ORR	Office of Research and Reports (USA)
OSO	Office of Special Operations (USA)
OSS	Office of Strategic Services (USA)
PCI	*Partito Comunista Italiano* – Italian Communist Party
POW	prisoner of war
PSB	Psychological Strategy Board (USA)
PSLI	*Partito Socialista Italiano* – Social Democratic Party
R & A	research and analysis
RCMP	Royal Canadian Mounted Police
RIAS	*Radio im Amerikanischen Sektor* – Radio in American Sector

SAC	Strategic Air Command (USA)
SBZ	*Sowjetische Besatzungszone* – Soviet Occupation Zone (Germany)
SD	*Sicherheitsdienst* – Security Service (Germany)
SED	*Sozialistische Einheitspartei Deutschlands* – Socialist Unity Party of Germany
SfS	*Sekretariat für Staatssicherheit* – Secretariat for State Security (East Germany)
SIGINT	signals intelligence
SPD	Social Democratic Party (Germany)
SSU	Special Services Unit (USA)
Stasi	*Staatssicherheit* – Ministry for State Security
TASS	Soviet news agency
UfJ	*Untersuchungsausschuss freiheitlicher Juristen der Sowjetzone* – Investigative Committee of Free Jurists
USFET	US Forces European Theater (USA)
USAF	United States Air Force
USIG	Administration of Soviet Property in Germany
VDA	*Verein für das Deutschtum im Ausland* – League for Germans Abroad

Foreword

Considering the very large number of twentieth century historians who participated in the Second World War, and had been indoctrinated into secret intelligence sources, it is astonishing that the true impact of intelligence on the successful prosecution of the conflict was not documented very much earlier. In fact the first mention of the contribution of Allied code-breaking in the Battle of the Atlantic and the defeat of the U-boats did not occur until 1968, and the vital role played by cryptanalysts at Bletchley Park was not revealed for a further six years. Historians of the calibre of Sir Harry Hinsley, Hugh Trevor Roper and Ronald Lewin, who knew all too well about what has often been called 'the missing dimension' opted for discretion, and even David Kahn's *Codebreakers,* released in 1966, omitted any reference to the German Enigma cipher machine. Understandably Winston Churchill's magisterial account of *The Second World War* could not have been expected to disclose secrets, but the result was that, fed on a diet of sanitised biographies of Eisenhower and Montgomery, the public was given no clue about the wartime contributions made by Britain's secret agencies.

Gradually, the truth began to emerge. After Fred Winterbotham received official permission in 1973 to write *The Ultra Secret* in an effort to stymie Anthony Cave Brown's *Bodyguard of Lies,* and Sir John Masterman had released *The Double Cross System* in 1972, exposing the extent of MI5's domination of its Abwehr adversary, the walls of secrecy in Whitehall began to crumble. The Foreign Secretary, David Owen, gave permission in 1977 for veterans of ULTRA to discuss the application of their special skills, but not to explain precisely how they had achieved technical mastery of the enemy's cipher systems. Finally, the entire five volumes of the official history of *British Intelligence in the Second World War* were published, seven years after they had been commissioned in 1972, but the last volume, written by Sir Michael Howard, was held up for ten years before it was declassified in 1990.

Why the reluctance to impart the very significant influence of intelligence over the momentous events of the last century? Intelligence was crucial throughout the First World War, and Nigel de Grey's breaking of the Zimmermann Telegram in 1917 has been widely regarded as a turning-point in the conduct of the war, and perhaps the one single event that propelled the United States into the conflict. Is it simply that espionage, cryptography and strategic deception have not been considered respectable subjects for study by *bona fide* historians, or is it that weapons of such potential should only be mentioned sparingly in case unreliable politicians, ever accused of not playing the long game, seek a short-term advantage and thereby compromise a source? Such breaches of security are not unknown. The direct quotation in 1923 of Soviet diplomatic telegrams in a government white paper led to a change in Soviet cipher procedures which closed off the source for a further two decades. The astonishing outburst of a former Foreign Office minister, Ted Rowlands, during a Commons debate on the Falklands campaign in 1982 alerted General Galtieri to the fact that Argentina's most sensitive communications had been routinely intercepted and decrypted.

It may well be that intelligence played no greater part in the history of the twentieth century in comparison to earlier millennia, but the difference is the amount of documentation now available in the archives for study, and the new-found willingness of the actual participants to describe their own work. Whereas it was considered almost unpatriotic, during the first half of the Cold War, to undertake research projects into topics impinging on nuclear, security and intelligence topics, it would now be impossible to be taken seriously without offering some insight into those areas. Indeed, no worthwhile analysis of the events of the last century could be contemplated without the inclusion of references to SIS, the CIA, MI5, OSS, GCHQ, the NSA and their Soviet counterparts. Could the Great War be discussed sensibly without reference to the code-breakers of Room 40? What effect did the Russian revolution, and the West's attempts to isolate the spread of Communism, have on history between the wars? Might the raid on Pearl Harbor have been prevented if the White House had grasped the meaning of the MAGIC intercepts? Could the Nazis have won the war if they had exploited their technical advantages, and developed jet fighters, ballistic missiles and an atomic bomb? How long would it have taken Moscow to acquire a nuclear weapon without the assistance of spies? Did Soviet defectors help or hinder the West's understanding of Soviet strategy? If the VENONA texts had been released thirty or forty years earlier, would the Cold War have taken a different course? Did the action of well-placed moles help persuade the Kremlin that they were never at risk of a surprise attack by NATO? Such speculation has no historical value, but it does serve to illustrate the influence of the clandestine world over what we now understand to have been our recent history.

This collection of writing, in the pages that follow, casts light on the role of secret intelligence in our times, and amounts to a provocative analysis of an era of super-power confrontation which never developed into a hot war.

Nigel West
Centre for Counterintelligence and Security Studies
Washington DC
January 2002

Introduction

Secret intelligence is not an invention of the twentieth century. Probably as long as states have existed, they have sought information not openly available about real, potential, or imagined internal and external enemies. Individual agents, internal police forces, or small secret service organizations have collected and analysed intelligence to provide guidance to policy-makers in foreign and domestic affairs and to the armed forces for military purposes. With the increasing globalization of international relations and in particular with the rise of modern, electronic means of communication during the last 80 years, however, the need has arisen for well-funded and well-equipped intelligence agencies capable of coordinating the various sources of information and able to digest an ever increasing amount of raw data. The two world wars, the ideological conflict between totalitarian and democratic states in the 1920s and 1930s, and especially the Cold War have led to the rapid expansion of information gathering, propaganda warfare, and covert operations.

Secret intelligence and special operations have always fascinated the general public. Spy novels, avidly read by hundreds of thousands all around the world; movies featuring James Bond and Maxwell Smart; and sensationalist accounts of agents' exploits, however, have long discouraged scholars from seriously considering the history of intelligence as an integral part of the history of international relations, military history, and social history. Thus, intelligence has long been the 'missing dimension' in historical research. This has changed dramatically in the course of the last two decades. It is today increasingly accepted that serious research in international relations and particularly military history must take secret intelligence into account. The gradual opening of archives and records and the declassification of massive numbers of documents, particularly in the USA and the former German Democratic Republic (GDR), have shifted a once elusive and tainted field to centre stage.

In an effort to broaden the scholarly research on secret intelligence, the International Intelligence History Association (IIHA) devoted its second and third annual conferences, which took place in Hamburg in 1996 and in Strausberg in 1997, respectively to aspects of secret intelligence. The IIHA was founded in 1993 by German historians as the *Arbeitskreis Nachrichtendienstgeschichte*, and it has since grown into a large international organization promoting scholarly research on intelligence organizations and their impact on historical development and international relations. Its international membership consists of historians, political scientists, cryptologists, active and former intelligence officials, and members of the armed forces.

Most of the contributors to this volume are members of the IIHA, and the papers published here were originally presented at the annual meetings in Hamburg and Strausberg. The conferences placed special emphasis on two aspects. The first aspect was the domestic and societal context in which secret intelligence is being gathered and in which intelligence organizations operate. Several of the essays in this volume shed light on the bureaucratic infighting between different intelligence agencies and on the relationship of intelligence organizations with other governmental departments and society at large. The motivations and objectives of politicians and officers are analysed, and the impact of secret intelligence on governmental policy and military strategy is investigated.

Second, specific attention was paid to the integration of the history of secret intelligence and the history of international relations. Particularly for the twentieth century, the writing of diplomatic history without the consultation of all available intelligence records is no longer feasible. During World War II, but especially during the Cold War, politicians and military leaders relied on secret information provided by intelligence agencies as an indispensable tool for their decision-making, and they used propaganda and covert operations to achieve their goals. In addition, what secret information was gathered, how it was linked to other relevant data, how it was evaluated, and what projects were undertaken by intelligence organizations reveal much about the mentality and perception of the intelligence officers, politicians, and military leaders involved, and are thus of great interest to the historian of international relations.

The essays in this volume are arranged in chronological order with a section on Germany during the Weimar Republic and World War II first, a number of papers on the USA and its allies in World

War II and in the Cold War, a third part on the GDR and the USA in the late 1940s and early 1950s, and, finally, reflections on the present and future of intelligence and reports by eyewitnesses, two former members of the CIA and a former officer of the Soviet intelligence service (KGB), who recount their intelligence activities in Germany. The volume closes with a reflective piece by a Canadian scholar of intelligence history.

Providing an outline of the history of information-gathering organizations in Germany from World War I to the Weimar Republic, Ludwig Richter furnishes an overview of the origins of the German intelligence services. When Germany began organizing a secret intelligence and counter-espionage division in 1912, the intelligence services of other nations could already look back on a long and successful tradition; but the Germans soon learned the lesson war was to teach them. Gerhard L. Weinberg's paper deals with intelligence in World War II and the possibilities for further research. He presents an overview of available sources and the process of declassification of yet unreleased records in US archives, with special emphasis on radio decodes.

For the World War II era, Cornelia Wilhelm delineates how German intelligence organizations and the Nazi party extensively used the personal and organizational networks of ethnic Germans as a so-called fifth column. This historically unique cooperation was the result of a process that had taken several years to develop and that increased after the USA had entered the war. Connecting World War II with the post-war era, Petra Marquardt-Bigman looks at the development of US intelligence strategy. She examines how the analysis of both readily accessible and secret intelligence, that was accomplished very successfully by the Research and Analysis Branch of the OSS, quickly gave way to the nearly exclusive focus on espionage and covert operations executed by the CIA in the post-war era. Mario Del Pero continues this line of analysis by establishing a typology of 'covert actions'. He demonstrates the continuity of this concept in US foreign policy and calls for a more critical approach towards covert operations. Horst Boog shows how the USA also took advantage of other sources of information before strategic air reconnaissance became possible sporadically in 1951 and on a more regular basis in 1956. Mainly relying on 'human intelligence' (HUMINT), during this period, the US Air Force initiated in 1949 a systematic interrogation of German and Austrian prisoners of war returning from

Soviet captivity in the so-called Wringer project. With the escalation of the Cold War, intelligence began to branch out into the economic field. Frank Cain explains how the Western industrial nations tried for decades to stop the export of militarily useful technologies to Eastern bloc countries. His paper shows in detail how intelligence officials at US embassies and at the COCOM headquarters in Paris compiled information to uncover companies and countries trying to trade with communist countries in prohibited goods, despite the embargo.

While the USA re-established an intelligence agency in 1947, the official beginnings of a security service in East Germany date from 1948. The political police K-5 had already prosecuted war criminals and prominent members of the Nazi party in 1945. Its transformation into the Ministry for State Security (MfS), which Monika Tantzscher traces in detail in her contribution, took until February 1950. That the uprising of 17 June 1953 in the GDR came as a surprise to the CIA is pointed out by Christian Ostermann. On the basis of recently declassified CIA and NSC (National Security Council) reports, he argues that the USA did not engage in aggressive psychological warfare as a result of the revolt, but rather continued its soft propaganda approach.

Some of the intelligence activities in Germany are discussed in the final section from the perspective of eyewitnesses. David E. Murphy, a former member of the CIA's Berlin operations base, explains the set-up of the CIA headquarters in the former German capital and supports Christian Ostermann's argument that the uprising of 17 June 1953 took the CIA by surprise. Murphy maintains that US agents had no part in the eruption of the revolt. The CIA did assist, though, in the creation of the West German intelligence service. James H. Critchfield recounts how, in 1948, he had to decide whether Reinhard Gehlen was to be supported in building an intelligence organization. With US help, the *Bundesnachrichtendienst* (BND) was finally established in 1956. The Soviet side of the story is provided by the former KGB general Sergei A. Kondrachev who offers insight into some internal discussions of the Soviet intelligence services from the 1940s to the 1960s. He asserts that the KGB repeatedly warned of the deteriorating conditions in the GDR but was ignored by the political leadership until the revolt of 17 June 1953 brought the discontent suddenly into the open.

An overview of the activities of intelligence services from the

Canadian point of view by Wesley K. Wark concludes the volume. Reflecting on the current situation, he explains the connection between the 'information age' and the 'intelligence revolution', listing five features of the latter, and providing a prospect for the future when he argues that the Canadian intelligence system established on the basis of historical tradition, will hardly suffice for the twenty-first century.

Scholarly research in secret intelligence is a fast growing, developing, and fascinating field and no compilation of essays can cover all the aspects it touches upon. We are certain, however, that the information and new analytic approaches provided in this volume will help to stimulate new research in the field of intelligence history. The two IIHA conferences and this volume would not have been possible without the generous financial support provided by the *Deutsche Forschungsgemeinschaft* and the *Deutsche Gesellschaft für Amerikastudien*, which enabled us to invite many internationally renowned colleagues specializing in intelligence history as well as former intelligence officers. Reinhard R. Doerries and Jürgen Heideking, who organized the conferences in Hamburg and Strausberg, have provided much encouragement and pivotal support, which we gratefully acknowledge. We are also indebted to Thomas Meeh for his help with a number of papers.

Jürgen Heideking died in a car accident in the spring of 2000 before he could see the publication of this volume that he so ardently supported. Mourning the loss of a great scholar, teacher, and friend, we dedicate this volume to his memory.

Heike Bungert, Cologne
Jan G. Heitmann, Hamburg
Michael Wala, Munich

1

Military and Civil Intelligence Services in Germany from World War I to the End of the Weimar Republic

Ludwig Richter

When Germany began organizing a secret intelligence and counter-espionage division in late 1912 as part of its general staff, the military intelligence services of Britain, France and Russia could already look back on a long and great tradition.[1] The Reich lacked a political intelligence service comparable to those of the great European powers because the German general staff stubbornly objected to using any form of police investigation methods or political espionage and opposed the intermingling of political and military affairs in general.[2]

Only in the face of the undeniable increase in military intelligence activities by France and Britain after 1906 did the German general staff and the Ministry of War finally agree to a fundamental reorganization of Germany's institutions for gathering military intelligence.[3] This was accomplished under Major Heye, later the Army's Supreme Commander, who was appointed chief of the military intelligence service known as 'Department III B' in 1910. He was succeeded by Major Walter Nicolai in the spring of 1913.[4]

Information related to military intelligence had previously been gathered by intelligence officers collaborating with district officers stationed at the Reich's borders and special intelligence departments within the police force. Not until 1910 were these officers assigned to the General Commands (*Generalkommandos*). The creation of an independent military intelligence service thus marked a major shift in policy. Although Germany's intelligence service had no political arm whatsoever before World War I, the Foreign Ministry kept a wary eye on the intelligence service to make sure its activities remained strictly within the confines of the armed forces. When the war broke out, Department III B consisted of about 80 officers whose field of activity was restricted to military affairs. The department's activities were initially directed mainly towards France but were later extended to Russia as well.[5] Division III B had an annual budget of 350,000 marks until 1913; this was increased to 450,000 marks in 1914 – a very moderate sum indeed compared to Russia's 13 million roubles.[6]

In the prewar years, neither the Supreme Command nor the government understood that a well-functioning intelligence service ultimately depends on clear political directives. This lack of a uniformly directed military and political intelligence service had dire consequences, most notably that Department III B had no reliable information on the morale or objectives of the Entente Powers in 1914. Even when, in the course of the war, the Foreign Ministry finally established a political foreign intelligence service,[7] there was very little cooperation between Division III B and the Foreign Ministry's agencies. On the contrary, the two services frequently worked side by side with no effective communication taking place between them. Moreover, disputes over jurisdiction often led to heated confrontations between the Supreme Command and the Foreign Ministry.

The power of Department III B was dramatically enhanced by the declaration of war, which transferred executive authority to the Supreme Command. As head of the department, Colonel Nicolai was now in charge not only of the intelligence and counter-espionage service, but of press censorship and domestic propaganda as well. In the end, however, this proved to be a Herculean task far in excess of the department's personnel and financial resources. Before and during the war, its main field of operation was intelligence, with special emphasis on developments within the French and Russian armies, as well as on the British fleet and its plans of operation. This focus on intelligence was intensified by Colonel Nicolai's conception of his duties. Nicolai believed his main task lay less in the technical management of intelligence operations than in counselling the Supreme Command on the basis of information gained from these operations. He thus functioned primarily as a general staff officer.[8]

The so-called 'Lichnowsky memorandum' aptly illustrates the strict separation between military and political affairs. Probably completed in August 1914,[9] this treatise by the former German

2

ambassador to Great Britain, Karl Max Fürst von Lichnowsky, placed the responsibility for the July 1914 succession of war declarations leading to World War I squarely on the shoulders of the German government. The author had sent the work to some close political allies under the pledge of secrecy. However, it was passed on to Captain Hans von Beerfelde by Richard Witting, managing director of the National Bank of Germany. Von Beerfelde, who worked as an auxiliary intelligence officer for the political division of the Deputy General Staff in Berlin, duplicated the memorandum and circulated it among pacifist circles he was affiliated with in Germany and abroad.[10] This incident induced Major Nicolai to issue the following directive in August 1917:

> Insofar as officers of Department III B are required to deal with political questions in the line of duty, they may only act within their orders, and may only report to their superiors. If matters of political concern come to an officer's knowledge, he may only pass them on through official channels. Independent political activities by officers must be stopped immediately by their superiors and are to be reported to the Head of Department III B.[11]

In the course of the war and in the face of rapidly growing political and social pressures on the German government, this strict separation of political and military affairs and the voluntary restriction of Division III B to matters of military importance had become increasingly difficult to maintain for intelligence officers working in Germany. Major Nicolai was thus compelled to issue this directive in March 1918:

> Lately intelligence officers have shown an inclination to include matters in their reports which have no bearing on their actual assignment. Their job involves the surveillance of conditions in the military of our adversaries and on their home-front. Nevertheless, events and circumstances in Germany itself or views and rumours voiced abroad about Germany or individual Germans have repeatedly found their way into reports. ... I ask you to examine these reports very carefully before passing them on to ensure that we [Division III B] do not disseminate propaganda or gossip.[12]

3

It is not easy to evaluate the achievements of German military intelligence during World War I. To be sure, the transfer of executive authority to the Supreme Command at the outset of the war gave Department III B a level of power unknown to the intelligence services of the Allies. Nevertheless, Department III B was substantially inferior to the Allies' intelligence and counter-intelligence services in more ways than one. It was never sufficiently funded or staffed and was encumbered with an excessive workload that included such activities as propaganda and censorship of the German press. As a matter of fact, Department III B's endeavours were not even particularly successful in the area of military affairs. On the contrary, it failed to detect such portentous events as the mutiny of several units of the French Nivelle army in the spring of 1917 or the formation of powerful tank battalions in Britain prior to their unexpected mass deployment at Cambrai.

One of the main reasons for Department III B's ineffectualness was the conflict between the military command and the government, which intensified as the war progressed. Above all, the creation of a political intelligence service within the Foreign Ministry headed by Matthias Erzberger was a source of constant strife between Division III B and the Foreign Ministry.

At the very beginning of the war, Erzberger had offered his services to the Foreign, War, and Navy ministries in any capacity they might consider appropriate. The Admiralty and the Foreign Ministry wanted him to act as head of German propaganda for neutral countries.[13] Despite Erzberger's lack of experience in foreign policy, Chancellor Bethmann Hollweg found him useful in a wide variety of strategically important functions.[14]

Erzberger's job was anything but easy. By the third week of August, foreign public opinion had turned against Germany in the wake of the unprovoked invasion of Belgium – celebrated at home as a triumph of military expediency. Another problem was Germany's complete lack of any prewar conception of a foreign propaganda policy. In 1910, the Foreign Ministry had made a perfunctory attempt to raise additional funds for its public relations department for the purpose of shaping foreign public opinion. But a coalition of socialists, liberals, and centre representatives had refused to appropriate the money.[15] Fully understanding the rationale behind the Foreign Ministry's request, Erzberger introduced a motion in 1911 to establish a fund of 300,000 marks for 'the dissemination of German news abroad', which was then passed by the *Reichstag*.[16]

The Foreign Ministry had failed, however, to develop a network of contacts. The first job of the newly created Propaganda Office – financed with Foreign Ministry funds[17] – therefore entailed creating a mailing list of several thousand foreign addresses. Erzberger, an extremely adroit and rapid worker, managed to produce this list within a few days.[18]

Aware that the success of the Propaganda Office very much depended on its access to inside knowledge, Bethmann Hollweg issued instructions to allow Erzberger to attend all secret meetings of the Foreign Ministry, the Ministry of War, and the Admiralty. Although the Propaganda Office was given complete freedom to use all information it acquired during these meetings, the rigidness of the German Supreme Command proved a severe obstacle to any ambitious propaganda initiatives. The Military Press Office (*Kriegspresseamt*) posed a particular problem. Directly subordinate to the Supreme Command in October 1915 and led by Lieutenant Colonel Deutelmoser until 1916–17 (followed by Major Stotten and Major Würz), this agency made repeated attempts to frustrate the political objectives of the Propaganda Office. The efforts of the Propaganda Office were also greatly handicapped by its lack of exclusive authority: it was by no means the only institution established to influence public opinion. After the beginning of the war, the inertia of the prewar years gave way to an excessive proliferation of official, semi-official, and unofficial propaganda agencies. Caught up in a hopeless bureaucratic entanglement, the main organizations (apart from Erzberger's Propaganda Office) forced to compete with each other were the News Section of the Supreme Command under Nicolai (Department III B), the Military Liaison Office within the Foreign Office under von Haeften, the News Section of the Foreign Office under Hamman, and the Military District Commander's Office of Censorship.[19] The creation of the Military Press Office in October 1915 did little to improve this chaotic situation.

It is therefore extremely difficult to evaluate the activities of the Propaganda Office in any conclusive manner. It was not able to prevent public opinion in neutral foreign countries from turning violently anti-German, nor did it succeed in influencing public opinion in Italy and Romania sufficiently to prevent those two countries from entering the war on the side of the Allies. Thus, the efforts of the Propaganda Office do not bear comparison with the achievements of Lord Northcliffe in Britain and George Creel in the USA. Still, it must be emphasized that the Propaganda Office never had the advantage of an exclusive, or even clearly defined, domain. Its activities were hindered by the military authorities – especially by the Supreme Command – throughout the war, whereas both Northcliffe and Creel served governments under which civilian supremacy went unchallenged.

The collapse of Germany in November 1918 led to the dissolution of existing military intelligence and counter-espionage structures.[20] Under the stipulations of the Treaty of Versailles, Germany was allowed to maintain neither a general staff nor a military intelligence service. Several spectacular cases of espionage, such as the Winiker case,[21] however, strengthened the German Supreme Command's determination to circumvent these restrictions. Consequently, a counter-espionage office was established inside the Ministry of Defence (*Reichswehrministerium*). It was called *Abwehr* (counter-espionage service) by its first director, Major Gempp, who had worked for Nicolai as intelligence officer 'Oberost' during the war. The name *Abwehr* was chosen to convince the interallied military commission of the purely defensive objectives of the new office. It maintained only a small staff over the next few years. The counter-espionage service first formed part of the statistics division of the Army Office (*Truppenamt*) and only later came under the direct authority of the Minister of Defence. It consisted of just two to three general staff officers and five to seven junior officers occupied as clerks. The *Abwehr* was divided into two sections: East and West.[22] Executive bodies were established within each of the army's seven military district commands (*Wehrkreise*), which were initially staffed with only a general staff officer and an auxiliary officer.

Largely because of a lack of staff and funding, the *Abwehr*'s activities in the Weimar Republic were generally restricted to two main areas:[23] counter-espionage directed mainly against the former enemies Britain and France[24] and the observation of the rearmament of the Polish army. It was only under the leadership of Navy Captain Patzig (whose appointment was a minor sensation; up to that time, the *Abwehr* had been the exclusive domain of the army) that the *Abwehr*'s scope of activities and self-conception underwent a change. The *Abwehr* had previously functioned primarily as an agency responsible for the internal affairs of the Ministry of Defence; now it was gradually converted into a regular military intelligence service, thus shifting its focus to foreign policy. This development gained substantial momentum after 30 January 1933 and following the appointment of Colonel von Reichenau as head of the *Truppenamt* and Lieutenant General von Blomberg as Minister of Defence. The *Abwehr*'s budget was boosted considerably on orders from Hitler, who was influenced by his admiration for the traditions and the institutions of the British Empire. Hitler dreamed of establishing a comprehensive intelligence service modelled after the British Secret Service.[25]

This brief outline of the development of the *Abwehr* in the Weimar Republic should not cause us to lose sight of other equally important intelligence services that existed alongside this military organization mainly concerned with counter-espionage. These include the Political Police (*Politische Polizei*), the National Office for the Maintenance of Public Order (*Reichskommissariat für Überwachung der Öffentlichen Ordnung*), and its counterpart, the Prussian State Office for the Maintenance of Public Order (*Staatskommissariat für Öffentliche Ordnung*), to name only the most significant institutions.

Between 1871 and 1918, the Political Police formed an integral part of the police forces in the German states (*Länder*). During World War I, it was able to expand its influence by cooperating closely with the military authorities, who had assumed executive power.[26] The social democrats had long demanded the disbandment of the Political Police due to its repressive actions against the growing Social Democratic Party (SPD).[27] Department V, the political arm of the Berlin police authority, which had simultaneously functioned as the local and state police authority since 1880, was officially dissolved by Emil Eichhorn in the wake of the revolution of 1918. Eichhorn was a member of the Independent Social Democratic Party and also served as the People's Commissar for the Public Security Service (*Volkskommissar für den Öffentlichen Sicherheitsdienst*). Privately, Eichhorn remained convinced of the necessity of a political police force. However, in order to sever the historical links to the detested Imperial Secret Police on the staff level at least, he appointed members of the workers' and soldiers' councils (*Arbeiter- und Soldatenräte*) to the force.[28] Eichhorn's successor, Eugen Ernst (SPD), shared Eichhorn's views despite officially calling for the dissolution of the Political Police. He consequently sought to disguise its existence by integrating it – as a subordinate department – into Division

I of the Berlin police authority.[29] Not until 20 May 1925[30] did it become the independent 'Division I a' of the Berlin police department. The rejection of plans to create a national department of criminal investigation (*Reichskriminalamt*) and a national department for political affairs (*Landeszentralbehörde für Politische Angelegenheiten*) prompted a decision to integrate the Political Police units into the general police force.[31] In actuality, the newly created Division I simply continued where its predecessor had left off, namely, by operating as an intelligence-gathering agency for matters of interest to the Political Police, not only for Prussia but for the entire Reich.

The process of consolidation was expedited by the ministerial decree of 12 December 1928,[32] which incorporated all levels of the Prussian police apparatus into an Administrative Police Department, a Municipal Constabulary, and a Criminal Investigation Department (*Verwaltungs-, Schutz- und Kriminalpolizei*) on the local and the regional level. Political affairs formed part of the responsibilities of Division I of the Administrative Police Department. The Prussian Criminal Investigation Department in Berlin (*Landeskriminalamt*), which was put under the direct control of the Prussian Minister of the Interior, functioned as a central intelligence office. An amendment to the above-mentioned decree of 12 December 1928 expressly assigned counter-espionage activities to the Political Police – in addition to the responsibility for domestic security, constitutional affairs, and the surveillance of the press, associations, and assemblies.[33]

In the Weimar Republic, the intelligence activities of the Political Police were of extraordinary importance, especially in light of the fact that the independent intelligence service of the Municipal Police (*uniformierte Polizei*), dating from 1918, had been dissolved by the Allies in 1921 in connection with the abolition of the Security Police (*Sicherheitspolizei*).[34] As a result, the Municipal Police were entirely dependent on information provided by the Political Police divisions. The Political Police consisted of both full-time and 'unofficial' members (undercover agents). Yet staff shortages prevented the Political Police from fully covering even Berlin, where there were only 300 full-time officers. Between 180 and 280 of these were assigned to field service.[35] Similar figures applied to all other German states.[36] Unfortunately, no reliable data are available on the exact number of undercover agents. Even though the authorities designated their employment as 'indispensable', they were constantly warning against overestimating their importance.[37]

The practical work of the Political Police mainly centred on the observation of elements hostile to the republic. It gleaned information from publicly accessible sources, such as newspapers, magazines, and pamphlets. The surveillance of public meetings was also of great importance.[38] Other principal sources of information were denunciations by individual citizens and the deployment of undercover agents. The fact that intelligence activities were restricted to general preventive or suppressive police assignments was not an obstacle to effective intelligence operations, since neither term was narrowly interpreted when it came to reconnaissance and surveillance. The loose interpretation of high treason,[39] the Acts on the Protection of the Republic (*Republikschutzgesetze*),[40] and the Emergency Acts (*Notverordnungen*)[41] provided the authorities with a broad legal basis for the surveillance of political opponents and counter-espionage activities. In addition to providing evidence for criminal charges against suspicious elements, surveillance activities were used as the basis for reports on the 'state of the nation', which were exploited for both criminal and political investigations. These reports, an important source of information on domestic policy in the Weimar Republic, have been largely ignored by historians to date.[42] There was one particular obstacle to the surveillance activities of the Political Police which proved insurmountable in the end: the *Reichswehr* (German armed forces). The military tenaciously defended its exclusive right to monitor and combat illegal activities, denying the police any authority over cases involving army units (illegal ones included), on *Reichswehr* territory or in army barracks.[43]

The gathering of political intelligence to provide early warnings of potential threats was primarily the job of the Political Police. Special agencies were established to coordinate these activities in Prussia and the *Reich* at an early stage in the Weimar Republic. A fundamental problem remained the aforementioned struggle between the *Reichswehr* and civil authorities over the responsibility for internal security and the question of a political intelligence service controlled by the government. Even after the revolution of November 1918, the *Reichswehr* Supreme Command continued its activities in the field of domestic intelligence. In a report to the military authorities and general staff in May 1919, the Supreme Commander of the *Reichswehrgruppe* 1, General von Lüttwitz, emphasized the necessity of 'intelligence activities assiduously organized down to the last detail in the face of continuing threats of riots in the *Reich*'. At that time, he reported, such activities were being conducted by a well-organized military domestic intelligence service, which was also in charge of propaganda and influencing the press.[44]

All army section commands (*Reichwehrgruppenkommandos*) and their respective army brigades (*Reichswehrbrigaden*) maintained political intelligence units. Major General von Möhl, Supreme Commander of *Reichswehrgruppe* 4, defined his work as 'clever, inconspicuous surveillance conducted by persons especially suited to the job, discussions with particularly suitable civil servants and well-informed private citizens'. The objective of these operations was to gather 'useful evidence to enable an accurate assessment of the situation in different parts of the country'.[45] In the ensuing months, the individual *Reichswehrgruppenkommandos* put considerable effort into procuring staff and funding for their political domestic intelligence services.[46] By late in the summer of 1919, their efforts had proved so successful that Major General von Hübner, chief of *Reichswehrbrigade* 23, even courted the 'active cooperation' of the district presidents (*Regierungspräsident*) of Upper and Lower Franconia. He stressed:

> The *Reichswehr* shall constitute one of the essential pillars of government authority and public security. Its mission is to prevent and, if necessary, to suppress riots and rebellions. The *Reichswehr* can best meet these demands if it is never caught by surprise by the unforeseen activities of subversive elements. Besides maintaining a certain degree of preparedness, this means that the *Reichswehr* must keep its finger on the pulse of public opinion and have access to the latest information on all aspects of political life. From this follows the necessity for the *Reichswehr* to maintain a political intelligence service, which in the interest of public security must be expanded. ... I therefore propose that the district presidents advise their subordinate authorities to send weekly reports to their respective post commanders.[47]

Nevertheless, the district president of Upper Franconia, von Strossenreuther, followed the example of the Bavarian government under Prime Minister Johannes Hoffmann (SPD) and distanced himself from this attempt to bring about the cooperation of civil and military authorities in matters of political intelligence.[48]

As it happened, the reports from the political intelligence divisions of the General Command came under severe criticism in the course of 1919, mainly from the Prussian government and civil authorities. The Prussian Minister of Agriculture, Otto Braun, dismissed the reports sent to him by the General Command of the Second Army corps as 'superficial and therefore worthless and superfluous'. Moreover, he asked the General Command to 'confine its activities to military affairs'. This view was seconded by the district president of Pomerania, Lippmann.[49] In the summer of 1919, the Prussian government took steps to complement – and eventually replace – the military service's one-sided reports. This, however, entailed creating a civil intelligence service within the police force. In August 1919, the Prussian government set up a special agency to supervise and coordi-nate the activities and (re)organization of such an institution: the State Office for the Maintenance of Public Order.[50] This office shared nothing but its name (*Staatskommissariat*) with other Prussian state offices.[51] The only reason for calling it a *Staatskommissariat* was to emphasize its independence of the ordinary structures of the state bureaucracy. As central agencies operating on the state level, these offices were subordinate only to the Prime Minister and the Minister of the Interior. Nominally, the new agency contained three divisions: the intelligence office, an executive office, and a press bureau. The last two, however, were of little relevance. The activities of the State Office were confined to informing the Prussian government and other authorities of potential threats to public security. This was accomplished by way of individual dispatches and periodical reports on organizations, persons and activities hostile to the republic.[52]

A secret memorandum from December 1919 (probably written by the Permanent Under Secretary to the Chancellery, Heinrich Albert) reveals the scale of the office's intelligence operations at that time. The memorandum describes the agency's area of responsibility as 'the surveillance of any activities in Prussia whose aim is the disturbance of public safety and order, economic sabotage or the unlawful incite-ment of seditious activities'. The director of the *Staatskommissariat* had already created a

> complex intelligence-gathering network. This makes him the best informed man on the political climate ... in Prussia and its provinces, as well as in all other parts of Germany. This in turn provides him with the means to correlate the various forms of intel-ligence and arrive at an accurate assessment of the overall situation.[53]

In 1923, however, the State Office lost its extensive executive powers when it was stripped of its responsibility for protecting the president and members of the national government.[54]

The *Staatskommissariat* primarily utilized undercover agents to complete its tasks, though it also relied on information gathered by the Political Police and the 'reporting centres' (*Meldestellen*), which had been created at Divisional Police Headquarters (*Oberpräsidien*) expressly for this purpose. Yet the original idea to have the State Office for the Maintenance of Public Order displace the *Reichswehr* as the political intelligence service failed. This was partly due to the continuing rivalry between military and civil authorities, though the main reason was apprehension about eroding the authority of the central government. The *Reichswehr* maintained the only nation-wide political intelligence service, and the government, for all its concern about the one-sidedness of the reports, did not want to lose this instrument.[55]

The efficiency of the newly created State Office was largely dependent on its director, yet the first *Staatskommissar*, Herbert von Berger,[56] failed miserably. He was the former head of Department VII, the Higher Office of Police and Press Affairs (*Höheres Polizei- und Pressewesen*) at the Berlin police headquarters, and had then worked for the Prussian Ministry of the Interior. His reports seemed to indicate that the republic was threatened only by left-wing elements. He was unable to perceive any possible danger from the right and failed to predict the impending Kapp putsch. As a result, precautionary measures either were not taken at all or were taken much too late.[57] After the suppression of the putsch, von Berger was replaced by Robert Weisman, First Public Prosecutor with the Department of Public Prosecution Berlin I.[58] It was Weisman who succeeded in turning the *Staatskommissariat* into a well-organized and efficient political intelligence service. He consistently managed to recruit informants from political and administrative quarters in most parts of Prussia. Moreover, he gained recognition for himself and his agency against all competitors by providing the Prussian government with quick, precise, and comprehensive situation reports.

As an institution, however, the *Staatskommissariat* remained a foreign element within the Prussian executive, as it was directly subordinate to the Prussian Prime Minister. In addition, Weismann had retained his function as Public Prosecutor for political cases, in which capacity he was answerable to the Department of Justice. This convergence of competing authorities and levels of hierarchy inevitably resulted in considerable confusion. Some police headquarters, government administrations (*Regierungspräsidien*), and divisional police administrations reported to both the Ministry of the Interior and the State Office for the Maintenance of Public Order.[59] Only the appointment of Weismann as Secretary (*Staatssekretär*) to the Prussian Ministry of State put an end to this persistent conflict, though it coincidentally ended any hope of autonomy on the part of the *Staatskommissariat*. On 1 October 1923, it was assigned to the Ministry of the Interior. Full integration followed in April 1924.[60] As part of the Ministry of the Interior, the political intelligence unit was simply called 'Intelligence Service' (*Nachrichtenwesen*). It belonged to the political division of the police department, which was directly answerable to the chief of police. From that point on, the *Staatskommissariat* had no practical relevance as an independent body. All of its principal duties, including the preparation of reports, were carried out by the political division at the Berlin police headquarters.[61] It is thus incorrect to speak of the end of the *Staatskommissariat* as the end of the political intelligence service as such, although it does mark the end of its administrative independence. Prussia had merely completed a development which had already taken place in other states or soon would. By 1925, 16 of the 18 states had created so-called *Nachrichtenstellen*, intelligence agencies organized either as divisions of the police force or as independent bodies (*Nachrichtenzentralen*).[62]

The development of a national intelligence service soon followed Prussia's example. It began with efforts by the Minister of the Interior to become independent of the *Reichswehr*'s political intelligence service. The Minister of the Interior, Erich Koch-Weser (German Democratic Party) originally intended to turn the Prussian State Office for the Maintenance of Public Order into a national authority. Late in the autumn of 1919, the cabinet resolved to allocate funds and assign two national government officials to the Prussian Office.[63] In the wake of the Kapp putsch, however, this policy was abandoned, mainly due to strong opposition in the southern states, though Berger's inferior reporting was also a factor. After overcoming initial opposition in Prussia,[64] the central government created an independent National Office for the Maintenance of Public Order in May 1920.[65] Hermann Kuenzer, a lawyer from Baden, was named the

13

director (*Reichskommissar*). On the administrative level, this office was directly answerable to the national Ministry of the Interior and became part of its Department IV (police affairs) – also headed by Kuenzer. It nevertheless maintained its autonomy as a political intelligence service.

The activities of the newly created *Reichskommissariat* more or less corresponded to those of the Prussian office: the surveillance of elements hostile to the republic, the exchange of information with other authorities, and the preparation of regular reports to the central government.[66] In most cases, readily available sources were used, in particular newspaper and magazine articles, as well as notes taken at meetings by police officers working as guards. In addition, all associations had to submit their statutes to the National Register of Associations. Internal documents, however, could be demanded only in exceptional cases.[67]

Several circumstances hampered the *Reichskommissariat* in the fulfilment of its wide range of duties. The Weimar Constitution apportioned very limited police power to the national authorities,[68] a fact which in turn restricted the competency of the *Reichskommissar*. Moreover, there was a constant struggle between the *Reichskommissariat* and other national and state institutions. Finally, the *Reichskommissariat* suffered from a shortage of staff: in 1923, it had only 23 full-time qualified employees.[69] Although several undercover agents had been added by 1925, they were apparently only employed on a case-by-case basis. All in all, the number of undercover agents must have been rather insubstantial, as the budget provided for their employment was considerably lower than the corresponding Prussian budget.[70] While the Prussian *Staatskommissar* had a closely knit network of intelligence sources at his disposal, the *Reichskommissar* was almost entirely dependent on third-party information – mainly provided by the states. Prussia soon charged that the *Reichskommissariat* was neglecting its duties due to insufficient staffing and inadequate organizational structures.[71] Whereas relations with Prussia were strained yet functional, relations with Bavaria could not have been worse. After a second attempt was made to assassinate Philip Scheidemann, an SPD delegate to the German parliament and former chancellor, only an undercover *Reichskommissariat* agent, among all the original suspects, was arrested, tried, and sentenced.[72]

With its limited authority and means, the *Reichskommissariat* more suitably functioned as a mediating body between various agencies than as an independent intelligence service. It succeeded, for instance, in coordinating the intelligence activities of state and federal authorities by organizing 'Intelligence Conferences' (*Nachrichtenkonferenzen*). Separate meetings were held for northern and southern Germany from 1924 to 1926; from 1927 on, there were unified meetings under Prussian leadership. At these events, the responsible case officers gave detailed reports on their most recent findings. In addition, measures to improve the cooperation between different police authorities were extensively discussed.[73]

As an intelligence service, however, the *Reichskommissariat* remained substantially dependent on third-party information submitted to it voluntarily by the individual states. This meant that one of the primary objectives behind the creation of the *Reichskommissariat* was never achieved: freeing the national government from its dependence on the states' political intelligence services. A plan to turn the *Reichskommissariat* into a National Department of Criminal Investigation also failed.[74] In 1929, the Minister of the Interior, Carl Severing (SPD), reorganized the office along the lines of the Prussian model. The *Reichskommissariat* ceased to exist as an independent body and was integrated into Department I of the Ministry of the Interior, which was also put in charge of intelligence activities.[75] This meant that the Ministerial Director (*Ministerialdirektor*) of the department, initially Menzel (SPD) and subsequently the nationalist Gottheiner, was now also head of the intelligence service. The creation of a new intelligence agency within the Ministry of the Interior (*Nachrichtensammelstelle im Reichsministerium des Innern*) led to the dismissal of the *Reichskommissar* and a substantial number of his staff. Above all, the new *Nachrichtensammelstelle* no longer gathered any intelligence itself and no longer possessed undercover agents of its own. It was a body purely devoted to processing information either gathered from overt sources or provided by the states.

The quarrels between the military and civil authorities, already present during World War I, continued undiminished even though the political and military institutions changed with the creation of the republic. In the end, the civil authorities did not succeed in replacing the *Reichswehr*'s domestic political intelligence service. Consequently, there was no cooperation between civil and military authorities in this area. Even though the Prussian Office for the

Maintenance of Public Order and the Prussian Political Police managed to create a closely knit network for the surveillance of unconstitutional activities, the dualism created by competing federal and state authorities persisted. Moreover, the political intelligence agencies were highly dependent on information provided by the Political Police. Yet if the Political Police could no longer adequately carry out their surveillance work because of increased assignments in other areas, the comprehensiveness of their reports naturally suffered.

This outline of the history of information-gathering institutions in the Weimar Republic paradigmatically illustrates that an intelligence service without support structures is like a knight without a sword. Furthermore, the effectiveness of intelligence operations is contingent upon the use which high-ranking officials make of their reports. In the end, intelligence reports can only aid and support political decisions – while conversely functioning as a mirror of political decision-making.

NOTES

1.   For England, cf. M.G. Richings, *Espionage: The Secret Service of the British Crown* (London: Hodgins, 1935); G. Aston, *Secret Service 1914–1918* (London: Faber & Faber, 1930); E.H. Cookridge, *Secrets of the British Secret Service* (London: Sampson Low Marston & Co, 1948). For France, cf. M.H. Gauché, *Le Deuxième Bureau au travail* (Paris: Gravier, 1954) and M. Gunzenhäuser, *Geschichte des Geheimen Nachrichtendienstes. Literaturbericht und Bibliographie* (Stuttgart: Klett Cotta, 1968), p. 34. For Russia, cf. – apart from Gunzenhäuser, pp. 28–31 – see also A.W. Gerasimoff (chief of the Political Police in Petersburg), *Der Kampf gegen die erste russische Revolution: Erinnerungen* (Leipzig: Gröner, 1934).

2.   For the secret intelligence and counter-espionage departments in imperial Germany 1871–1918, cf. *Gunzenhäuser*, op. cit., pp. 23, 40. Cf. also the instructive book by A.K. Graves, *The Secrets of the German War Office* (London: Platt, 1914); J. Dyssord, *L´Espionage allemande a l´oeuvre* (Paris: Trués, 1915); and R. Boucard, *Les dessous de l´espionnage allemande. Des documents – des faits* (Paris: Trués, 1931).

3.   Cf. the short surveys by G. Buchheit, *Der deutsche Geheimdienst* (München: List, 1966) pp. 17–19 and W. Görlitz, *Der deutsche Generalstab. Geschichte und Gestalt 1657–1945* (Frankfurt/Main: Haude & Spener, 1950), pp. 267–9. Between 1908 and 1914, 1,056 persons were arrested for espionage. 135 of those were sentenced for high treason. Cf. W. Nicolai, 'Einblicke in den Nachrichtendienst der Feindstaaten im Bereich der Mittelmächte', in F.

Felger (ed.), *Was wir vom Weltkrieg nicht wissen* (Berlin and Leipzig: Andermann, 1929), pp. 120–1.

4. Cf. especially his books *Nachrichtendienst, Presse und Volksstimmung im Weltkrieg* (Berlin: Mittler, 1920) and *Geheime Mächte: Internationale Spionage und ihre Bekämpfung im Weltkrieg und heute* (Leipzig: Meyer, 1923). The fact that the management of the intelligence service, at Ludendorff's insistence, was handed over to the only 39-year-old Nicolai, who had just been promoted to the rank of major, caused 'some shaking of heads' within the general staff. W. Berg, 'Interessante Fälle aus der Arbeit der Geheimen Feldpolizei', in Felger, op. cit., p. 105.

5. Nicolai, op. cit., pp. 8ff.; cf. also the chart in Buchheit, op. cit., p. 82.

6. Nicolai, op. cit., pp. 118–31 (pp. 119f).

7. Matthias Erzberger, a Centre Party delegate to Parliament, offered to take over the job.

8. Nicolai consequently transferred the entire executive management of the counter-espionage service to Police Commissioner (*Polizeirat*) Bauer; cf. Nicolai, op. cit., pp. 5f. and the report by Elsbeth Schragmüller (head of Section France in the *Kriegsnachrichtenstelle Antwerpen*), 'Aus dem deutschen Nachrichtendienst', in Felger, op. cit., pp. 138–45.

9. There are three different versions of the memorandum: 'England vor dem Kriege' (August 1914); 'Wahn und Wille' (January 1915) and 'Meine Londoner Mission 1912–1914' (August 1916). The versions of 1914 and 1916 are reprinted in F. Thimme, 'Fürst Lichnowskys "Memoirenwerk"', *Archiv für Politik und Geschichte*, 10 (1928) pp. 36–54. For the version from 1915, cf. J.C. Röhl (ed.), *Zwei deutsche Fürsten zur Kriegsschuldfrage. Lichnowsky und Eulenburg und der Ausbruch des Ersten Weltkrieges. Eine Dokumentation* (Düsseldorf: Schwann, 1971), pp. 39–65. For the 'Lichnowsky case', cf. also the heated debates of the German parliament's *Hauptausschuß* on 23 August 1917 and 16 March 1918, R. Schiffers and M. Koch (eds.), *Der Hauptausschuß des Deutschen Reichstags 1915–1918* (Düsseldorf: Droste, 1981), doc. nos. 173; 219.

10. On 12 July 1918, Lichnowsky was expelled from the Prussian *Herrenhaus* for his conduct. In the end, however, criminal proceedings against the ambassador and proceedings under martial law against von Beerfelde were halted by the November revolution.

11. Nicolai, op. cit., p. 9.

12. Ibid., p. 10.

13. M. Erzberger, *Erlebnisse im Weltkrieg* (Stuttgart: Deutsche Verlagsanstalt, 1920), p. 4; K. Epstein, *Matthias Erzberger and the Dilemma of German Democracy* (Princeton, NJ: Princeton University Press, 1959), pp. 98f.

14. For the congenial cooperation between Erzberger and Chancellor von Bethmann Hollweg up to 1917, cf. K.H. Jarausch, *The Enigmatic Chancellor. Bethmann Hollweg and the Hubris of Imperial Germany* (London: Macmillan, 1973); G. Wollstein, *Theobald von Bethmann Hollweg* (Göttingen: Musterschmidt, 1995). Erzberger's position within the Catholic Centre Party during the war is described by R. Morsey, *Die Deutsche Zentrumspartei 1917–1923* (Düsseldorf: Droste, 1966), pp. 53–61.

17

15. Nicolai, op. cit., p. 53; W. Schoen, *Erlebtes* (Berlin: Andermann, 1921), p. 117.
16. Erzberger, op. cit., p. 3; cf. also *Reichstag Debates*, vol. 284 (24 April 1912), p. 1378.
17. Later, many rumours arose in connection with the sums involved in the operations of the Propaganda Office. According to Erzberger's figures (which were never convincingly refuted), they totalled 'less than a dozen million marks', *Erzberger*, op. cit., p. 21. The question of financing was also discussed in *Der Erzberger-Prozess. Stenographischer Bericht über die Verhandlungen im Beleidigungsprozess des Reichsfinanzministers Erzberger gegen den Staatsminister a.D. Dr. Karl Helfferich* (Berlin: Hobbing, 1920), pp. 645–55, 824–6, 1030–3.
18. Erzberger, op. cit., p. 5. Cf. also Nicolai, op. cit, pp. 166–72 and P. Elzbacher, *Die Presse als Werkzeug der Auswärtigen Politik* (Jena: Meyer, 1918), pp. 48–52.
19. In October 1914, Erzberger counted 27 such agencies (Erzberger, op. cit., p. 5). He was instrumental in setting up a central coordinating body, the *Zentralstelle für Auslandsdienst*, under the direction of the former ambassador to Tokyo, Baron von Mumm (directors: Erzberger, Paul Rohrbach, Ernst Jäckh). Erzberger; Hammann, the Foreign Office press chief; Solf, the Colonial Secretary; Wahnschaffe, Bethmann's Chancellery chief; and Stein, the Berlin correspondent to the (liberal) *Frankfurter Zeitung*, met daily at the Foreign Office to discuss the general war situation and work out propaganda directives. Cf. O. Hammann, *Bilder aus der letzten Kaiserzeit* (Berlin: Hobbing, 1922), pp. 113–26; H. Stegemann, *Erinnerungen aus meinem Leben und aus meiner Zeit* (Berlin: Meyer, 1930), pp. 273–5. For the overall organization of German propaganda cf. H.D. Lasswell, *Propaganda Technique in the World War* (New York: Trent, 1927), pp. 22–4 and especially W. Vogel, 'Die Organisation der Presse und amtlicher Nachrichtenstellen von Bismarck bis 1933', in W. Heide and K. D'Ester (eds.), *Die Zeitungswissenschaft*, vol. 16 (Berlin: Meyer, 1941), pp. 26–34.
20. Apart from brief comments in the books by Buchheim, op. cit., pp. 33–42; P. Leverkuehn, *Der geheime Nachrichtendienst der deutschen Wehrmacht im Kriege* (Frankfurt: Schmidt, 1957); and O. Reile, *Geheime Westfront* (München: List, 1962); *Geheime Ostfront* (München: List, 1963), there is no description of the German military intelligence service in the Weimar Republic. Cf. also Gunzenhäuser, op. cit., pp. 24, 49–52, 284–90.
21. Winiker, radio operations specialist and (supposedly) lecturer at the Technical University of Berlin, was appointed army counsellor (*Heeresberater*) in the summer of 1919 in the code department of the German government. After obtaining detailed knowledge of military radio operations and the code system, he fled to Poland. See Reile, *Geheime Ostfront*, p. 42.
22. For the division of the *Abwehr* into three subgroups (1. Investigation, 2. Code Department, 3. Counter-espionage), cf. the diagram by Buchheit, op. cit., p. 33.

23. This was also true of its activities under Colonel Gempp's successors: Major Schwantes (June 1927), Colonel von Bredow (December 1929), and Navy Captain Patzig (June 1932).

24. The French spies were very alert and active once the former head of the Deuxième Bureau, General Dupont, had been appointed chief of the Interallied Military Control Commission (*Interalliierte Militärkontroll-kommission*). For German intelligence activities concerning Poland, cf. Reile, *Geheime Ostfront*, pp. 42–4, 96–100.

25. Cf. K.H. Abshagen, *Canaris. Patriot und Weltbürger* (Stuttgart: DVA, 1949), pp. 110–12.

26. For the origins of the Political Police in the nineteenth century, cf. A. Schweder, *Politische Polizei. Wesen und Entstehung im Metternischen System, in der Weimarer Republik und im nationalsozialistischen Staate* (Berlin: Hobbing, 1937); H. Schlierbach, *Die Politische Polizei in Preußen* (Berlin: Schmid, 1938); W. Siemann, *Deutschlands Ruhe, Sicherheit und Ordnung. Die Anfänge der Politischen Polizei 1806–1866* (Tübingen: Niemeyer, 1985); for the war, cf. B. Weiss, *Polizei und Politik* (Berlin: Dietz, 1928), pp. 50–8.

27. Cf. E. Ernst, *Polizeispitzeleien und Ausnahmegesetze* (Berlin: Dietz, 1911).

28. The re-entry of many former Political Police officials was facilitated by the fact that on 8 November 1918 the officers of Political Department V burned all files relating to their persecution of Social Democrats; cf. Ch. Graf, *Politische Polizei zwischen Demokratie und Diktatur. Die Entwicklung der preußischen Politischen Polizei vom Staatsschutzorgan der Weimarer Republik zum Geheimen Staatspolizeiamt des Dritten Reiches* (Berlin: de Gruyter, 1983), p. 7.

29. Weiss, op. cit., pp. 52–4; H. Buchheim, *SS und Polizei im NS-Staat* (Duisdorf: Trill, 1964), p. 31; S. Aronson, *Reinhard Heydrich und die Frühgeschichte von Gestapo und SD* (Stuttgart: DVA, 1971), p. 84.

30. Graf, op. cit., p. 11.

31. Cf. below and Note 74.

32. Graf, op. cit., p. 14.

33. The decree of 12 December 1928 and its annexes are cited by Weiss, op. cit., pp. 63–6.

34. Weiss, op. cit., p. 137. For the rivalry between the Prussian security police and the *Reichswehr*, cf. P. Lessmann, *Die preußische Schutzpolizei in der Weimarer Republik* (Düsseldorf: Droste, 1989), pp. 65–78. The situation of the police forces in Berlin is depicted by Hsi-Huey Liang, *Die Berliner Polizei in der Weimarer Republik* (Berlin: de Gruyter, 1977).

35. Graf, op. cit., p. 23; Liang, op. cit., p. 37.

36. Cf. the (very superficial) study by J. Schwarze, *Die bayerische Polizei und ihre historische Funktion bei der Aufrechterhaltung der öffentlichen Sicherheit in Bayern von 1919–1933* (München: Oldenbourg, 1977) pp. 146–50. For Hesse, cf. B. Klemm, ... *durch polizeiliches Einschreiten wurde dem Unfug ein Ende gemacht* (Frankfurt/Main: Biblio, 1982), pp. 27–9. Neither study contains exact figures on the staff of the Political Police.

37. Weiss, op. cit., p. 102. In metropolitan areas, in particular, the Political Police seem to have regularly employed undercover agents. In small towns and in the countryside there were apparently no equivalent structures. Klemm, op. cit., pp. 134, 170, 179.

38. Most of the documents reprinted in Klemm, op. cit., were taken from the press and public meetings.

39. Ch. Gusy, *Weimar – die wehrlose Republik? Verfassungsschutzrecht und Verfassungsschutz in der Weimarer Republik* (Tübingen: Niemeyer, 1991), pp. 107–15.

40. G. Jasper, *Der Schutz der Republik. Studien zur staatlichen Sicherung der Demokratie in der Weimarer Republik 1922–1930* (Tübingen: Niemeyer, 1963), pp. 56–92.

41. A. Kurz, *Demokratische Diktatur? Auslegung und Handhabung des Artikels 48 der Weimarer Verfassung 1919–1925* (Berlin: Duncker & Humblot, 1992); Gusy, op. cit., pp. 125–9. After the *Reichsgericht* had prohibited the observation of public meetings without special authorization in 1932 (*Reichsgericht* verdicts in criminal cases, vol. 66, pp. 228–37), Section 2 of the emergency act of 12 December 1932 expressly permitted them again (cf. *Reichsgesetzblatt* [1932], p. 548).

42. A few of those reports are reprinted in Klemm, op. cit., pp. 65–9. For Prussia cf. also E. Ritter, *Lageberichte und Meldungen* (München: Oldenbourg, 1979), p. xxix.

43. Little attention has been paid to this point; cf. the letter from *Reichswehrminister* Geßler to Oeser (Secretary of the Interior) on 29 January 1923, in which Geßler insisted 'that the military administration as a sovereign administration (*Hoheitsverwaltung*) cannot be subordinated to the police authorities like a private person. On the contrary, it has a similar status to the police authorities', H. Hürten (ed.), *Das Krisenjahr 1923. Militär und Innenpolitik 1922–1924* (Düsseldorf: Droste, 1980), doc. no. 3. Cf. also General von Seeckt's (Chief of the Military Supreme Command) order for the protection of official military installations against 'infringements' by the police on 18 May 1923, as well as the complaints by the *Reichswehr* about police forces allegedly 'spying' on a Saxon infantry regiment on 28 May 1923, ibid., doc. nos. 15, 17.

44. H. Hürten (ed.), *Zwischen Revolution und Kapp-Putsch. Militär und Innenpolitik 1918–1920* (Düsseldorf: Droste, 1977), doc. no. 38; cf. also Major Hierl's memorandum on 23 June 1919 about his experiences during the suppression of the Munich '*Räteregierung*'; ibid., doc. no. 49.

45. Ibid., doc. no. 63.

46. Cf. the request by Group Commando 4, for example, to the *Reichswehr* command post Bavaria on 9 September 1919 for the assignment of 70,000 marks per month, ibid., doc. no. 93.

47. Ibid., doc. no. 134 (24 November 1919).

48. Stroeßenreuther's refusal; ibid., doc. no. 135. The Bavarian Minister of the Interior decided on 18 December 1919 that 'the contents of the weekly reports which are now being sent to the government are not suitable for

transmission to any military stations. The presidents of the administrative districts are instructed to inform the *Reichswehr* brigades monthly on the political and economic situation with regard to its effects on public security', H. Nusser, 'Militärischer Druck auf die Landesregierung Johannes Hoffmann von Mai 1919 bis zum Kapp-Putsch', *Zeitschrift für Bayerische Landesgeschichte*, 33 (1970), p. 834; cf. also D. Hennig, *Johannes Hoffmann. Sozialdemokrat und Bayerischer Ministerpräsident* (München: Saur, 1990).

49. Cf. the letters by Braun (25 August 1919) and Lippmann (31 August 1919) to the Supreme Command of the Second Military Corps, Hürten, *Revolution*, op. cit., doc. nos. 79, 86.
50. Decree by the Prussian government on 21 July 1919; for the term *Staatskommissariat*, cf. the decree of 9 December 1919, Bundesarchiv Koblenz, Reichskanzlei R 43 I/2305; cf. also Ritter, op. cit., p. x. The German government supported its work financially and delegated two representatives.
51. For their competencies, cf. Gusy, op. cit., pp. 7–13.
52. The collected Prussian reports for the Weimar Republic are contained in the Bundesarchiv (Berlin); some of them are also in the Staatsarchiv Bremen.
53. Top secret memorandum by Albert, Bundesarchiv Koblenz Reichskanzlei R 43 I/2305.
54. Ritter, op. cit., p. xi.
55. Bundesarchiv Koblenz, Reichskanzlei R 43 I/2305.
56. For von Berger's political conviction, 'which lay in the rightist antidemocratic forces', cf. D. Orlow, *Weimar Prussia 1918–1925* (New York: Addison-Wesley, 1985), pp. 146–8; K.H. Pohl, *Adolf Müller. Geheimagent und Gesandter in Kaiserreich und Republik* (Köln: Bund, 1995), pp. 260–5.
57. Cf. for this point and for von Berger's attempts to bring about an agreement between Lüttwitz and the government during the insurrection, J. Erger, *Der Kapp-Lüttwitz-Putsch* (Düsseldorf: Droste, 1967), pp. 123–6.
58. On Weismann's activities, cf. (unjustifiably critical) H. Schulze, *Otto Braun oder Preußens demokratische Sendung* (Frankfurt: Propyläen, 1977), p. 377; more balanced is the characterization by A. Brecht, *Aus nächster Nähe. Lebenserinnerungen 1884–1927* (Stuttgart: DVA, 1966), p. 327.
59. Cf. the detailed depiction in E. Eimers, *Das Verhältnis von Preußen und Reich in den ersten Jahren der Weimarer Republik 1918–1923* (Berlin: Dietz, 1968), p. 341.
60. Ibid., p. 346.
61. Graf, op. cit., p. 21.
62. For individual organizations cf. Ritter, op. cit., p. xiii.
63. Ibid., Reichskanzlei R 43 I/2305 and the observations of G. Schulz, *Zwischen Demokratie und Diktatur* (Berlin: de Gruyter, 1963), p. 243.
64. M.Vogt (ed.), *Akten der Reichskanzlei. Das Kabinett Müller I* (Boppard: Boldt, 1971), doc. nos. 24, 88.
65. For the decree, cf. Reichsgesetzblatt 1920, p. 918; for Kuenzer, cf. Brecht, op. cit., p. 411.

66. The National Commissioner's reports, one of the most important sources of information on the history of domestic policy in the Weimar Republic, were published (on microfiche) in Ritter, op. cit. Although O.E. Schüddekopf used some parts for his book, *Linke Leute von Rechts* (Stuttgart: DVA, 1960), German historians have as yet underestimated the importance of these files.

67. See, for example, an internal memorandum of the Communist Party, Bundesarchiv Koblenz, R 134, vol. 2, pp. 17–20 or the confidential guidelines of the 'Organization Roßbach', which differed from its statutes, ibid., vol. 57, pp. 12–15.

68. G. Anschütz, *Die Verfassung des Deutschen Reiches vom 11. August 1919* (Berlin: Hobbing, 1933), pp. 289–95. In the event of a real threat to the *Reich*'s internal security, the national government was entirely dependent on the *Reichswehr* forces; R. Liepmann, *Die polizeilichen Aufgaben der deutschen Wehrmacht* (Berlin: Andermann, 1926), pp. 59-65.

69. Bundesarchiv Koblenz, R 134, vol. 54, p. 15 and Ritter, op. cit., p. xvi.

70. In 1919 the national government bore 2.5 million marks of the costs for the Prussian Office, yet in 1920 the national budget appropriated only 150,000 marks, and in 1929 only 413,500 marks for the National Office; ibid., vol. 67, pp. 111–19.

71. Weiss, op. cit., p. 110.

72. Cf. the detailed description of this case by W. Heine, *Sozialistische Monatshefte*, 45 (1926), pp. 203–5.

73. The news conferences of 28 and 29 April 1930 and of 14 December 1930 are reprinted in I. Maurer and U. Wengst (ed.), *Staat und NSDAP* (Düsseldorf: Droste, 1977), doc. nos. 6, 49.

74. Erich Koch-Weser, the Secretary of the Interior, had in 1919 already planned the establishment of a national criminal investigation office; this plan was thwarted by the opposition in the Federal Council. After Rathenau's assassination in 1922, the Act on the Organization of a National Criminal Investigation Department (*Reichskriminalpolizeigesetz*) was approved as part of the Act on the Protection of the Republic (*Republikschutzgesetze*) by the National Council; in the following years, however, the states prevented the law from coming into force, cf. Eimers, op. cit., pp. 344–6.

75. C. Severing, *Mein Lebensweg*, vol. 2 (Cologne: Bund, 1950), p. 164.

Unresolved Issues of World War II: The Records Still Closed and the Open Records Not Used

Gerhard L. Weinberg

More than half a century after the end of World War II, numerous questions and controversies about that great conflict are still shrouded at least partly in darkness because important records are still closed to research. Exactly whom these materials are being kept from and why is frequently hard to understand. By this time, one would think that secrecy serves little purpose. Privacy considerations concerning some records about individuals will remain for a few years yet, but national security? Whose, and from whom? The far greater danger, to which I have called attention repeatedly, is that the records themselves will have degenerated physically beyond recall before they are microfilmed or made accessible, or both;[1] but I suppose that this possibility is of little concern to those who insist that some files of the 1930s and 1940s cannot yet be seen by scholars.

In discussing the records still closed, recently released, and long since open but inadequately utilized, the discussion here is limited to materials which relate to intelligence in the broadest sense, including espionage and signals intelligence. The largest and most obvious collection of records still closed is that of the former Soviet Union. As David Glantz and Jonathan House make clear in their recent comprehensive study of the war on the Eastern Front, the archives of the former Soviet Union are steadily closing, not opening; and most of the operational records, to say nothing of the intelligence records, are simply not accessible to scholars on a regular and equal basis. Those with enough hard currency to dole out can get access to certain items, but nothing approaching real scholarly access on the sort of basis one is accustomed to in many Western archives is possible.[2] That leaves open innumerable questions, not only in regard to what the Soviet government learned, and what, if anything, it did with the knowledge, but also a host of other questions. When did the Soviet Union begin reading German Enigma traffic? When, if at all, did its decoders break into the traffic of the German teletypewriter enciphering machine, the *Geheimschreiber*? To what extent were the Soviets reading British and US codes, which ones, and when? Were they able to break into the machine codes of their Allies? Did their spies in Britain and the USA provide them with entry into machine codes? And if so, when?

A related set of questions concerns those records captured by the Red Army during and at the end of the war but not, as we now know, turned over to the former German Democratic Republic or the other European countries from whom the Germans had previously seized those records. Some of these materials have been microfilmed by the US Holocaust Memorial Museum – and those films are accessible in Washington (though often without the needed guides) – and some others have been made accessible to missions from other countries. There are several German projects which have been allowed access, and records have also been opened to other countries – Belgium for example.[3] What is at this stage by no means clear, however, is the extent to which the Soviets seized records of German and other intelligence agencies as well as whether any such archives will ever be made accessible.

Let me turn now to the Western Powers. Sir Harry Hinsley explained in the official history of *British Intelligence in the Second World War* that the authors of that multi-volume set did not provide citations for many important documents quoted or utilized in preparing their text because these documents were never to be opened.[4] Why statistical reports on German concentration and death-camp inmate numbers, for example, must be kept closed indefinitely is puzzling, to say the least. There have been hints that more sensible approaches will yet prevail, but there is surely much of interest still secret. With many of these messages there is an issue that will be referred to repeatedly: the intercept, whether in German or in translation, is frequently likely to be the only surviving version of a text of which the original has not survived in the German archives.

There have been substantial and important additions to the 'Ultra' materials opened up in the UK Public Records Office in Kew in recent years, such as the regular reports on Ultra for Prime Minister Churchill.[5] Nevertheless, my impression is that vast quantities remain closed, and this applies to other aspects of British World War II intelligence operations as well. This is also true for much pre-1939 material. My own experience in working on the origins of World War II has been that the records pertaining to British intelligence in the 1930s were almost invariably marked as closed into the second decade of the twenty-first century.

The USA has been more forthcoming than the other Allied powers of the war, a subject discussed further in this chapter; and under the impact of the Nazi and Japanese War Crimes Disclosure Legislation, important OSS and other materials have been and are in the process of being released. However, a major issue concerns captured German records about efforts to break into Allied codes. Since 1945, there has been a large collection of differing provenances, but all dealing with this subject, under joint British–US control. After a lengthy process, which culminated in the winning of a case by a committee I chaired before the Inter-Agency Classification Review Board in the 1970s, a massive quantity of these records was opened. The German navy's intelligence service (the *B-Dienst*) material in this opened material concerning German successes and failures in solving Allied naval and convoy codes, certainly provided important new insights into the Battle of the Atlantic, to mention only one example. But a substantial portion of this collection has remained closed; at different times I have heard estimates of 10,000 folders and 200,000 pages, estimates that sound rather similar to each other. When the secrecy on these records is lifted, we are likely to get some interesting new insights into the war.

It is possible that these records may become accessible before too long. On 4 April 1996, the National Archives made accessible to research a newly declassified addition to Record Group 457, the records of the National Security Agency (NSA), the organization that inherited materials pertaining to code-breaking from the US predecessor organizations in this field. The approximately million and a half pages in this collection, held in 1,479 cartons, deal overwhelmingly with codes and code-breaking in World War II. Included are massive amounts of material on German, Japanese, Italian, and US codes and code-breaking, as well as documents pertaining to World War II neutrals, from 1900 to 1950 with overwhelming emphasis on the World War II years.

Before discussing this collection further, let me explain why its release leads me to think that more may well be coming out in regard to the collection in joint British–US custody. The records now declassified by the NSA include important unpublished British histories of intelligence activities; like the collection as a whole, such materials would not have been released in Washington without concurrence by London. Since that concurrence was obviously forthcoming for this huge collection – in which there are all kinds of things that had been very closely guarded until then – it seems safe to assume that similar materials still closed on both sides of the Atlantic may be opened before too long. The 2000 and 2001 releases under the War Crimes Disclosure legislation constitute a good start, and they include intelligence records provided to the USA by the British and opened up with London's consent. There is, to mention only one example, a run of British intercepts of German Security Service (SD) messages from and to their office in Rome in 1943. Perhaps, one day, the British government will authorize the release of those intercepts that were not shared with the USA and for the release of which the US government therefore could not ask on the basis of holding copies.

Let me return to the collection opened in 1996. Obviously, I am in no position to describe it in detail; in fact, it is doubtful that anyone is in such a position. But some things can be said. The collection is entirely open without restrictions. There is a 112-page list of the collection that is also open to use and to copying and that is expected to be made available on the World Wide Web. This list, however, is quite summary in form and gives only the vaguest indication about the contents of individual files. It does help by providing some important clues to the general nature of what is included.

In the collection are massive quantities of documentation on German, Japanese, and Allied code-making and related activities. A substantial proportion is evidently of a highly technical nature, but this will not invariably be evident from the descriptions in the currently available inventory. A large number of items are in the form in which they were originally captured. In other words, we have here, at least for the time being, numerous folders in the original, captured in the field or at the end of the war. There are files of both cleartexts (deciphered texts) and intelligence summaries. Thus, Boxes 205 and 206 contain German OKW/Chi (High Command of the Armed Forces/Cryptography Unit) cleartexts of US State Department low-level diplomatic traffic from 1943–44, while Box 22 has summaries of economic intelligence about the Soviet Union issued by the Chief of the HNV *(Heeresnachrichtenwesen* – German Army Intelligence), 1943–45. The latter item illustrates a very important aspect of this collection: there are great masses of records concerning German signals intelligence on the Eastern Front. Included among the documents in this category are items which certainly appear from the descriptions to be Soviet materials captured by the Germans, integrated into their records, and then in turn captured from them by the Western Allies.

A most important group of documents included in the release is the run of British decodes of German Order Police *(Ordnungspolizei)* reports on the mass shooting of Jews in the first weeks and months of the German invasion of the Soviet Union. When these documents were referred to in the work by Professor Hinsley, it looked as if they were summaries of the notorious periodic reports of the special murder squads *(Einsatzgruppen)*. It now turns out that they emanated from an entirely different set of units and that those assigned the task of murdering Jews were vastly more numerous than had been thought previously. Here is a major way in which the release of intelligence records opens new perspectives on the Holocaust.[6]

In addition to enormous quantities of records from and pertaining to Japanese codes and code-breaking, there is also in this collection interesting documentation on Italy; thus, Box 147 has a file of Swiss diplomatic documents intercepted by the Italians in 1944–45.

It must be noted that the collection is by no means confined to the Axis side. There is extensive material on British and US code-making and -breaking activity. And the records on code-breaking by the USA are not confined to work on the codes of the Axis. Thus, Box 881 has a collection of US intercepts of low-level French diplomatic traffic of 1944–45. Some of this, as well as some other records, clearly goes into the early post-war period as well. And I must admit to having been a bit surprised to see considerable documentation on the code systems of most neutrals, including the Vatican, and as well as the codes of many Allied nations.

As the materials in this collection are worked over by scholars in the coming years, it seems quite likely that we will not only get a better picture of the intelligence activities, especially the signals intelligence activities, of all World War II participants and neutrals, but may well also have to revise widely held views of specific events and individuals. Let me mention just one example. The evidence available to Admiral Dönitz in the summer of 1943, as now further illuminated by material in this newly released collection, pointed with extraordinary clarity to the Allied ability to read German naval Enigma messages. Neither he nor key figures around him were willing to believe this or to take the necessary measures to alter the basic system that was no longer secure; measures of the sort the Allies took at about the same time when they discovered that the British convoy code was being read by the *B-Dienst*. In the reckless sending out of U-boats in the face of a compromised code system, we may now see a new reading of the title of the famous Nazi propaganda film, *The Triumph of the Will*.

One further comment has to be added on the subject of decrypts of German radio traffic. In the past it had been my opinion, based on what hints there were in the open record, that there was also a separate collection of intercepted German diplomatic messages grouped under the collective cover name of 'Floradora'. I am now tending to the view that these documents may well be included in the records already released but without any special designation identifying them as derived not from the reading of German Enigma systems but from *Geheimschreiber* transmissions and/or German misuse of one-time pads.[7]

Before we leave this whole complex of questions, at least brief reference needs to be made to other powers involved in the war. French World War II intelligence records are accessible in substantial quantities, even if they are by no means complete, evidently because of wartime losses.[8] Italian archives are also increasingly becoming accessible.[9] There will be plenty to do for all interested researchers. However, what seems to me especially troubling is the evident reluctance of scholars to exploit as extensively as possible records emanating from the field of intelligence that have been open for years, in some instances for decades. The time has come to turn to this aspect of intelligence records.

Beginning more than 25 years ago, the NSA opened for research massive collections of translations of intercepts of Axis messages, a high proportion Japanese but a substantial quantity German. These huge collections, with several of the series running to over 100,000 messages, have been utilized by a small number of scholars such as Professors Jürgen Rohwer, Edward Drea, and Carl Boyd, but most who work on the era of World War II have ignored them. Several of these series are a gold mine on an enormous variety of topics that many evidently have not thought of in connection with them. Japanese military and civilian diplomats were located all over Europe from Portugal to the Soviet Union, and they reported to Tokyo. These reports were frequently intercepted and decoded. And they cover all sorts of subjects. If you want insight into what was going on in Hungary during World War II, for example, here is a fine place to start because Japanese reports from there provide a picture which is difficult to obtain anywhere else. If you are interested in Pierre Laval's efforts to persuade the Germans to make a compromise peace with the Soviet Union so that the *Wehrmacht* could beat off an Allied invasion and keep France under German occupation, you need to read the reports of Mitani, the Japanese representative in Vichy. For new light on the situation in several countries of Latin America during the war, the Japanese reports from capitals such as Buenos Aires will be most helpful.

Professor Boyd has shown how the Allies benefited during the war from their reading of Japanese diplomatic traffic from Berlin.[10] Hinsley's history of British intelligence, previously mentioned, shows how that traffic helped the Allies keep track of significant developments in the field of new German weapons. What has not been sufficiently appreciated is the extent to which Japanese reports provide information on all sorts of internal developments in all the Axis countries; I would only mention the conversation between Mussolini and the Japanese Ambassador in Rome (Quirinal) on the day Mussolini was voted down in the Fascist Grand Council, the report on which is cited in my own history of the war.[11] Furthermore, Japanese diplomats and other representatives in the Soviet Union reported at great length on developments there as they saw them at the time. It must also be noted that for many of the conversations with high-level Germans, from Hitler on down, in the last year of the war, there are no surviving German records and no surviving Japanese records; the US translations of the intercepts appear to be the sole existing record.

In recent years, there has begun to be more sustained interest in the vast areas under Japanese control as a result of early Japanese victories, first in China and then in southern and Southeast Asia. Massive quantities of messages pertaining to all aspects of the history of Burma, Thailand, what was then French Indo-China, the Philippines, and the Dutch and British colonies of Southeast Asia may be found in the intercept collections. The course of the war between

Japan and China as well as Japanese policy in and toward the occupied portions of China and the puppet government Japan had established there can certainly be illuminated by the use of the intercepts. And it should also be noted that there are big runs of German diplomatic and military intercepts in these collections as well. A substantial proportion of the originals of these documents may not be found in the German records because of their loss or destruction during the war.

If one asks why this material has not been exploited to the extent that its importance warrants, I would offer three suggestions. The first reason may well be inherent in what has just been spelled out: those who work on any number of topics of the kind mentioned simply do not think of the vast collection of Japanese and German intercepted messages as a place to look for relevant information.

The second reason is that scholars have been as much misled as informed by what are called the 'Magic Summaries'. This massive series of contemporary summaries of the intercepts, prepared at the time for higher Allied authorities, has been widely publicized and extensively used. There is nothing wrong with using them unless one confuses them with the full collection and assumes that what intelligence experts at the time thought their masters needed to see quickly is all that the historian has to know about today. A striking example of this sort of confusion may be found in Ingeborg Fleischhauer's book on the secret German–Soviet soundings for a separate peace on the Eastern Front.[12] While finding all sorts of new and significant materials in Swedish and other archives, she badly misconstrued the soundings as a result of relying on the snippets included in the Magic Summaries instead of canvassing the collections of intercepts with their very extensive additional documents on the topic.

A technical aspect of these collections must also be recalled by historians who use them: messages were not always decoded right away for any number of reasons, but they were numbered and filed in the sequence of decoding and translating. Other messages might be thought to require prior attention from the limited number of available decoders; there could be garbles cleared up subsequently; there could be all sorts of other reasons for substantial delays in decoding messages which had actually been intercepted and could be read at least in part. References to such messages would generally not make it into the summaries at all when translated weeks, months, or even years later, because, whatever their significance, they were no longer

30

timely and therefore not worth calling to the attention of busy high-level officials. But the historian, though needing to know just when a piece of information became available to individuals in high positions in Allied governments, may still find that the contents are significant for what they tell us about the events recorded in them. Having spent what seemed like endless days and nights going through these lengthy runs of intercepts, I can sympathize with a preference for using the summaries; but a rich harvest will reward the diligence of patient scholars.

The third reason why so much of this material has not been taken into consideration by some historians is not quite so nice. Some of it simply will not fit into the preconceptions that have become established as something akin to revealed truth, and few are prepared to revise their most cherished interpretations. Let me illustrate this with one example, but a dramatic one. As Professor Rohwer demonstrated on the basis of some of the Ultra material many years ago, the British and US high commands used information from their reading of German naval Enigma to route their convoys around the U-boat lines in 1941 in order to avoid sinkings and incidents to the greatest extent possible.[13] It should be obvious that the information could have been utilized for exactly the opposite purpose: the bringing about of innumerable incidents between US ships and Germans submarines in the Atlantic.

If President Roosevelt had been as eager to involve the USA in the war as some imagine, here was the real as opposed to the imaginary back door to war.[14] With almost no exceptions, both US and German historians have preferred to ignore this dramatic evidence of the erroneous character of their preconceptions about Roosevelt. A recent 30-page discussion of the research and publications on US relationship to the war in 1939–41 in the leading US scholarly journal in the field makes no reference whatever to the Ultra material, then open for two decades, or to a single publication which takes it into account.[15] The idea of a US president hoping and trying to keep the country out of active hostilities while assisting others to defeat Germany is just too contrary to the cherished preconceptions of many to be allowed to intrude upon their constructs.

I conclude with a hint for those who may be working on the history of the last two years of the war. As the surviving German and Japanese record thins out, the collections of intercepts get thicker and better. The Western Allies were getting better at reading German and Japanese codes, and their intercept stations were moving closer to the transmitters and hence were less likely to miss whole messages or portions of them because of atmospheric conditions. Furthermore, as a by-product of the strategic bombing offensive, first the Germans and later the Japanese were obliged, because of the destruction of transportation and communications systems, to rely far more heavily on radio than they would have liked. Messages that earlier in the war would most likely have been sent by cable, mail, or messenger now had to be entrusted to the air in spite of the interception risks known to be involved. We now know that those risks were even greater than the Axis powers ever imagined.

A striking example of this was the Japanese plan code-named 'Damocles'. In what proved to be the final months of World War II, the Japanese planned to land a special suicide regiment on the islands of Tinian and Saipan in the Marianas in order to destroy the US B-29 bombers and their bases there. Many of the relevant orders and reports were sent by radio and therefore were intercepted by the US decoders. The USA then proceeded – in the last great wave of World War II air raids, in August 1945 – to destroy most of the Japanese planes designated for this operation on their bases on the ground. It was only after the war was over that the US high command learned that originally this same Japanese regiment was to have been landed by submarine on the coast of California, and was then supposed to storm inland to destroy the factories where the B-29s were being built. In the preparations for that earlier project, all the messages could still be sent by secure cables or similar means not subject to interception; but, by the summer of 1945, those means of communication had been so damaged by the bombing offensive that they could not be relied upon and the radio had to be utilized instead.[16]

But this process of increasing dependence by the Axis powers on radio as the means of communication even for the most sensitive types of messages and reports has had a compensatory effect for historians. Even as they lament the loss of such a high proportion of the German and Japanese records of 1944 and 1945, they are very likely to find translated intercepts of many highly important reports, orders, and other messages in the Public Records Office or the National Archives. That may well require rather more distant travel than some had anticipated – but then London and Washington are interesting places to visit.

32

NOTES

1. G.L. Weinberg, *Germany, Hitler, and World War II* (New York: Cambridge University Press, 1995), pp. 323–36.
2. D.M. Glantz and J. House, *When Titans Clashed: How the Red Army Stopped Hitler* (Lawrence, KS: University Press of Kansas, 1995).
3. D. Martin, 'Les archives de Moscou', *Bulletin de nouvelles du Centre de Recherche et d'Études Historiques de la Seconde Guerre Mondiale*, 30–50, 26 (1995), pp. 8–11.
4. F.H. Hinsley, *British Intelligence in the Second World War*, vol. 2 (New York: Cambridge University Press, 1981), Appendix 5 and pp. x–xi, 671, 673.
5. F.J. Harbutt, 'Recently Released Files from British Intelligence Records, 1943–1945', *Society for Historians of American Foreign Relations Newsletter*, 27, 1 (1996), pp. 27–31.
6. A very important book utilizing this new evidence is Richard Breitman, *Official Secrets: What the Nazis Planned, What the British and Americans Knew* (New York: Hill & Wang, 1998).
7. In a one-time pads system encoder and decoder of a message are the only ones who have access to a random book or pad of encryption they should use only once. There is a discussion of the attack on the German diplomatic code named 'Floradora' in *Stephen Budiansky, Battle of Wits: The Complete Story of Codebreaking in World War II* (New York: The Free Press, 2000), pp. 218–20.
8. Note the material from the Service Historique de l'Armée de Terre cited in M. Spivak, 'Vichy und der deutsch-sowjetische Krieg. Eine Chronik aus dem Untergrund', in R.G. Foerster (ed.), *'Unternehmen Barbarossa': Zum historischen Ort der deutsch-sowjetischen Beziehungen von 1933 bis Herbst 1941* (Munich: Oldenbourg, 1993), pp. 123–36.
9. See, for example, the book by R. Lamb, *War in Italy 1943–1945* (New York: St Martin's Press, 1994).
10. C. Boyd, *Hitler's Japanese Confidant: General Oshima Hiroshi and Magic Intelligence, 1941–1945* (Lawrence, KS: University Press of Kansas, 1993).
11. G.L. Weinberg, *A World at Arms: A Global History of World War II* (Cambridge: Cambridge University Press, 1994), p. 598 and note 43.
12. I. Fleischhauer, *Die Chance des Sonderfriedens: Deutsch-sowjetische Geheimgespräche 1941–1945* (Berlin: Siedler, 1986).
13. J. Rohwer, 'Die USA und die Schlacht im Atlantik 1941', in J. Rohwer and E. Jäckel (eds.), *Kriegswende Dezember 1941* (Koblenz: Bernard und Graefe, 1984), pp. 81–103.
14. This was the title of a particularly silly book by C.C. Tansill, *Back Door to War: The Roosevelt Foreign Policy, 1933–1941* (Chicago, IL: Regnery, 1952).
15. J.D. Doenecke, 'US Policy and the European War, 1939–1941', *Diplomatic History*, 19 (1995), pp. 669–98. Doenecke cites only a single work not in English in this lengthy bibliographic article – and the editors of the journal

evidently did not see a problem with this. But Rohwer's findings have been cited repeatedly in my own works published in English; perhaps that is what disqualified them from inclusion in the survey.

16. Weinberg, *A World at Arms*, p. 876.

3

Ethnic Germans as an Instrument of German Intelligence Services in the USA, 1933–45

Cornelia Wilhelm

From 1933 to 1945, the National Socialist Party (NSDAP) and the German intelligence services extensively used the organizational and personal networks of ethnic Germans and ethnic politics as a means for their political goals. The so-called fifth column had developed as a new factor during World War I, when German-Americans had been a target and a source of recruitment for the German intelligence services.[1] During the Nazi era, German intelligence again utilized recently immigrated Germans as 'ethnic agents' who were guided by political enthusiasm rather than by professional experience or by profound knowledge of their newly adopted country. Thus, they often tended to be a source of misunderstanding and acted unprofessionally. Accordingly, German intelligence in the USA was not very successful during either war. The Nazi party considerably overestimated these agents' potential as spies and saboteurs, partially because Nazi ideology assumed a superior 'racial value' in such 'folk Germans'. Desperately seeking politically reliable 'experts' on the Americas to help establish an infrastructure for a German spy network, they depended on contacts among recent immigrants.[2]

This chapter tries to shed some light on the role these ethnic Germans in the USA played in the recruitment and placement of agents and the planning of and participation in intelligence activities. Their actions are closely connected with German 'cultural work' abroad because the NSDAP redefined German culture as 'folk culture' (which valued 'blood, soil, and race'), rather than as high culture and traditional cultural refinement.

Intelligence work by German-Americans developed in three phases. The first phase was characterized by several first-time contacts of German Nazis or the German military intelligence agency, the *Abwehr*, with German-Americans in a series of decentralized and badly coordinated efforts. The driving force behind these contacts was fanatical devotion to the Nazi cause rather than a well-organized plan. The recruitment of agents was accidental, often depending on old political contacts of some of the immigrants with a strong NSDAP orientation who had worked as political propagandists. At this point, it was not the German officials who had a plan to recruit German-Americans, but ardent Nazi supporters in the USA who wanted to serve the adored party.

The second phase was launched when the USA devised strong measures to eliminate Nazi propaganda from the ethnic community. Government initiatives caused a small return migration of Germany's politically most reliable activists and intelligence spearheads in the USA. After their return to Germany, they were quickly incorporated into the party hierarchy and played a key role within a larger concept of information gathering and intelligence planning that also involved members of other fascist groups in the USA. In this concept, traditional academic research institutes and 'folkdom' organizations, which were well acquainted with the ethnic Germans' situation abroad and their ties to the old homeland, became a seedbed for the dissemination of propaganda, intelligence gathering, the establishment of secret organizations, and the recruitment of agents.

The third phase started with the beginning of World War II in 1939, when Germany initiated the repatriation of as many German-Americans to the Reich as possible – supposedly to support Germany's workforce – and in many cases thus recruited the actual agents, who were trained and then sent back to carry out intelligence operations. At that time, intelligence was mainly centralized in the hands of the party and the *Abwehr*. They tried to work professionally but could hardly achieve any successes because of the unprofessional behaviour of the German-Americans who had been recruited on the basis of their political convictions.

Although the USA was highly appealing to the leaders of the NSDAP in terms of the US *Lebensraum*, the 'racial potential of the white farmers in the USA', and its industrial productivity,[3] they lacked political supporters familiar with the USA and its people. Because of the Nazi ideology of a *Volksgemeinschaft*, the ethnic Germans' loyalty to another nation or state was ignored, and the political potential of German-Americans as part of a wider German community was misjudged.[4] Under their notion of 'folkdom', the party leaders totally disregarded the German-American immigrant experience, which involved an extremely fast assimilation into US society and values.[5] Very few German-Americans still felt any political ties to Germany in the 1920s, but Hitler assumed the German-Americans to be a culturally and politically active 'German' group of 20 million.[6] The only group Hitler could actually rely on in his plans to unify the diverse German-American groups under National Socialist ideology and revive the German-Americans' loyalties to the Reich,[7] was an organization of fanatical German Nazis in the USA, the German-American Bund. It consisted of Germans who had come to the USA in the 1920s and who perceived themselves as front-line fighters for Nazi ideology in North America and within the German-American community.[8]

Flattered by the political enthusiasm and idealism of this particular German immigrant organization, party officials believed that the Bund could motivate the already well-established German-American community. They did not realize that, precisely because their supporters were driven by fanaticism and idealism, they were hard to control, both in German-American diplomatic relations and in intelligence operations. Besides its propaganda activities, the German-American Bund was designed from its very founding in 1933 to work as a seedbed for intelligence activities and for the installation of a network of informants in the USA.

The *'Bunaste'* (*Bundesnachrichtenstelle*), the intelligence section of the Bund, was established under the control of the recent immigrant and ardent Nazi, Walter Kappe, who had been appointed head of *'Abwehr und Aufklärung'* in the USA.[9] Kappe was notified of this official decision by Heinz Spanknöbel, the first Bund leader in 1933. Spanknöbel had been one of the earliest and most fervent Nazi leaders in the USA, and he managed to win official recognition from the NSDAP during a short trip to Germany in early 1933, where he quickly established personal contacts with party officials. The two Nazi supporters had first met in Chicago in the 1920s, in the Germania Club, where they shared their political convictions with the recent immigrant Oscar Pfaus.[10] Although we do not know who granted 'official recognition' to Kappe – whether it was the party or the *Abwehr* – we know from other sources that the *Bunaste* between 1934 and 1935 had contacts with the *Abwehr* and started to establish a network of informants in the German-American community and in other pro-fascist US groups. Among those early agents was Count Friedrich Sauerma, alias Douglas or 'Dinter', a famous German pilot officer of World War I, who worked for his friend, Dr Schnuch (Spanknöbel's successor), as intelligence officer until the end of 1935, when an internal crisis disrupted the organization and Sauerma had to sever his affiliation with the Bund. Nonetheless, he continued to work for the *Abwehr* in the USA until 1941.[11]

At the same time, Dr Ignatz Griebel, another close friend of Spanknöbel in New York City, had offered his services to Goebbels and started an additional intelligence enterprise on the East Coast. This physician, who had emigrated from Munich in 1925, lived in Yorkville, New York's German quarter, as a much respected member of the community. He had belonged to the Steuben Society and the United German Societies of Greater New York, and he joined the Bund in 1932.[12] Together with Axel Wheeler-Hill, whose brother James was a leading Bund member, and the Philadelphia Bundist and Lutheran minister Kurt Molzahn, he took up intelligence work for the Gestapo and in 1934 switched to the *Abwehr*. Basically, Griebel used his popularity and his social network in the German-American community to recruit German-American engineers working in US defence plants to spy on the war industries.[13]

When Griebel and his spy ring were detected in early 1938, he fled to Germany on a North German Lloyd liner.[14] While Griebel opened a doctor's office in Vienna and seems to have withdrawn from intelligence work, we unfortunately have very little information on what happened to the first leader of the Bund when he returned to Germany, other than that Spanknöbel was hired by Goebbels's Propaganda Ministry.[15]

Apart from Spanknöbel, Walter Kappe stayed in the USA until 1936/37 and continued his work, which at that time merely meant passing on information on political aspects of the German-American community. Thus, he became a central figure for communications within the US network. At the same time, a few other agents were placed in the community and in US pro-fascist organizations with whom the Nazis considered cooperating in the future. Among them were Carl Günther Orgell, who officially served as the representative of the League for Germans Abroad (VDA) and who was well connected with the German-American community as secretary of Victor Ridder, the publisher of the largest German-American daily in New York City. In addition, he was a member of the Bund in New York City and worked also for William Dudley Pelley, the 'leader' of the Silver Shirts, a US fascist group which imitated the Nazi party.[16] Theodor Kessemeier, head of the Fichte-Bund in Hamburg and editor of the *Auslandsdeutscher Beobachter,* lived in Philadelphia, worked for the North German Lloyd company from 1933 on, and was a member of the Bund. He was in constant contact with Orgell and with Alexander von Lilienfeld-Toal,[17] who became Pelley's 'foreign adjutant' in 1933, while officially being employed by North German Lloyd in the USA. Lilienfeld-Toal relied on his very friendly relations with Kessemeier to funnel information home.[18]

In the following years, between 1934 and 1936, these individuals established social and informational networks, became well-known members of the German-American community, and regularly trans-mitted information to Germany on US politics, fascist groups in the USA,[19] and the German-American community. Because the German-American Bund openly admitted to being the US branch of the NSDAP and recruited US and German members in the USA as a predominantly political organization, the US government quickly responded with numerous official complaints to the German Embassy in Washington, DC.[20] Thus, by 1936, the NSDAP had to sever all official contact with the German-American Bund to prevent further diplomatic complications.[21]

But the NSDAP was far from actually giving up its idea of main-taining contacts with the German-Americans and from directing the work through such well-organized groups as the German-American Bund: from 1936 on, the party officially handed over its contacts with the Bund to 'cultural' organizations in Germany experienced in working with Germans abroad.[22]

These 'cultural' organizations became important primarily because they were sources of information, channels of influence, and means for the utilization of ethnic Germans by the German intelli-gence services. Because the Nazi *Weltanschauung* maintained that those Germans had emigrated and successfully survived in a foreign environment were the most valuable and energetic members of Germandom, it was only natural that the Nazis concluded that ethnic Germans, especially those who were convinced of their task, would be ideally qualified to undertake dangerous missions for their people and their home country. Supposedly, it was not always the decision of the *Abwehr*'s professionals to involve ethnic agents in actual sabotage and espionage but rather a matter of the political influence the party exercised on the *Abwehr*, contributing to the selection of ethnic agents and a growing involvement of 'folkdom' institutes in intelligence operations.

German 'folkdom' organizations, such as the *Verein für das Deutschtum im Ausland* (VDA [League for Germans Abroad]), the Fichte-Bund in Hamburg, and the *Deutsche Ausland Institut* (DAI [German Foreign Institute]) in Stuttgart had had close ties with Germans in the USA for decades. They were familiar with German-American communal structures because of their research materials and collections, and it was easy for them to supply information on geography, industry, and politics to German intelligence organizations. In the years between 1933 and 1936, these institutes had already operated intensively in the USA, albeit without much coordination and often competing with each other. But by 1936/37, the party had finally acquired firm control over all kinds of 'folkdom' work.

Among all these organizations, the DAI was of pivotal importance for the Nazi party. While other organizations often resisted strict party control, the DAI willingly cooperated and was eventually 'upgraded' in the party hierarchy to the status of major think-tank for Nazi 'folkdom' politics. The DAI was excellently connected in the USA and, unlike other institutions, it worked with both Germans who lived abroad and folk Germans. This was very important for the NSDAP, because its *Auslandsorganisation* (FO [Foreign Organization]) under Ernst Wilhelm Bohle was officially entitled to organize only Germans abroad who still were German citizens. In gaining political control over the folk Germans who were now US citizens, the party needed a trustworthy mediator. Richard Csaki, the director of the DAI in Stuttgart, as well as other employees, such as Gustav Moshack and Karl Klingenfuß, worked very closely with the FO of the NSDAP. Klingenfuß even switched to the FO. For the NSDAP, this cooperation seemed to be beneficial for both sides: while it secured political influence for the DAI, it provided the party with a partner that was reliable politically and in its actual propaganda and information work. At the same time, competition for influence and power, as for example, with the VDA, or the Deutsche Akademie (GA [German Academy]), was eliminated. That Stuttgart was designated as the 'City of Germans Abroad', underscored the party's decision to centralize all efforts related to 'folkdom' work in Stuttgart and around the DAI. At least from 1936 onwards, when the centralization of Nazi 'folkdom' propaganda had nearly come to an end, the DAI closely worked with representatives of the *Wehrmacht*, the German Foreign Office, and the party's FO.[23]

Unfortunately, we have little information about the Fichte-Bund of Hamburg,[24] originally established by the *Deutschnationaler Handlungsgehilfenverband*, and its destiny under the party's plans for reorganization. Most of what we know is based on the key position that Theodor Kessemeier held in the communication between the NSDAP, the Bund, and the Silver Shirts in the USA.[25] We do not have records to prove its connection with *Ast X* (*Abwehrstelle X*, a sub-branch of the *Abwehr* located in military district X, Hamburg, which was responsible for espionage in Britain and the USA), but, in 1939, the *Oberkommando der Wehrmacht* (OKW [German High Command]) made it clear how important the Fichte-Bund and the DAI would be in the event of a future war and in regard to eventual post-war planning, revealing how heavily its work was based on the two institutes' information and their networks.[26]

Parallel to the reorganization of *Volkstumspolitik* in the Reich, another development was triggered by the US government's open opposition to the Bund. Some of the most fanatical and idealistic Nazi activists returned to Germany in early 1936 because they felt they could help the National Socialist cause more in Germany than in the USA. We do not know whether they had at this point been 'encouraged' by the NSDAP to return, but this is highly likely. Almost all return migrants received positions in the party's foreign departments dealing with the USA. They were well connected with one another and made up for the lack of US specialists that had existed in the NSDAP. Among them were Fritz Gissibl, Sepp Schuster, Walter Kappe, Hugo Haas, and Ernst Vennekohl, all of whom had become members of the Bund very early on. Fritz Gissibl, supported by Ernst Wilhelm Bohle, started to work for the *Reichspropagandaamt* in Württemberg and soon became interoffice coordinator of the FO in the 'City of Germans Abroad'. At the same time, Mayor Karl Strölin, who was president of the DAI, rewarded him with an important position in the administration of the institute, while he also served as deputy for matters related to Germans living abroad for the city of Stuttgart. The accumulation of all those posts made Gissibl a very

41

central figure in any project on Germans or German-Americans in the USA involving the city, the party, or the institute.[27] Similarly, other former Bundists filled key positions in the party's hierarchy: Ernst Vennekohl led the US department of the VDA; Hugo Haas, who had formerly organized the Bund's youth group, now became head of the US department of the Hitler Youth; Sepp Schuster, a participant in the Hitler Putsch in 1923, was given a position at the *Reichs-ministerium für Volksaufklärung und Propaganda* (Ministry of Propaganda and Enlightenment);[28] Walter Kappe continued collecting 'news' in the DAI in Stuttgart as head of the press department;[29] Emil Goppelt became head of the division for return migration of the party's FO in Hamburg; and Georg Nebbe was given a post controlling the process of repatriation at the *SS-Volksdeutsche Mittelstelle*.[30]

In the following two years to 1938, the DAI in Stuttgart began to serve as the central think-tank for Nazi 'folkdom politics' in the USA and continued to do so even after the *Volksdeutsche Mittelstelle* had taken over all matters related to Germans abroad in 1938. In 1938, the DAI became *the* central element in the *Volksdeutsche Mittelstelle*'s planning in relation to the USA.[31] At the beginning of the year 1938, the *Volksdeutsche Mittelstelle* had launched the establishment of a North America department within the DAI. This new department was supposed to have two branches, one branch for 'practical work' and one 'research branch', which enabled it to contact directly German-Americans in the USA. Within this system, the newly founded *Kameradschaft USA* was to play a central role in transmitting information and as a major link between German bureaucracy and the USA.[32]

Staff members of the DAI, such as Heinz Kloss, Otto Lohr, Gustav Moshack, and Katharina Reimann, were responsible for the 'research' on North America. They established 'regional research groups' on ethnic Germans in the USA and made use of all available contacts and knowledge to produce information for the party and the military. They were also cooperating with the German-Americans in Cleveland, Ohio, and the NSDAP-funded *Deutsch-Amerikanisches Komitee* (German-American Committee), which was called the *Heimatkundeausschuss* and was organized rather loosely.[33] Several newly founded smaller research institutes in Germany were supposed to gather as much information on Germans abroad as possible. Those institutes focused on a number of regional ethnic German groups, such as the Swabians, the Lower Saxonians, or the Rhinelanders, who had tended to settle in distinct regions of the USA. The names of these new institutes associated with the DAI in Stuttgart were *Forschungsstelle Niedersachsen im Ausland, Forschungsstelle Schwaben im Ausland, Rheinländer in aller Welt,* and *Schlesier in aller Welt*. German researchers in the USA could thus gather detailed information on specific regions in the USA and were able to claim they had found 'scientific evidence' for German cultivation of the soil and German culture in the USA.[34] The DAI in Stuttgart and its affiliates produced elaborate regional maps of German settlements, German language islands in the USA, and the American surroundings. These maps supposedly provided evidence for the political reliability of German-American settlements in the USA,[35] and furnished information on their social and political organizations, lists of such organizations, and personal records of immigrants and their employment.[36] In Hamburg, Heinz Kloss, one of the most active 'researchers' of German-Americans on the payroll of the DAI in Stuttgart, was to become director of the *Publikationsstelle-Übersee*, a joint effort of the Foreign Office and the DAI established in 1941[37] and charged with publishing research material related to the USA for 'internal use of the party'. The material was to inform the foreign departments of the party and the *Wehrmacht* on details of US politics, society, and economy potentially useful for German propaganda.[38] They also continually worked on directories of German emigrants to the USA and their German relatives in order to be able to stay in touch with these emigrants and possibly to blackmail German-Americans into loyalty to the Reich.[39]

For the so-called practical work, the *Kameradschaft USA* was officially designated by the *Volksdeutsche Mittelstelle* as a social club of returned migrants, and it was associated with the DAI in Stuttgart where it had its offices. Its first head was Fritz Gissibl. He was succeeded by Walter Kappe, who had also decided to return to Germany in 1936/37 and continued to be a key figure in the establishment of a German-American intelligence network. As leader of the *Kameradschaft*, he was supposed to coordinate communications with the Bundists in the USA. Some of the individual members of the *Kameradschaft* had assumed important positions in party organizations central to the recruitment of agents. Besides Kappe, who never stopped working for the *Abwehr*, these were Emil Goppelt and Georg Nebbe. By providing this network, the *Kameradschaft* served two aims of the NSDAP. It provided a solid network for communications with politically reliable German-Americans and, because all members were enthusiastic and highly idealistic Nazis well connected with the party's organization, the *Kameradschaft* seemed to guarantee strict political control of the Nazis abroad.

But keeping the German-American Bund under control worked only to a limited degree: the idealism and energy of the movement and its leaders created their own dynamics. While the 'American Leader Fritz Kuhn' spent most of his energy on 'Hitler-like' aggressive appearances instead of carrying out 'cultural work', concern about German-American loyalty increased among the US public and within the US government. From 1936 to 1941, the state and federal agencies in the USA were intensively dealing with the problem of how to prevent the likely actions by possible 'German Agents in the United States'.[40] Officials never tried to 'outlaw' the ordinary German-American, but it was not easy for the US government to react to the threat of a possible fifth column. In light of Germany's increasing aggressiveness in Europe, fear of an uncontrollable fifth column in the USA mounted, particularly after the German annexation of the Sudetenland in 1938.[41]

After the beginning of World War II in Europe in September 1939, Germany's aim was to keep the USA out of the war. Thus, open sabotage by German agents had to be avoided because it might endanger US neutrality.[42] During this period, the *Abwehr* merely tried to establish a well-working but 'sleeping' web of agents, informants, and potential saboteurs, for which it recruited a number of German-Americans, all of whom were more or less connected with the Bund.

The only activities German agents did carry out were strictly political and designed to keep the USA out of the war. After the 'Nazification' of the larger German-American community had failed and the US government started to scrutinize seriously all German-Americans whose loyalty was questionable, the German government severed all official contacts with the Bund. 'For tactical reasons, direct German propaganda in the United States is not to be carried out. This is why intelligence work has to be carried on as long as possible. ... It seems to be necessary to act through indirect and covert actions to rock the basis of the political mood of all Anglo-American attempts at union',[43] Dr Adam von Trott of the German Foreign Office declared, outlining the basis of the German political planning that was to prevent the USA's entry into the war as a British ally.

In the following years, the German government continued a World War I pattern of propaganda: the German chargé d'affaires, Hans Thomsen, contacted the Kaiser's former agent, Georg Sylvester Viereck, who had been secretly pulling the strings for the Bund over the past years, setting up connections with well-established German-American societies. Viereck had stayed away from ardent political speeches and the militaristic image of the Bundists, although he had long been on the payroll of the NSDAP and acted as correspondent of the *Münchener Neueste Nachrichten* in the USA. He was paid by the German Foreign Office and the 'German Library of Information'.[44] He was now approached to help the German officials,[45] whose former concepts had failed, and his publishing company Flanders Hall as well as the Irish newspaper *The Leader*, with which Viereck had established contact, printed Nazi propaganda.[46] This setup was lucrative for the publishers: the potential publisher of a proposed weekly publication with the title *From the Heart of America to the Hearts of Americans* was offered a weekly payment of $17,000.[47]

Viereck also contacted members of Congress to support isolationist propaganda.[48] With the approval of Senator Hamilton Fish, long-standing member of the Steuben Society, and supported by Viereck, George Hill, who served as Fish's secretary in Congress, mailed over one million postcards, on the stationery of the US Congress, expressing profoundly anti-Roosevelt propaganda. This initiative was paid for by the US taxpayer.[49] The biggest coup Viereck arranged, however, was the launching of an isolationist committee during the Republican Party convention in the summer of 1940, which was meant to work actively against the Committee to Defend America by Aiding the Allies.[50] Already one week after Thomsen had contacted Viereck, he could report to the German Foreign Office how successful the German agent had been in arranging that 'isolationism' had become part of the Republican platform for the upcoming election.[51]

In addition, one of these networks established connections with the Ukrainian Hetman Organization, a fascist organization, whose leader Anastase Andreevich Vonsiatsky had become a very close friend of the Bund leader Fritz Kuhn and his successor Gerhard Wilhelm Kunze. A supporter of tsarist Russia, Vonsiatsky had left the Ukraine in 1920 after the Bolshevik revolution. While in exile in Paris, he had contacted secret organizations that were fighting the communists, as did many Russian refugees of the time. He gathered a group of White Russian, Lithuanian, and Ukrainian followers and established contacts with early members of the NSDAP, such as Emil von Scheubner-Richter and Alfred Rosenberg.[52] Coming to the USA after marrying a millionairess from Chicago he had met in Paris, he founded the Hetman Organization. In the early 1930s, Vonsiatsky presided over a Japanese–White Russian–Ukrainian intelligence network in the USA, which also helped the *Abwehr* to funnel money to German agents. This might suggest that the money Vonsiatsky in 1939 spent on bail for Fritz Kuhn, who had been sentenced for the misappropriation of the Bund's funds, actually came from Germany. The major gun-running and communications operations Vonsiatsky conducted to Latin America took place on the Pacific coast, and the most active members of the German-American Bund working with Vonsiatsky were Gerhard Wilhelm Kunze, Wolfgang Ebell from El Paso (who served as a contact with Mexico), Kurt Molzahn, and Otto Willumeit, a Chicago Bund leader. The Vonsiatsky–Kunze group was held responsible for several minor accidents on the East Coast in 1941 and for the sabotage of four plants of the Brewster Aeronautical Company and a warship plant in New York, where over 30 employees, belonging to the Bund and to the Hetman Organization, were arrested.

Problematic for the Ukrainian–German intelligence cooperation in the USA proved to be the year 1939, when Hitler decided to sign the non-aggression treaty with Stalin, formerly a common enemy of both groups and the initial rationale of their cooperation. But although Vonsiatsky did not officially attend any meetings with the German-American Nazis after the treaty was signed, he continued his intelligence cooperation intensively until this operation was broken up by the US authorities in 1942.

Even more important for the development of a network of informants in the USA than this cooperation was the German-American return migration in 1939 and 1940 and Kappe's *Kameradschaft USA*. Since 1938, the German embassy in Washington, DC, had organized a large campaign for the remigration and resettlement of German-Americans from the USA in Germany.[53] Officially, remigration was offered to German-Americans who still held German citizenship and who, under the new US laws, had to register as 'agents of foreign principals'. But the campaign was also addressed to German-Americans who were already naturalized

Americans. Meant to 'save' German nationals from US government registration, it depicted a shining image of the 'New Germany' and offered jobs to those willing to return to Germany. Officially labelled by the German Foreign Office as a 'labour recruiting campaign' among well-trained German workers in the USA, it was to provide a chance for returnees to contribute to Germany's new wealth and to plans for German settlement in occupied Poland.[54] Those few German-Americans who actually decided to return to Germany were often Bundists who wanted to avoid registration and were highly attracted by Nazi Germany.

The German consulates, which were responsible for the organization of the return migration, registered the migrants' names, their former place of residence, relatives in Germany, and the intended places of migration in Germany.[55] Although the programme targeted only a relatively small number of the 250,000 Germans living in the USA, German officials perceived it as a chance to recruit those who had not been critical of the Reich and who felt uncomfortable with the new registration laws.[56] For the return migrants, it seemed only natural that German authorities also requested information on former employment, skills, and details concerning possible future employment. Once the German-Americans arrived in Germany, they were taken care of by the FO, the VDA, or the *Volksdeutsche Mittelstelle*. Those party organizations tried to help them find a job, settle down, and reclaim citizenship, if this was necessary. As has already been pointed out, it was former Bundists such as Nebbe and Goppelt who were in charge of the departments handling return migration from the USA as part of the *Kameradschaft*'s network of gathering information on possible agents for the *Abwehr*. George John Dasch, later a German agent in the USA, described his arrival and registration in Berlin in the following words: 'The final step in my processing was a lengthy interview with two men, both of whom had lived many years in the United States. One of them, who introduced himself as Mr Walter Kappe, suggested I give up the idea of going to work for the Farben Trust. "A man with your knowledge of English and of America in general does not come to Germany every day and would be wanted by almost every department of the German government"'.[57]

The most important cases of recruitment of German-Americans were the following. One of the 'return migrants' was Oscar Pfaus, whom I have already mentioned as a companion of Kappe and

Griebel. In the 1930s, he was active in the Chicago Bund and edited the German *Weckruf und Beobachter*, the Nazi newspaper of Chicago, until he decided to return to Germany in 1938. There, he first became director of the Fichte-Bund in Hamburg and got in direct contact with the *Abwehr*. In 1939, he was sent to Ireland to recruit IRA terrorists for the *Abwehr* and to learn about the Irish underground in New York City and Boston, getting in personal touch with the head of the IRA in the USA, Sean Russell.[58] This contact, he suggested, could serve as a new base for operations in the USA for the *Abwehr*. The proposed plan suited the *Abwehr* very well, because, as has been pointed out earlier, for political reasons German sabotage was prohibited by the Foreign Office. Shortly thereafter, Admiral Wilhelm Canaris and General Erwin Lahousen of the *Abwehr* actually sent Karl Franz Rekowski as contact person, or V-man, to the USA to arrange sabotage operations to be carried out by the IRA. In autumn 1940, the Hercules powder plant in Kenvil, New Jersey, was the operation's first target with 52 persons killed and 50 injured in the sabotage; three war plants in New Jersey and Pennsylvania were to follow.[59]

Another returnee was Axel Wheeler-Hill, the brother of James Wheeler-Hill, a high-ranking Bund functionary working in the German Foreign Office, who returned to Germany in 1938 to join his brother. Here, James Wheeler-Hill recommended his brother for a training programme in the *Abwehr* in which Axel learned how to transmit coded messages. Although Axel Wheeler-Hill did not prove very talented at this job, the *Abwehr* sent him to New York in 1940 to establish an *Abwehr* network together with another young German-American, Felix Jahnke; they were both naturalized Americans. Once in New York, Wheeler-Hill quickly activated his transmitting station with the help of friends of the German-American Vocational League, but, in 1941, the FBI arrested all 29 German agents belonging to the Wheeler-Hill/Jahnke ring, a major setback for German operations in the USA. The wave of arrests of German agents by the FBI in 1941 and the political pressure to secure American neutrality caused Lahousen in 1941 to state that now 'all bridges to the US were destroyed'.[60]

Thus, the *Abwehr* did not have a functioning network for sabotage in the USA at the beginning of the war. This might in part explain why experienced men of the *Abwehr* finally accepted a project which did not impress them from the very beginning and that turned out to be the biggest failure of the *Abwehr* in the USA. Again, return migra-tion explains how Walter Kappe, who had advanced in the intelligence hierarchy and who was now servicing the *Abwehr* Section II 'Sabotage', recruited George John Dasch for the *Abwehr*. Kappe, a newcomer in the *Wehrmacht* and a 'party man', had been trying for some time to interest Captain Dr Richard Astor and General Lahousen in 'his plan' and 'the friends he would have at hand'.[61] Dasch was one of them: a German-American return migrant, who, like many of them, did not have an easy time adjusting and finding the job in Germany the German campaign had promised.

When Kappe interviewed return migrants applying for new papers, he met Dasch, as well as ten other men, whom he recruited for his project. Although Canaris and Lahousen were very sceptical of Kappe's plan, they finally had to accept it. Kappe, who, as Lahousen put it, 'spoke like a circus manager, who was offering the tricks of his artists', was obviously not experienced with the planning and organizing of such an operation. Both Canaris and Lahousen knew this well, but had to give their consent, because Kappe was strongly supported by members of the NSDAP. At that time, right after Germany had declared war on the USA in December 1941, the party pushed for sabotage actions there. Therefore, the *Abwehr*, which had lost its more professional agents in the arrests by the FBI in 1941, had little choice but to agree to Kappe's plan.

In the spring of 1942, after some training at Quenzsee, Operation Pastorius[62] was launched. In addition to George John Dasch, it included seven other ethnic Germans from the USA: Ernst Peter Berger, Heinrich Heinck, Edward Kerling, Herman Neubauer, Richard Quirin, Werner Thiel, and Herbert Haupt. Two submarines each landed four men on the US coast in June 1942. The German agents were to sabotage a hydroelectric plant in New York and aluminium factories in Illinois, Tennessee, and New York, as well as a few other targets, such as railways and water-supply systems. While one submarine arrived in Florida, Dasch and three other men landed on Long Island. Until today, it is not clear why Dasch and his men landed in full German uniform and spoke German to each other when they were first discovered by a member of the US Coast Guard. Was it just their lack of professionalism? Or was it part of Dasch's 'bigger' plan? This plan, which he claimed to have had right from the beginning of his recruitment, was as follows. Shortly after getting ashore, Dasch would leave his fellows and tell the FBI about the

German operation, and he would thus contribute to one of the most embarrassing setbacks for German intelligence work in the USA. While Dasch persistently claimed that he had had the intention to surrender to the FBI right from the time Kappe hired him, his 'honourable' motives leave much to be explained because the operation cost the lives of six of his companions.[63] One of the victims of Kappe's failure was Herbert Haupt, whose behaviour demonstrates how unprofessionally the so-called 'agents' of Operation Pastorius acted. Haupt came from a Chicago German-American family. His father was already known to the OSS as one of those German-Americans who, even after the beginning of the war, actively supported the 'German cause'. His enthusiastic son had left the USA to make his fortune in the old homeland and to work for the party his father so admired. There, like Dasch, he had been recruited by the *Abwehr*. Once back in the USA in the service of German intelligence, he so wanted to see his parents that he visited them in Chicago.[64] The result was not only his arrest and later execution, but a spectacular lawsuit and three sentences for 'high treason', which involved not only the actual German agents, but also a number of families that were related to the Haupts in Chicago.

Because of the embarrassing failure of this operation, the *Abwehr* made no further attempts to recruit German-Americans. Operation Pastorius marked the end of German-Americans' involvement in German intelligence efforts in the USA. Kappe joined the *Wehrmacht* and was killed in action before the end of the war. The actual effect of the use of ethnic agents turned out to be, on top of the failure of the actual operations, highly counter-productive in a wider sense: the entire German-American community in the USA increasingly was perceived as 'potential, if not actual, spies'.[65]

NOTES

1. Reinhard R. Doerries, *Imperial Challenge: Ambassador Count Bernstorff and German-American Relations, 1908–1917* (Chapel Hill, NC: University of North Carolina Press, 1989), pp. 39–76, 141–4, 155–90.
2. Ernst Hanfstängel, *Zwischen Weißem und Braunem Haus* (München: Piper, 1970). Kurt G.W. Lüdecke, *I Knew Hitler* (London: Jarrolds, 1938), pp. 290ff.
3. Gerhard A. Weinberg, 'Hitler's Image of the United States', *American Historical Review*, 69 (1964), pp. 1006–21; Gerhard Weinberg, *Hitlers*

Zweites Buch (Stuttgart: DVA, 1961), pp. 160f; Institut für Zeitgeschichte, ed. *Hitler: Reden, Schriften, Anordnungen, Februar 1925–Januar 1933. Volume 2*, 2 (München: Sauer Verlag, 1992), p. 447; Gerhard Weinberg, 'Von der Konfrontation zur Kooperation, Deutschland und die Vereinigten Staaten 1933–1949'; Frank Trommler, ed., *Amerika und die Deutschen. Bestandsaufnahme einer 300jährigen Geschichte* (Opladen: Westdeutscher Verlag, 1986), pp. 393–405.

4. Heinz Kloss, *Um die Einigung des Deutschamerikanertums. Die Geschichte einer unvollendeten Volksgruppe* (Berlin: Volk und Reich, 1937), p. 13. See also Colin Ross, *Unser Amerika* (Leipzig: F.A. Brockhaus 1936), p. 25.

5. Reinhard R. Doerries, 'Organization and Ethnicity: The German-American Experience', *Amerikastudien*, 33 (1988), pp. 309–17; Cathleen Neils Conzen, 'The Paradox of German-American Assimilation', *Yearbook of German-American Studies* 16 (1981) pp. 153–60. Lüdecke, *I Knew Hitler*, p. 270.

6. Ross, *Unser Amerika*, p. 25; Kloss, *Um die Einigung des Deutschamerikanertums*, p. 13.

7. Sander A. Diamond, *The Nazi Movement in the United States* (Ithaca, NY: Cornell University Press, 1974), pp. 55ff.

8. 'Zum Geleit' *Vorposten*, 1 (1 October 1930), p. 1: American Jewish Archives, Cincinnati (AJA), Mss. Coll. # 202 Jewish Community Relations Committee, Cincinnati, Box 1.

9. Heinz Spanknöbel to Walter Kappe, 6 July 1933, Politische Abteilung III (Vereinigte Staaten von Amerika), Po 26, vol. 21, Politisches Archiv, Auswärtiges Amt (PA AA), Bonn.

10. Oscar C. Pfaus was born in Illingen, Germany, in 1901, and emigrated to the USA (Chicago) in the early 1920s. He founded the Chicago 'Germania Club' together with Heinz Spanknöbel and possibly Walter Kappe, a member of the Friends of the New Germany and the German American Bund. For his wartime career, see below. After 1945, he lived in Hamburg. Enno Stephan, *Geheimauftrag Irland. Deutsche Agenten im irischen Untergrundkampf 1939–45* (Oldenburg: Gerhard Stalling Verlag, 1962), pp. 19ff; John P. Duggan, *Neutral Ireland and the Third Reich* (Dublin: Gilland Macmillan, 1985), pp. 59–63, 149; Julius Mader, *Hitlers Spionagegenerale sagen aus* (Berlin: Verlag der Nation, 1971), p. 169.

11. Ladislas Farago, *The Game of the Foxes* (London: Pan Books, 1971), pp. 333ff.

12. Dr Ignatz Theodor Griebel was born in Würzburg, Germany, in 1899. He was an artillery officer in World War I, became a US Army reservist and worked as a physician in Yorkville, Manhattan. He was recruited in the 1920s by Paul Kraus of the *Abwehr X* in Hamburg and had close contact with Josef Goebbels through his brother Karl. Farago, *The Game of the Foxes*, pp. 42ff; William Breuer, *Nazi Spies in America* (New York: St Martin's Press, 1989), pp. 10ff.

13. Farago, *The Game of the Foxes*, pp. 42ff, and Breuer, *Nazi Spies in America*, pp. 14ff.

14. Breuer, *Nazi Spies in America*, pp. 94ff.
15. Breuer, *Nazi Spies in America*, p. 13. Both Griebel and Spanknöbel were in close contact with the Nazi Propaganda Ministry and Dr Hellmuth von Feldmann, who was responsible for the US division of the ministry and had contacted the Bundists on his frequent visits in the USA.
16. Heinz Nixdorf, Reichsführerschule Bernau near Berlin, without address, 30 September 1933: Bundesarchiv, Koblenz (BA), Slg. Schumacher 420; and testimony by Paul von Lilienfeld-Toal and Theodor Kessemeier, HUAC, 73rd Congress, 2nd Session, *Public Hearings at Washington, DC, June 5–7, 1934*, (Washington, DC: GPO, 1934); Paul von Lilienfeld-Toal to 'Bob' (Bob Summerville), 14 August 1933, Exhibits, Tray 13420; Records of the Committee to Investigate Nazi and Other Propaganda Activities, RG 233, National Archives.
17. Hans Adolf Jacobsen, *Nationalsozialistische Außenpolitik 1933–1938* (Frankfurt/M.: Metzner, 1968), p. 94. For information on Kessemeier's background see Iris Hamel, *Völkischer Verband und nationale Gewerkschaft* (Frankfurt/M.: Europäische Verlags-Anstalt, 1967), pp. 125ff.
18. Testimony by Paul von Lilienfeld-Toal and Theodor Kessemeier, HUAC. Lilienfeld-Toal was born in the Baltic states.
19. The NSDAP was mainly interested in William Dudley Pelley's group, the Silver Shirts; Suzanne G. Ledeboer, 'The Man Who Would be Hitler: William Dudley Pelley and the Silver Legion', *California History*, 65 (1986), pp. 126–36.
20. Memorandum of the Legal Adviser of the Department of State, 21 October 1933: Department of State Central Files, Box 4729, RG 59, NA; Cordell Hull to Ambassador William Dodd, 6 February 1934, US Department of State, *Foreign Relations of the United States, 1934*, vol. 2, p. 530 (hereafter cited as *FRUS* with year and volume number). William Dodd to President Roosevelt, 15 August 1934, Franklin D. Roosevelt Papers, President's Personal Files (PPF) 1043, Roosevelt Presidential Library, Hyde Park, NY; memorandum by Cordell Hull 28 June 1935, *FRUS, 1935*, vol. 2, p. 482; memorandum by Cordell Hull 7 September 1935, *FRUS, 1935*, vol. 2, p. 486; memorandum by the Chief of the Division of European Affairs, 29 July 1935, *FRUS, 1935*, vol. 2, pp. 483f.
21. Hans Luther to German Foreign Office, 29 December 1934: Politische Abteilung III (Vereinigte Staaten von Amerika), Po 26, vol. 23, PA AA; memorandum Alexander v. Fuehr, 16 October 1933, *Akten zur deutschen Auswärtigen Politik. Aus dem Archiv des Auswärtigen Amts* (hereafter cited as *ADAP*), Series C, vol. 2, pp. 5ff; telegram from Hans Luther to German Foreign Office, 11 February 1934, *ADAP*, Series C, vol. 2, p. 248, 256f; circular letter to all Party Members in the USA, 1 February 1934, by Ernst Wilhelm Bohle, Politische Abteilung III (Vereinigte Staaten von Amerika), Po 26, vol. 17, PA AA. Memorandum referring to 'Der Bund der Freunde des Neuen Deutschland', by Alexander v. Führ, 13 December 1935, Politische Abteilung III (Vereinigte Staaten von Amerika), Po 26, vol. 27, PA AA.
22. Hans Luther to German Foreign Office, 28 June 1935, including

'Niederschrift über kulturpolitische Fragen in den Vereinigten Staaten', *ADAP*, Series C, vol. 4, pp. 374ff; memorandum of Hans Wilhelm Freytag in the German Foreign Office, 11 October 1937, Politische Abteilung IX, Po 25, vol. 3, PA AA.

23. Ernst Ritter, *Das Deutsche Ausland Institut* (Wiesbaden: Steiner, 1976) pp. 41, 60, 108ff, 121, 131ff, 145; Hans Adolf Jacobsen, *Hans Steinacher, Bundesleiter des VDA 1933–1937, Erinnerungen und Dokumente*, Schriften des Bundesarchivs 19 (Boppard: Boldt, 1970), pp. 289ff; Donald McKale, *The Swastika Outside Germany* (Kent, OH: Kent State University Press, 1977), p. 115; memorandum 'Über die Volkstumsarbeit deutscher Stellen in den Vereinigten Staten von Amerika', by Twardowski, 4 April 1940: Politische Abteilung 6A, Deutschtum Nr. 1, Deutschtum in Nordamerika, vol. 16, PA AA.

24. Although there was some research on the Fichte-Bund done by Nelson Edmundson, he very much underestimated its importance and activity, especially during the Nazi period. Nelson Edmundson, 'The Fichte Society: A Chapter in Germany's Conservative Revolution', *Journal of Modern History*, 38 (1966), pp. 164–80. Much more reliable is the information on the Fichte-Bund provided by Iris Hamel in her study of the Deutschnationaler Handlungsgehilfenverband; Hamel, *Völkischer Verband und nationale Gewerkschaft*, pp. 125ff.

25. John Roy Carlson (alias Arthur Derounian), *Undercover: My Four Years in the Nazi Underworld of America* (Philadelphia: E.P. Dutton and Co., 1943), pp. 72f. Theodor Kessemeier to German Foreign Office, 24 June 1932, Politische Abteilung, Presseabteilung, Fichte-Bund, vol. 1; Theodor Kessemeier to Adolf Hitler, 10 February 1933, ibid.

26. Protocol of a meeting of representatives of the OKW, Reichsministerium des Inneren (RMI), Reichsministerium für Volksaufklärung und Propaganda (Promi), Stellvertreter d. Führers, Foreign Office, Winterhilfswerk (WHW), Adolf Hitler-Spende (AH)-Spende der Dt. Wirtschaft am 6 April 1939, gez. Ehrenkauf, Kulturabteilung, Geheim, Dt. Fichte-Bund, vol. 1, PA AA.

27. Witness of Fritz Gissibl in Nürnberg, 2 January 1948: Institut für Zeitgeschichte Archives, (IfZ), Nürnberger Prozesse (NG) 4624. Ritter, *Das Deutsche Ausland Institut*, pp. 111ff.

28. Letter to K. Strölin, 28 July 1939 (most probably by F. Gissibl), Hauptarchiv der NSDAP, NS 41/13, BA. M. Sgt. Ransom Taylor to Lt. Col. Hans W. Helm, 21 January 1946, NS 20/127-14, BA.

29. Letter to K. Strölin, 28 July 1939 (most probably by F. Gissibl): NS 41/13, BA.

30. Order of the Kameradschaftsleitung, no date, gez. Walter Kappe, NS 20/127-15, BA; Ernst Schuster and Ernst Vennekohl, 11 December 1939, NS 20/127-9, BA; also Raymond E. Murphy, *National Socialism* (Washington, DC: GPO, 1943), p. 89.

31. Memorandum on the meeting with Ogruf. Werner Lorenz, Volksdeutsche Mittelstelle (VOMI), 23 May 1937: Captured German Records (CGR), DAI, Reel 443, Library of Congress (LC), Washington, DC. See also Karl Strölin

to Werner Lorenz, 24 May 1937, ibid.; Strölin to Lorenz, 27 May 1937, ibid.; and 'Aussprache nach der Besichtigung', Strölin to Lorenz, 27 May 1937, ibid.

32. Memorandum for Gissibl ('zur beliebigen Verwendung in seinem Memorandum an den Verwaltungsausschuß des DAI'), no date [after April 1938], without signature [most probably by Otto Lohr], private collection of S.A. Diamond.

33. Memorandum on German 'folkdom' work in the USA by Twardowski, 4 April 1940, Politische Abteilung VIA, Deutschtum, Nr. 1, Deutschtum in Nordamerika, vol. 16, PA AA. See also Heinz Kloss to Stahmer, VOMI, 15 February 1938, CGR, DAI, Reel 474, LC. See also Klaus Kipphan, *Deutsche Propaganda in den Vereinigten Staaten 1933–1941* (Heidelberg: C. Winter, 1971), pp. 44ff. See also 'Gründung eines Ausschusses für Heimatkunde', *Deutscher Weckruf und Beobachter (Chicago)* 4, 12 (27 March 1937), p. 1; and 'Grosser Erfolg der amerikadeutschen Heimatkundetagung in Cleveland', *Deutscher Weckruf und Beobachter* 4, 11 (20 April 1937), p. 1. The organizing committee of the Heimatkundeausschuss was composed of Dr Glasser, Dr Reichle, Prof. Krüger, Pastor John Foisel, Karl T. Marx, Theo Breuer, Fritz Kuhn, and Carl Günther Orgell.

34. Norbert Zimmer, *Der Siedlungsweg der Niedersachsen über die Erde* (Hannover: Selke, 1934); Norbert Zimmer, *Deutsche 'buten und binnen', Ein Bericht über Weg und Ziel volksdeutscher Forschungsarbeit in Niedersachsen* (Hannover: Selbstverlag 1938).

35. Heinz Kloss, *Atlas der im 19. und frühen 20. Jahrhundert entstandenen deutschen Siedlungen in den US* (Marburg: Elwert, 1975). See also O.A. Isbert, 'Kartographische und statistische Methoden im Volkstumskampf', *Deutschtum im Ausland*, 25 (1942), pp. 21–5. Roswitha Czollek, 'Nationale Minderheiten.im Konzept imperialistischer Expansionsstrategie. Zur Rolle des Deutschen Ausland-Institutes Stuttgart (DAI) in den Jahren der faschistischen Kriegsvorbereitung', *Jahrbuch für die Geschichte der sozialistischen Länder Europas*, 19 (1975), p. 144. Heinz Kloss, 'Über die mittelbare kartographische Erfassung der jüngeren deutschen Volksinseln in den Vereinigten Staaten', *Deutsches Archiv für Landes- und Volksforschung*, 3 (1939), pp. 453–74.

36. Fritz Konrad Krüger, Wittenberg College, Springfield, OH, to Hans Steinacher, VDA, 16 November 1937, printed in Jacobsen, ed., *Hans Steinacher*, doc. 142, pp. 478ff.

37. *Innerdienstliche Mitteilungen des Deutschen Ausland-Institutes* 9 (18 December 1941), CGR, DAI, Reel 373, LC. See also Heinz Kloss to Dr Goeken, German Foreign Office, 6 June 1940, Politische Abteilung VIA, Deutschtum Nr. 1, Deutschtum in Nordamerika, vol. 16, PA AA.

38. *Innerdienstliche Mitteilungen des Deutschen Ausland-Institutes* 9 (18 December 1941), CGR, DAI, Reel 373, LC. Compare with the letter of H. Kloss to Regierungsrat Ferdinand Goeken in Foreign Office, 6 June 1940. The letter refers to the distribution of Kloss's study 'Sippenkundliche Amerikadenkschrift', which was to be mailed to 26 departments as strictly

confidential matter; Politische Abteilung VIA, Deutschtum Nr. 1, Deutschtum in Nordamerika, vol. 16, PA AA. In 1940 the study was printed and published for interoffice distribution; Kloss's name was not mentioned. Deutsches Ausland-Institut, ed., *Vorschläge für die sippenkundliche Erfassung der Reichsdeutschen Amerikawanderer des 19. Jahrhunderts* (Stuttgart: DAI, 1940). Martin Dies, *Die Propaganda totalitär gesinnter Gruppen in den Vereinigten Staaten 1917/18.* Schriftendienst Übersee 2 – nur für den Dienstgebrauch! (Stuttgart/Hamburg: Publikationsstelle Übersee, 1942). Compare also Alfred-Ingemar Berndt, Ministerialdirektor, Propaganda-ministerium, to Reichsministerium des Inneren, 19 April 1943, Politische Abteilung Inland IIC, Deutschtum Nr. 2, DAI, vol. 14, PA AA. Katharina Reimann, Publikationsstelle Stuttgart-Hamburg to Foreign Office, Inland IIC, 11 May 1944: Politische Abteilung, Inland IIC, Deutschtum Nr. 2, Überseedt. Forschungsgemeinschaft, vol. 6, PA AA. Haupt-schuljungsamt der NSDAP, ed., *Amerika als Zerrbild europäischer Lebensordnung.* Schulungs-Unterlage 19 (München: NSDAP, 1942). Wilhelm Feldner, *Europa und Amerika, Fehlerquellen im Aufbau des amerikanischen Volkstums.* Schulungs-Unterlage 18 (München: NSDAP, 1942); Reichsorganisationsleiter, Hauptschulungsamt der NSDAP, ed., *Lebensraum – Schlagwort oder Notwendigkeit?* Schulungs-Unterlage 26 (München: NSDAP, 1944); Ernst Schmitz, *Die deutsche Leistung in den Vereinigten Staaten von Nordamerika.* Schulungs-Unterlage 17 (München: NSDAP, 1942).

39. FBI report by W.H. Caver at Albany, NY, 6 September 1940, RG 59, Box 3023, NA. See also Kipphan, *Deutsche Propaganda in den Vereinigten Staaten 1933–1941*, p. 37.

40. FDR to Cordell Hull, 15 August 1942, Franklin Delano Roosevelt Papers, President's Secretary's Files (PSF), Confidential File, State Department 1941–1942, Box 9, Roosevelt Library.

41. Francis MacDonnell, *Insidious Foes. The Axis Fifth Column and the American Home Front* (Oxford: Oxford University Press, 1995) pp. 29ff; Louis De Jong, *Die Deutsche Fünfte Kolonne im Zweiten Weltkrieg* (Stuttgart: DVA, 1959), pp. 108ff. Major Truman M. Martin, Infantry, Assistant Chief of Staff, G-2, to Assistant Chief of Staff G-2, War Department, E.R. Warner McCabe, 17 June 1940, War Department, Military Intelligence Division, RG 165, Box 2857, NA. Harold Ickes to FDR, 11 September 1939, Franklin Delano Roosevelt Papers, PSF, Departmental Files, Box 55, Roosevelt Library. Dorothy Thompson, 'How Shall We Meet Nazi Propaganda?', *The Nation*, 20 December 1933, pp. 70ff.

42. Thomsen to Foreign Office, 18.9.1939, Politische Abteilung IX, Po 23, vol. 1, PA AA. Farago, *The Game of the Foxes*, p. 90. MacDonnell, *Insidious Foes*, p. 69. The Rumrich spy case, which involved also Ignatz Griebel, contributed heavily to this caution.

43. Memorandum re 'Amerikapropaganda', Dr von Trott, 19 November 1940, Kulturabteilung, Geheim, Nordamerika, vol. 1, PA AA.

44. John O. Rogge, *The Official German Report: Nazi Penetration 1924–1942* (New York: Yoseloff, 1961), pp. 131, 135.
45. Thomsen to Foreign Office, 13 July 1940, *ADAP*, Series D, vol. 9, doc. 422. Rogge, *The Official German Report*, pp. 259–73.
46. State Department Special Interrogations Commission, Testimony Heribert von Strempel, 18 November 1945, IfZ, Mikroverfilmte Akten (MA) 1300/3, Blatt 539–546. Telegram, Thomsen to Foreign Office, 26 November 1940, Politische Abteilung, Kult Pol. Geheim, Nordamerika, vol.1, PA AA; telegram, Stahlecker to Dr Werth, 13 January 1941, ibid.; telegram, von Altenburg, German Consulate General San Francisco, to Foreign Office, 29 November 1940, ibid.
47. Telegram, Thomsen to Foreign Office, 22 July 1941, ibid., vol. 2, PA AA.
48. Rogge, *The Official German Report*, pp. 266, 269. Lundeen, Fish, and Viereck had been friends for years.
49. Rogge, *The Official German Report*, 160ff. Sumner Welles to FDR, 27 July 1942, Franklin Delano Roosevelt Papers, PSF, Confidential File, Box 9, Roosevelt Library; Thomsen to Foreign Office, 30 July 1941, Kulturabteilung, Geheim, Nordamerika, vol. 2, PA AA.
50. Thomsen to Foreign Office, 12 July 1940, Büro des Staatssekretärs (St.S.), USA, vol. 2, PA AA. For the Committee to Defend America, see also Michael Wala, 'Selling War and Selling Peace', *Amerikastudien/American Studies*, 30 (1985), pp. 91–105.
51. Telegram, Thomsen to Foreign Office, 19 July 1940: Büro des Staatssekretärs (St.S.), USA, vol. 2, PA AA. Farago, *The Game of the Foxes*, pp. 420ff.; Breuer, *Nazi Spies in America,* pp. 178ff.
52. Charles Higham, *American Swastika* (Garden City, NY: Doubleday, 1985), pp. 123–7; Georg Franz-Willig, *Die Hitlerbewegung. Der Ursprung 1919–1922* (Hamburg: von Decker, 1962); and Walter Laqueur, *Deutschland und Russland* (Berlin: Propyläen, 1965), pp. 72ff.
53. Green H. Hackworth, Legal Adviser, Department of State, to Cordell Hull, 28 January 1938, RG 59, Box 4730, NA.
54. Weizsäcker to Thomsen, 31 December 1938, Büro des Staatssekretärs (St.S.), USA, vol. 1; FBI report by J.R. Morrison on Labor Recruiting Campaign conducted in the US by German Volkswagen Werke, 26 June 1944, Records of the Army Staff, RG 319, Entry 47, Box 464, NA; Sydney B. Redecker, Consul General, Frankfurt am Main, to Secretary of State, 3 July 1946, RG 59, Box 6727, NA; Hermann Göring to Governments of the Länder, Foreign Office, Stellvertreter des Führers, Oberpräsidenten in Preußen, den Staatspräsidenten der Reichshauptstadt Berlin, re 'Weiterbehandlung von Einbürgerungsverfahren', 11 January 1940, NS 20/127-8, BA.
55. Hans Borchers to German Foreign Office, 6 December 1940, Büro des Staatssekretärs (St.S.), USA, vol. 1, PA AA; Borchers to German Foreign Office, 22 November 1940, Kulturabteilung, E, vol. 1, PA AA. See also memorandum Schellenberg, 24 January 1940, Inland IIg, Berichte und Meldungen zur Lage in und über Amerika, vol. 1, PA AA; and Schellenberg to Neuwirth, 9 February 1940, ibid.

56. Memorandum of the Ansiedlungsstäbe Posen und Litzmannstadt, Abteilung Planung, 10 February 1941, IfZ, MA 225, Blatt 9332-9339.
57. George John Dasch, *Eight Spies Against America* (New York: Robert M. McBride Co., 1959), pp. 37ff.
58. Stephan, *Geheimauftrag Irland*, pp. 22f.
59. Farago, *The Game of the Foxes*, p. 559.
60. Interview with General A.D. Erwin Lahousen: IfZ, ZS 658.
61. Ibid.
62. The name of the operation refers to the first group of German immigrants to the British North American colonies in 1683, who were led by Franz Daniel Pastorius.
63. Dasch, *Eight Spies Against America*, pp. 76, 219ff. Dasch's autobiography is highly criticized in Jürgen Thorwald, *Der Fall Pastorius* (Stuttgart: Steingrüben Verlag, 1953), pp. 116ff. Thorwald is very suspicious of Dasch's motives for his betrayal. On this issue, see also Eugene Rachlis, *They Came to Kill: The Story of Eight Nazi Saboteurs in America* (New York: Random House, 1961), pp. 291ff.
64. Otto Richard Wergin was a member of the Germania Club in Chicago, of which Oscar Pfaus, Heinz Spanknöbel, and Walter Kappe had been members. Obviously, the membership of this club had been a seedbed for later intelligence activity. Foreign Nationalities Branch of the Office of Strategic Services (FNB) – report by Albert Parry on the German-Americans of Chicago, 25 August 1942, Records of the Office of Strategic Services, RG 226, Int. 13 GE 345, NA. Shirley J. Burton and Kellee Green, 'Oaths of Allegiance, Acts of Treason: The Disloyalty Prosecutions of Max Stephan and Hans Haupt', *Prologue* 23 (1991), pp. 242ff.
65. J. Edgar Hoover to Marvin H. McIntire, 27 July 1942, Franklin Delano Roosevelt Papers, PSF, Departmental File, Box 57, Roosevelt Library.

4

Pioneering Research and Analysis: The R & A Branch of the Office of Strategic Services and Its Legacy

Petra Marquardt-Bigman

The idea that the standard index card might well have been 'the most powerful weapon'[1] in the arsenal of the US wartime intelligence agency, the Office of Strategic Services (OSS), will hardly conform to the prevalent image of this agency which – not without reason – has been blamed for having 'set a precedent for each and every malodorous operation of its successor organization, the Central Intelligence Agency (CIA)'.[2] However, the conduct of questionable clandestine operations was by no means the only or most enduring legacy of the OSS. Rather, I will argue that those OSS members who made skilful use of their index cards and pioneered intelligence research and analysis set a precedent, which was emulated in the CIA and is still evoked in debates about reforms of US intelligence. Yet, their achievements did not change the fact that 'Starting with the OSS and continuing into the early CIA, Intelligence lost out to Operations in the struggle to set the fundamental mission of American intelligence.'[3]

The following outline of the history of the OSS Research and Analysis (R & A) Branch[4] will therefore not only describe the accomplishments of this branch, but also address some of the historical reasons for the institutional marginalization of intelligence analysis. Discussing how R & A's achievements as well as its problems continued to influence the organization and conduct of US intelligence after the dissolution of the OSS in September 1945, I will attempt to highlight a legacy that has been overshadowed by the

James Bond glamour of clandestine operations not only in the intelligence community, but also in history books.

When William J. Donovan tried to convince President Roosevelt in spring 1941 that the USA needed a 'central enemy intelligence organization' in order to cope with the threat of war, he emphasized the vital importance of an 'effective service for analyzing, comprehending, and appraising ... information'.[5] Perhaps the most innovative aspect of Donovan's proposal was his suggestion to recruit for this task 'carefully selected trained minds', namely, scholars from all academic fields.

While Donovan's ambitions went far beyond heading an expert intelligence research and analysis service, this was the role which was – at least officially – assigned to him, when Roosevelt established the Coordinator of Information (COI) in July 1941.[6] With the help of Archibald MacLeish, the Librarian of Congress, as well as representatives of academic organizations, it took Donovan barely a few weeks to recruit an impressive number of Ivy League scholars. Having thus laid the basis for a group which was later characterized as 'the most brilliant team of analysts in the history of intelligence',[7] Donovan turned his interest and energies to building up the branches he really felt passionate about: psychological warfare, sabotage, and subversion. His fascination with covert operations of any kind never diminished his genuine respect and appreciation for the work of R & A, but the branch that had ostensibly been meant as the centrepiece of the COI soon found itself relegated to a minor post in the COI budget, and under constant pressure to prove its usefulness.

However, how exactly the branch could and should prove its worth was a question which had no ready answer, since there had never been anything like a highly qualified staff of academic professionals working in US intelligence. Donovan had originally envisaged that the scholars assembled in R & A – historians, social scientists, linguists, economists, geographers, psychologists, and technical experts – would continue to work as they had before their recruitment for R & A, providing information and reports based on open sources available in their field. That they were also expected – and expecting – to utilize information gathered by the COI and other government agencies turned out to be one of the first and most persistent problems encountered by R & A: the wartime need for secrecy offered a perfect excuse for indulging in bureaucratic jealousies and misgivings. Moreover, the established government agencies tended to regard Donovan's COI as just another superfluous addition to a bureaucracy expanding in preparation for a war that many wanted to avoid. Making a contribution to the already ongoing war effort was – to say the least – rather difficult under these circumstances.

But despite these problems, R & A soon succeeded in demonstrating that scholars had indeed some contribution to offer. The staff were eager to refashion intelligence work by establishing rigorous academic standards; to their dismay, they found that even time-honoured methods such as the 'inductive and deductive processes of analysis' were 'surely and shamefully new' in this field.[8] R & A economists early developed creative methods of supplementing their meagre data, and already in December 1941, in one of their first studies of the 'German Economic and Military Position',[9] they presented results which could not easily be ignored, since they contradicted much of the accepted wisdom of the time (and, by the way, eventually proved correct).

When the Japanese attack on Pearl Harbor and the US' entry into the war triggered a debate about the reorganization of US intelligence in early 1942, R & A was already regarded in some quarters as 'a school of advanced research of the highest caliber which can readily be used effectively'.[10] But when the COI was eventually renamed Office of Strategic Services and subordinated to the Joint Chiefs of Staff, the military regarded Donovan's agency primarily as their 'shadow warfare' arm responsible for 'planning, development, coordination, and execution of the military program for psychological warfare'.[11] Covert operations such as sabotage, espionage, and the support of resistance groups thus gained clear priority over intelligence research.

R & A's official task now consisted of compiling and evaluating the information necessary for the conduct of covert operations, but the work of the branch was made no easier by its integration into the military apparatus. On the contrary, the access to up-to-date information became rather more difficult, since even within the OSS the colleagues who plotted secret airborne missions to drop agents behind enemy lines showed little inclination to share their 'secrets' with their 'chairborne' colleagues from the R & A 'Campus'. While R & A thus had little choice but to continue to focus on background research – which naturally was of limited value to current military operations – the branch still managed to gain a reputation as the most respected part of the entire OSS operation.

This success was partly due to a reorganization of the branch at the end of 1942. Reflecting the conviction that research neatly compartmentalized into established academic disciplines was inadequate to comprehend the 'total' war being fought, R & A's original division into functional and geographical units was abandoned in favour of integrated regional divisions, a change which anticipated the organization of area studies. Thus, for example, the newly established Europe–Africa Division under the direction of Yale historian Sherman Kent comprised subdivisions for political, economic, and geographical research. The potential for interdisciplinary cooperation created with this new structure soon proved essential for R & A's work. The branch also benefited from a change in leadership, when the historian William Langer took over its direction in autumn 1942, and with the recruitment of new staff, R & A eventually expanded to some one thousand men and women, among them future Nobel laureates, presidential advisers and many of those who shaped the US academe after the war.

In contrast to its first year of existence, when R & A had to work hard to establish its reputation and to interest potential clients in its products, the branch found itself now sometimes hardly able to keep up with its workload. One project which proved particularly work-intensive was the Civil Affairs Guides Program commissioned in July 1943 by the War Department in preparation for the occupation and military government of Germany.[12] But while this project put a heavy strain on R & A's resources, it also allowed the branch to become involved in post-war policy planning. This seemed particularly advantageous in view of the fact that the OSS with its focus on covert operations faced a rather uncertain future once the war ended. However, R & A soon had to realize that post-war policy planning was developing into a veritable minefield. The ambition of the branch to create professional standards for intelligence research and analysis by adapting scholarly methodologies was motivated in part by the contemporary optimism about the potential of the social sciences to produce 'objective' results, which could be used to formulate and implement rational, objectively 'right' policies. That there was, however, precious little agreement on what constituted objectively 'right' policies became all too obvious during the work on the Civil Affairs Guides Program that involved a variety of government agencies, each of which advocated its own point of view on what US policy objectives in Germany should be and how they could best be achieved. The rigid dictates of military necessity compelled R & A to accept many compromises and illustrated that R & A had to control carefully its scholars' ambition to influence policy on the basis of their professional expertise.

Internal guidelines for the preparation of political reports consequently emphasized that R & A had to avoid acting like a pressure group – 'no matter how strongly we may believe we are right'.[13] The staff were admonished to produce sober, objective, and informative studies, in which political recommendations – 'whether explicit or veiled' – had no place, because 'the readers of our political reports commonly have a prior conviction on the subject under discussion, convictions based on considerable knowledge of the material'. Taking into account that the recipients of R & A's reports were usually pressed for time and would find voluminous academic treatises of little value, the guidelines also demanded that each study be preceded by a concise summary highlighting the major issues of the subject as well as the conclusions drawn from the analysis; the study itself was to serve mainly as illustration and evidence.

Like these guidelines, some internal papers illustrate the confidence of the branch that it was ideally suited to meet Washington's demand for 'first-class political research on foreign countries'. However, some R & A members had come to doubt that Washington decision-makers were able to recognize or appreciate 'first-class research'. Indeed, while government agencies – particularly the Departments of War and State, as well as the Joint Chiefs of Staff (JCS) – made considerable use of R & A's services, the branch got little feedback and was left to guess the impact of its work. Least affected by this situation were R & A's economists, whose work, though not without faults, largely justified their lack of modesty. However, those R & A scholars who were working on political reports had ample grounds to feel frustrated: not only did they find it intellectually and psychologically impossible to follow their guidelines and work on post-war policy issues without formulating policy recommendations; but they also had to face the fact that Washington's debate on post-war policy questions had little to do with scholarly 'objectivity'.

While historians have tended to discount the contribution of their colleagues in R & A, President Truman awarded R & A director William Langer the highest civilian honour, the Medal for Merit, in recognition of his competent leadership 'in pioneering the production of vast quantities of studies, surveys, handbooks, and guides which were of inestimable value in the prosecution of the war'.[14] The president also decided that the branch should not be dissolved with the rest of the OSS in September 1945. In order to ensure 'that pertinent experience accumulated during the war will be preserved and used in meeting the problems of the peace', Truman ordered the transfer of R & A to the State Department, which was mandated to 'take the lead in developing a comprehensive and coordinated foreign intelligence program'.[15]

Even if critics charged that Truman showed a 'limited intelligence perspective',[16] it was by no means unreasonable to abolish the 'shadow warfare' capabilities of the OSS at the end of the war, while preserving the research and analysis function, which had clear (and proven) peacetime uses. However, the idea that the State Department would be capable of using R & A as a basis to create a foreign intelligence service, which would produce centralized intelligence research and analysis for all federal agencies including the military, soon proved quite unrealistic. Indeed, even though Under-Secretary of State Dean Acheson had convinced Secretary of State James F. Byrnes that R & A's work during the war had been 'invaluable' and that it would be 'disastrous' to abolish the branch together with the OSS,[17] R & A scholars found that most of their new colleagues regarded them as unwelcome competition and set out to marginalize them with considerable bureaucratic sophistication. Under these circumstances, many of those who had decided to stay on in Washington beyond the end of the war felt that their career as intelligence analysts offered little perspective and started to leave.

When it became obvious that the State Department was unable to establish a central foreign intelligence service, the debate about the organization of US post-war intelligence, which had started in mid-1944, was taken up again. Eventually those who advocated the establishment of a central intelligence agency more or less closely modelled after the OSS, gained the upper hand. As one historian put it: 'Harry Truman had killed the OSS in 1945 but had failed to drive a wooden stake through its heart; it rose again as the CIA.'[18] By mid-1947, when Congress passed the National Security Act and thereby also authorized the first peacetime US intelligence agency, many had become convinced that only the war, but not the peace had been won. In the unfolding 'Cold War', the 'shadow warfare' strategies developed in the OSS could easily appear as the perfect instrument to safeguard US security interests without fighting a 'hot' war.

However, the newly established CIA built not only on the legacy of the operational branches of OSS, but also on R & A's bequest. When the CIA director, General Walter Bedell Smith, decided to reorganize intelligence research and analysis after the agency had failed to predict the outbreak of hostilities in Korea in June 1950, he turned to William Langer. Arguing that 'national estimates were of the utmost importance as the basis for sound decision making',[19] he managed to convince Langer to take an extended leave from Harvard in order to set up an Office of National Estimates (ONE) within the CIA. Langer organized this office as a somewhat elitist, miniature 'Research and Analysis Branch' with a staff of some 50 scholars, whose responsibility was to provide Washington decision-makers with National Intelligence Estimates (NIE). The broader functions of intelligence research were assigned to a newly established Office of Research and Reports (ORR) with a staff of several hundred persons. However, neither the massive expansion of the CIA's intelligence capabilities in the early 1950s nor the fact that intelligence was formally established as one of the CIA's principal activities under the Directorate for Intelligence, which soon employed more than 3,000 people, meant that intelligence had finally gained priority – or even parity – with operations.

Yet, the ONE's authoritative position as the sole source of estimative intelligence gave it a very different standing within the CIA and the administration than R & A had ever enjoyed, and while NIEs may have been regarded as a new form of finished intelligence, they were in reality modelled on R & A studies. But R & A's most enduring legacy was probably the professionalization of intelligence research and analysis. In the CIA, this legacy was personified by Sherman Kent, who had directed R & A's Europe-Africa Division and succeeded Langer after the expiration of his leave from Harvard in early 1952 as head of the ONE, a position he held until his retirement in 1967.[20] Already in 1949, Kent had published a book on *Strategic Intelligence for American World Policy*,[21] which was one of the first systematic treatments of intelligence analysis and became the standard work read by students and practitioners in this field. As head of the ONE, Kent continued his efforts to establish intelligence analysis as an intellectual discipline with a well-ordered methodology reflecting the highest scholarly standards. In his view, that was indeed the only way to cope with the dilemma that had so plagued many R & A scholars and was inherent in the intelligence analyst's work: while he (or, rarely, she) was supposed to study thoroughly an issue and to apply his or her scholarship and expertise to arrive at conclusions, the analyst could not expect that the decision-maker would necessarily act in accordance with these conclusions. Reminiscent of the R & A guidelines, Kent warned his staff that all they should aspire to achieve was the decision-maker's confidence in the quality and objectivity of their work.

But while the NIEs did acquire a reputation for detached objectivity and intellectual integrity, they also became vulnerable to the criticism of irrelevance. This was again a problem that had already confronted R & A, and it resulted in part from the practice of initiating studies internally, which had been R & A's solution at a time when the branch still had to advertise its capabilities. However, even in R & A, the intelligence analyst's ambition to define his subject himself was not only motivated by necessity, but also by the – perhaps 'platonic' – aspiration of the scholar to guide the king, which, not surprisingly, was seen by some as intellectual arrogance. In any case, whatever intellectual arrogance the ONE displayed, it was matched when another scholar, National Security Adviser Henry Kissinger, began to ignore the – in his opinion 'Talmudic' – NIE.[22]

The dissolution of the ONE in 1973 perhaps marked the end of those aspects of R & A's legacy which implied a concept of intelligence as a primarily, or even exclusively, scholarly discipline. With the perceived acceleration of history, a new notion of intelligence developed, which has been characterized as owing more to journalism than to scholarship.[23] Since journalism does have standards of excellence, this characterization does not necessarily imply a negative judgement of quality. However, the re-emergence of age-old hatreds, tensions, and conflicts after the end of the Cold War, as well as concerns about a potential 'clash of civilizations', seem to warrant the conclusion that a scholarly perspective spanning centuries might still be able to contribute something to intelligence.

The end of the Cold War has also reopened the debate on the relative importance of intelligence and operations. This discussion has been carried on intermittently over the past decades and has produced several proposals to reform US intelligence by reducing covert operations and increasing intelligence research and analysis. The latest example is perhaps Roger Hilsman's article in the *Foreign*

Affairs issue of September 1995,[24] which calls for the transformation of the CIA into an 'independent research and analysis organization'. As Hilsman points out, his proposal goes back to ideas discussed in the early 1960s, when the Bay of Pigs fiasco triggered a debate about a reform of US intelligence. But the end of the Cold War has made it possible to consider even more fundamental reforms of the US intelligence community, not least because it has allowed the deeply rooted US mistrust of government secrecy to re-emerge. This traditional resentment joined forces with a new awareness that there is a need to re-examine how intelligence should be defined in the 'information age'.[25] In view of the proliferation of information processing throughout the government and society as a whole, it seems questionable whether it makes sense still to understand intelligence as it commonly is conceived, namely, as *all* the information necessary for the decision-maker. Thus, for example, the information gathered and processed by some big investment company may very well be essential for a political decision – but should it therefore be classified as intelligence? And, even more importantly, would a centralized government agency be able to provide it? As a member of the Working Group on Intelligence Reform has recently suggested, the information age might actually allow for a rather narrow definition of what constitutes intelligence – and therefore requires some measure of government secrecy – since much of the 'intelligence' needed by the decision-maker can readily be found where Donovan turned when he established the R & A Branch.

NOTES

1. R.W. Winks, *Cloak & Gown. Scholars in the Secret War, 1939–1961* (New York: Morrow, 1987), p. 63; cf. also B.F. Smith, *The Shadow Warriors. OSS and the Origins of the CIA* (New York: Basic Books, 1983), p. 361.
2. R.H. Smith, *OSS: The Secret History of America's First Central Intelligence Agency* (Berkeley, CA: University of California Press, 1981), p. xii.
3. C.D. Ameringer, *U.S. Foreign Intelligence: The Secret Side of American History* (Lexington, MA: Lexington Books, 1990), p. 396.
4. This outline is based on the relevant chapters of my book *Amerikanische Geheimdienstanalysen über Deutschland 1942–1949* (Munich: Oldenbourg, 1995); for references of source materials and literature see especially pp. 24ff., 53ff., 205ff.
5. This and the following quotation are from W.J. Donovan, 'Memorandum of Establishment of Service of Strategic Information', 10 June 1941, in T.F.

Troy, *Donovan and the CIA: A History of the Establishment of the Central Intelligence Agency* (Frederick, MD: Aletheia Books, 1981), pp. 419f.

6. The presidential order is reprinted in Troy, *Donovan*, p. 423.

7. William S. Stephenson, quoted in R. Dunlop, *Donovan: America's Master Spy* (Chicago, IL: Rand McNally, 1982), p. 309.

8. National Archives and Records Administration (NA), Record Group (RG) 226, Entry (E) 99, box (b) 76, folder (f) 45/46: History of the Research and Analysis Branch in the Office of Strategic Services, June 1941 – Sept. 1944 (R & A History): 'The Nature of Research and Analysis Activities', p. 4.

9. NA, RG 59, R & A 214 A, B, 12 December 1941. For a more detailed discussion of the work of R & A economists see B.M. Katz, *Foreign Intelligence: Research and Analysis in the Office of Strategic Services, 1942–1945* (Cambridge, MA: Harvard University Press, 1989), pp. 97–136; P. Marquardt-Bigman, *Geheimdienstanalysen*, pp. 35–43.

10. Quoted from a report commissioned by the Joint Chiefs of Staff to evaluate the potential usefulness of the various COI departments, in Troy, *Donovan*, p. 133.

11. JCS 155/4/D, 12 December 1942, in Troy, *Donovan*, pp. 431–4.

12. For more details on this, see P. Marquardt-Bigman, *Geheimdienstanalysen*, pp. 119–45.

13. For this and the following quotations, see NA; RG 226, E 1, b 3, 'Draft of proposed guide to preparation of political reports' (no date); ibid., b 9, f Political Reports (Preparation of): 'Guide to Preparation of Political Reports', 5 May 1944; NA RG 226, E 37, b 2, f Civil Affairs-Research and Analysis Civil Affairs Committee, minutes of the session of 31 July 1944.

14. W.L. Langer, *In and Out of the Ivory Tower: The Autobiography of William L. Langer* (New York: N. Watson Academic Publications, 1977), p. 199.

15. Letter from President Truman to Secretary of State Byrnes, 20 September 1945, quoted from Troy, *Donovan*, p. 463.

16. Ibid., p. 270.

17. Quoted from Troy, *Donovan*, p. 311.

18. Ameringer, *U.S. Foreign Intelligence*, p. 201.

19. Langer, *Ivory Tower*, p. 221.

20. On Kent's role as the head on ONE see D.P. Steury, ed., *Sherman Kent and the Board of National Estimates. Collected Essays* (Washington, DC: Center for the Study of Intelligence, Central Intelligence Agency, 1994), particularly the perceptive introduction of the editor, pp. ix–xxv.

21. Princeton, NJ: Princeton University Press, 1949.

22. Quoted from Steury, ed., *Sherman Kent*, p. xx.

23. Ibid., p. xxv.

24. R. Hilsman, 'Does the CIA Still Have a Role?', *Foreign Affairs*, 74, 5, (September 1995), pp. 104–16.

25. See A. Shulsky, 'What is Intelligence? Secrets and Competition Among States', in R. Godson, E. May and G. Schmitt, eds., *U.S. Intelligence at the Crossroads: Agendas for Reform* (Washington, DC: Brassey's, 1995) pp. 17–27.

5

The Role of Covert Operations in US Cold War Foreign Policy

Mario Del Pero

The decision by the US government to create a peacetime independent intelligence organization, the Central Intelligence Agency (CIA), was a natural product of systematic changes induced by the Cold War. Initially, the CIA was primarily concerned with intelligence and analysis, but it rapidly shifted its emphasis to covert operations.[1] This chapter deals with the role of covert operations in the Cold War strategies of the USA. It will be demonstrated how covert operations became crucial and indispensable tools of containment, adaptable to different strategic doctrines which, at least formally, were considered antithetical.

Over the last 20 years, the US historiography of the Cold War seems to have overcome the previously rigid and bitter polarization of 'orthodox' and 'revisionist' historians in favour of a presumed new and more objective synthesis known as post-revisionism. This approach, which comprises – it must be emphasized – many different positions, is especially characterized by increased attention to the strategic and geopolitical aspects of the dispute between the USA and the Soviet Union, as opposed to ideological explanations. The Cold War is consequently interpreted simply as a 'conflict for the balance of power'.[2]

The undeniable merits of the post-revisionist school, which promoted a more balanced analysis of post-World War II historical developments, should not prevent us from examining its limitations. First of all, the preoccupation with geostrategic and security issues has often caused the important ideological dimension of the Cold War to be underestimated in favour of a return to neo-orthodox realist positions.[3] Furthermore, numerous issues have not been adequately addressed, falling in the gaps between divergent and incompatible interpretations. The most important of these is probably the continuity/discontinuity of policies and, especially, of the strategic doctrines established by the various US administrations during the post-war period.[4] These historiographical deficiencies will probably be reduced when access is granted to important documents still classified at this writing, as well as through innovative methodological approaches focusing on aspects of the Cold War that have so far been neglected.

One of these aspects is undoubtedly intelligence. The great emphasis placed by post-revisionist historiography on the geostrategic and security dimensions of the Cold War inevitably contributed to increased scholarly interest in intelligence agencies, which represent one of the essential elements of every state's security policy. I personally believe – and have argued elsewhere[5] – that post-revisionism has also occurred in the historiography of intelligence. Put very simply, the case could be made that recent literature on intelligence and espionage was also preceded by an 'orthodox' consensual approach in the 1950s, and by radical revisionism which developed mainly in the 1970s. Whereas the former focused primarily on theoretical aspects of intelligence (as can be seen in the works of Sherman Kent and Roger Hilsman), the latter is clearly exemplified by the works of Philip Agee and Victor Marchetti.[6]

Post-revisionism in intelligence studies exhibits some of the traditional limitations of post-revisionism, such as neglecting the specific ideological and cultural aspects behind the Cold War polarization. At the same time, even the best works on the history of post-war US intelligence are not immune to a common tendency to concentrate almost exclusively on intelligence, therefore failing to establish a connection to a more general context. Yet the main risk – one that has already manifested itself – is that an overemphasis of the Cold War aspects of strategy and security will effect a return to the neo-orthodox paradigm. In the area of intelligence, this could lead to a decline in the critical spirit needed to deal with many of the actions initiated by US intelligence agencies, in particular the large number of unnecessary covert operations they have undertaken over the last 50 years.

One of the first and foremost challenges facing intelligence researchers is that of providing a definition of intelligence. This problem may be exacerbated in a foreign language: no equivalent exists in Italian, for instance, so the English word must be used instead. Allowing for a certain amount of unavoidable simplification and abstraction, we could define intelligence as the opposite of ignorance. It is derived by transforming 'raw' and factual information into real knowledge. This information is often gathered by clandestine instruments which may be either technological (such as satellites) or human (secret agents). Consequently, intelligence agencies often rely heavily on covert operations, defined as 'secret active efforts to alter political conditions in foreign countries through financial, paramilitary and other means'.[7]

If we may again simplify circumstances that in reality are quite complex, covert operations can be divided into four basic categories:[8]

1. *propaganda*, designated as 'white' propaganda when the source of the information is openly revealed, 'grey' propaganda when it is either unattributed or attributed to a third source, and 'black' propaganda when it is misleadingly attributed to an enemy

2. *political covert actions*, consisting of support for friendly political groups and representatives

3. *economic covert actions*, in which secret means are used to alter and weaken the adversaries' economies

4. *paramilitary covert actions*, the most controversial and hazardous type of secret operation.

Covert operations obviously constitute an indispensable instrument in the foreign policy of every great power. The gathering and processing of information – the analytical function of intelligence agencies – is aimed at acquiring knowledge of and understanding the situation in a foreign country. The goal of the intelligence agencies' operative arm is to alter and modify this situation (not necessarily through violence). In a way, covert operations represent the active and positive; analytical activity represents the negative and passive side of intelligence. Covert operations, also referred to as the 'quiet option', are therefore used in the wide 'grey zone' (or 'low-intensity war zone') between overt military intervention or no intervention at all.

The Cold War created the preconditions for an unprecedented development of covert operations, both qualitatively and quantitatively, thus increasing their relative importance in the arsenal of foreign policy instruments available to the USA. It is beyond dispute that in the early post-war years the USA was, both in absolute and relative terms, the premier world power. In fact, if only economic indicators are considered, it was the only world power. It is not surprising that the USA immediately placed an extremely high value on covert operations as useful tools in the international arena. This development has often been attributed to the influence of the policies and personnel of wartime intelligence agencies (in particular the Office of Strategic Services [OSS]). There is probably some truth to this assertion; the attitudes of OSS staff heavily influenced the Central Intelligence Group (CIG) and the CIA. But the legitimization of covert operations as 'normal' instruments of foreign policy, and the corresponding increase in their deployment, was primarily a consequence of the structure and nature of the international order inherited from World War II.[9]

The post-war international community was characterized by the rapid emergence of two ideologically opposed blocs based on antithetical and incompatible social systems. This ideological conflict produced a linguistic and conceptual code replete with standardized images that became entrenched in society's collective consciousness.[10] The role of propaganda – defined above as one form of covert operation – was greatly expanded. There were elaborate and explicit efforts to define an 'American model' capable of competing with the Marxist-Soviet model prevalent at that time. This task was assigned primarily to the various US intelligence agencies, and propaganda soon became one of the most characteristic and lasting features of the Cold War. But the interpretation of Soviet actions was also highly ideological, especially after George Kennan's views – though not completely understood – had become a dominant theme of US diplomacy.[11] The image of the Soviet Union was in fact strongly influenced by the considerations expressed in the 'long telegram' of February 1946. The pessimistic conclusions reached by Kennan, who believed that no collaboration was possible between the USA and the Soviet Union, were rapidly adopted as the official position of the Truman administration.[12] One of the most interesting aspects of the 'long telegram' is Kennan's distinction between the position of the Soviet rulers and that of the Soviet people. According to Kennan, the official party line does not represent natural outlook of Russian people. Latter are, by and large, friendly to outside world, eager for experience of it, eager to measure against it talents they are conscious of possessing, eager above all to live in peace and enjoy the fruits of their own labor. Party line only represents thesis which official propaganda machine puts forward with great skill and persistence to a public often remarkably resistant in the stronghold of its innermost thoughts.[13]

The covert operations undertaken in the early years of the Cold War by the USA and Great Britain in the 'denied areas' (the Ukraine and the Baltic states) were often motivated by this assumption.

The systematic progression of the Cold War and the particular characteristics of the enemy, the Soviet Union and communism, both contributed to the US decision to resort to covert operations. However, this was also a direct consequence of the extreme frustration of US diplomacy, unable to achieve its goals and anxious for some immediate results.

Though a number of the reasons usually put forward to justify the use of covert operations were already contained in the 'long telegram', Kennan explained this perceived necessity more explicitly in his 'X article' published in *Foreign Affairs* in the summer of 1947. There he reiterated some of the ideas expressed in his 'long telegram', in particular the convergence of ideological impulses and long historical developments in the making of Soviet foreign policy.[14] Kennan subsequently stressed the extreme weakness of the Soviet Union, devastated by the war and beset with an unbalanced and unstable socio-economic structure, but cautioned against illusions regarding the likelihood of the rapid demise of the communist regime. Instead, he called for a 'patient and vigilant containment of the Soviet expansive tendencies'.[15]

The real meaning and methods of 'containment' in the immediate post-war years are still a matter of discussion among historians (a discussion also fuelled by the contradictory positions assumed by Kennan at different times).[16] In any case, it is important to emphasize that covert operations rapidly became a very important instrument of 'containment'.

One month after the publication of the 'X article', Kennan, as chief of the State Department's Policy Planning Staff, wrote to the Secretary of Defense, James Forrestal, proposing the creation, within the military, of a 'guerrilla warfare corps' and training schools. Kennan believed this was necessary in order 'to fight fire with fire'.[17] Forrestal agreed on the necessity of establishing a programme of covert operations abroad, but believed it preferable to assign responsibility for these operations to the CIA. The opposition of CIA Director Roscoe Hillenkoetter – who feared that covert operations might compromise the CIA's intelligence efforts – and of his legal adviser, Lawrence Huston, were not sufficient to prevent the adoption of National Security Council (NSC) 4-A in December 1947. This represented a significant moment in the history of US intelligence: the CIA, initially created primarily as a defensive organ, was now provided with the means to conduct offensive operations. Active intervention in the internal affairs of foreign countries was to become one of the agency's distinguishing features.[18]

The willingness to resort to covert operations was strongly influenced by the political climate of the time, including the development of an anti-communist fervour that occasionally bordered on hysteria. A perfect example of this can be seen in the events that took place in Italy in 1947–48. An important facet of US policy in Italy – still extremely haphazard and incoherent at that point – was the fear that communists might be elected to power. It is ironic that George Kennan, the 'cold' and sober realist, went so far as to make such dangerous and unrealistic proposals as the outlawing of the Italian Communist Party (PCI) in order to start an open conflict and a civil war, which seemed preferable to a possible communist victory.[19]

Fortunately, more moderate opinions prevailed, though almost every means possible was used to influence the elections of April 1948. NSC 1–2 and NSC 1–3 of February and March 1948 directed the CIA to undertake covert activities to finance the Christian Democratic Party (Democrazia Cristiana [DC]) and the Social Democratic Party (Partito Socialista dei Lavoratori Italiani [PSLI]). The episode in Italy involved the use of both covert activities and 'white' propaganda (also definable as an 'overt action'), designed to create a positive image of the USA.

The US involvement in the 1948 elections clearly demonstrates the great importance which the Truman administration attached to events in Italy, though the US intervention was not a decisive factor in the Christian Democrats' victory. It is not possible, in fact, to distinguish between external and domestic factors in Italy, particularly where the Catholic Church is concerned.[20] The reluctant decision to support De Gasperi's Christian Democrats and the US faith in the centre–left parties (the Republicans behind La Malfa and Saragat's Social Democrats, who fared miserably in the elections) demonstrate both a lack of understanding of the situation in Italy and the inability to modify it.

According to James Miller, 'Americans reacted to the Christian Democracy's triumph with an orgy of self-congratulation'.[21] In reality, US officials in Italy were probably quite aware of the limited role they had played in determining the outcome of the 1948 elections. The paradoxical capacity of the 'junior party' (Italy) to exploit its weakness for diplomatic gain was also becoming evident to the USA. Nevertheless, the Italian elections of 1948 established an important precedent both for the CIA and for US foreign policy in general, as these operations were hailed as a model that could be universally applied, a model that furnished the definitive legitimization for covert operations as 'useful' and 'normal' instruments of containment.[22]

In the years that followed, the agencies responsible for covert operations were further strengthened by the creation of the Office of Special Projects (then Office of Policy Coordination) in June 1948, and the Central Intelligence Act of 1949.[23]

In January 1950, George Kennan resigned from the Policy Planning Staff. He was replaced by Paul Nitze, who soon thereafter collaborated with a group of officials from the Departments of State and Defense to compose one of the most important documents of the Cold War: NSC-68.[24] It is still a matter of discussion whether this document represented a turning point in the history of the Cold War, or at least in the political-military strategy of the Truman administration.[25] The conceptual and semantic similarities between this document and Kennan's analyses are often striking, yet the importance of NSC-68 lies in its effort to integrate political, economic, and military considerations into a definition of 'national security'. The US goal was the containment of Russia's expansionist tendencies (according to the authors of NSC-68, the Soviet Union was 'animated by a new and fanatic faith, antithetical to our own'[26]). The commitment had to be global because of the scale of the Soviet menace: 'The assault on free institutions is world wide now, and in the context of the present polarization of power a defeat of free institutions anywhere is a defeat everywhere.'[27] All means were considered appropriate to thwart Soviet intentions:

Our free society, confronted by a threat to its basic values, naturally will take such action, including the use of military force, as may be required to protect those values. The integrity of our system will not be jeopardized by any measure, *covert or overt, violent or non-violent* [emphasis by the author], which serves the purpose of frustrating the Kremlin design.[28]

NSC-68 thus contributed, even from a doctrinal perspective, to the further legitimization (assuming that was necessary) of covert operations as ordinary instruments of US foreign policy.

Three documents crucial to US post-war foreign policy – the 'long telegram', the 'X article', and NSC-68 – thus expressed a similar (though not identical) perception of the Soviet Union and the nature of the Cold War, a perception by virtue of which, when confronted with adversaries ready to make use of every means at their disposal, it was considered not only legitimate, but even necessary, to resort to covert operations.

It is ironic that this justification was the product of a presumed 'realist' approach (of which Kennan was one of the most important representatives), allegedly concerned primarily with the geopolitical aspects of the conflict between the USA and the Soviet Union rather than ideological considerations.[29] In actuality, it is impossible to overlook how the USA, in the name of this purported realism, initiated not only 'normal' propaganda activities and support for friendly political groups, but also a series of covert operations in the Soviet bloc. The latter were characterized by superficiality and carelessness, as seen in the joint British–US operation in Albania. The failure of those operations, probably due in part to the efficiency of Soviet counter-espionage, was not critically evaluated.[30]

Starting in the early 1950s, the relative stabilization of the Cold War in Europe reduced the number of covert operations undertaken in the Old World, while simultaneously leading to an increase in covert operations in what had been the 'peripheral' areas of the globe, into which the polarized conflict was now moving.

Even scholars usually sensitive to the requirements of intelligence agencies, and not a priori hostile to covert operations, have warned against their indiscriminate use. According to Walter Laqueur, clandestine activities have often been abused, leading to operations that were dangerous, morally debatable, foolish, and pointless.[31] US post-war foreign policy also seems to have succumbed to this temptation:

the USA approved and carried out many covert operations that were senseless, risky, and potentially harmful to its reputation.

Most surprisingly, despite the evolution and countless revisions of US strategies and military doctrines, the role of covert operations rarely changed, and they were always considered essential to the success of US foreign policy. They had rapidly become crucial instruments of containment; it would therefore be difficult not to agree with Loch K. Johnson when he maintains: 'From the Truman to the Reagan Administrations, this option has often been a favorite of presidents and their advisers in the pursuit of foreign policy objectives.'[32]

The conditions created by the Cold War and the polarization of international politics stimulated the development of covert operations. The particular nature of the post-war conflict between the USA and the Soviet Union legitimized the use of unorthodox diplomatic and military practices such as espionage and covert operations. The main arguments advanced in their defence were the impenetrability of the Soviet Union and the conviction that it had a powerful and global intelligence apparatus.

Be that as it may, it would be extremely reductive to explain covert operations only as the inevitable product of external pressures. We have already seen how their necessity had been theorized by George Kennan during his years as head of the State Department's Policy Planning Staff, and how the presumed success of the initial covert operations (such as the elections in Italy in 1948) had strengthened the planners' faith in them, as reinforced by NSC-68, regarding their effectiveness against the Soviet menace.

During the Eisenhower presidency, the CIA's clandestine activities reached their peak, due both to Allen Dulles's dynamism and the 'New Look' strategy, whose main goal was to reconcile a balanced budget with the demands of national security. Because they were relatively inexpensive, covert operations were the natural complement to 'brinkmanship diplomacy' based on the threat of 'massive retaliation'.[33]

The Kennedy administration devised a new 'flexible response' military strategy which more closely approximated the principles of NSC-68 (with which it shared a preference for an expansive and neo-Keynesian fiscal policy) than the principles of Eisenhower's 'New Look'. Even this approach assigned a very important role to covert operations.[34] In those years, the conflict with the Soviet Union was expanding into newly decolonized areas. The Kennedy administration viewed this as a global challenge between two antithetical political and economic models.[35] As a consequence of this 'peripheralization', the bipolar conflict lost the static nature of its European dimension. This process energized the conflict and produced a growth of covert operations in areas where the rivalry was fought out by means of wars 'by proxy'. This trend did not change either with the Johnson administration, which put into effect many of Kennedy's strategic elaborations, nor with that of Nixon, who presided over a comeback of some of the principles of the Eisenhower approach in tandem with extraordinary political and diplomatic unscrupulousness.

Covert operations continued to assume a central role in US foreign policy at least until the scandals of the 1970s, when US intelligence was accused of conducting illegal operations. Due to their extreme flexibility, covert operations assumed a kind of 'strategic ubiquity'. They became instruments adaptable to virtually any situation and usable within the framework of every political and military strategy. Even if we accept John Lewis Gaddis's interpretation of Cold War strategies,[36] according to which the implementation of containment measures requires dividing the various administrations' foreign policies into a universalist and symmetric model, on the one hand (providing for a general response to any Soviet action), and a particularist and asymmetric model, on the other hand (prescribing selective responses to specific Soviet actions), the fact remains that covert operations lent themselves quite well to both approaches. The symmetric model used various methods of graduating possible responses and emphasized a flexible military apparatus heavily dependent on covert operations. The asymmetric model, based on the possibility of choosing both the theatre and the modalities for the response to an enemy action, extolled the low cost of covert operations, which, in any case, often represented the only alternative to total war. Consequently, they were assigned a crucial role both in symmetric doctrines, such as NSC-68 and Kennedy's 'flexible response' concept, and in selective and asymmetric approaches such as those of Eisenhower and Nixon.

It therefore appears that covert operations developed a dynamic of their own, one not always in harmony with broader strategies and doctrines. In other words, their role in post-war US foreign policy has remained remarkably constant. This continuity is one argument in favour of historiographical approaches that, unlike that of Gaddis, tend to stress the similarities of the various administrations' foreign policies more than their differences.[37] But, of course, a conclusion of this kind must be corroborated by analyses and studies of other areas of US foreign policy besides intelligence and covert operations.

A final, critical assessment of the limits and dangers of the indiscriminate use of covert operations as a normal foreign policy instrument is nevertheless in order. During the Cold War, many US covert operations were guided by a blind fear of communism that often simplified and distorted intricate socio-political circumstances. Unorthodox tools such as covert operations were often administered through informal procedures, leaving wide discretionary powers to the men 'in the field'. The supposed success of early operations caused the executive to lose sight of the importance of maintaining formal channels of authorization and communication with the men responsible for covert operations. This established a dangerous precedent and encouraged imprudent 'voluntarism'. Finally, scant or no attention was paid to the potential long-time effects of a covert operation. All too often, shortsighted considerations prevailed, with planners being interested only in immediate results and oblivious to deeper structural problems. Inevitably, this lack of foresight eventually worked against the USA: an immediate success is seldom an enduring one.[38]

US covert operations must be analysed in the more general context of US foreign policy, not apart from it. Yet the link between covert operations and policies did not lie – as maintained by the radical and revisionist literature on intelligence of the 1970s[39] – in the joint planning and organization of covert operations. It was instead a natural outgrowth of the manner in which the priorities of US foreign policy were defined.

The initial successes of covert activities, combined with the frustrating slowness of diplomacy, transformed them into a sort of panacea thought capable of resolving extremely complicated issues. As time went by, many operations were undertaken without properly weighing their risks and advantages. As a result of this infatuation with covert operations, the US government lost sight of the actual goal of its policies, the containment of the Soviet Union. In the process, the CIA's overall reputation suffered, including that of the various units responsible for intelligence, previously renowned for the quality and accuracy of their analyses.

NOTES

1. See also the contribution by P. Marquardt-Bigman in this volume.
2. F. Romero, 'La Guerra Fredda nella Recente Storiografia Americana. Definizioni e Interpretazioni', *Italia Contemporanea*, 200 (December 1995), pp. 397–412; A. Stephanson, 'The United States', in D. Reynolds, ed., *The Origins of the Cold War in Europe* (New Haven, CT: Yale University Press, 1994), pp. 23–52. On post-revisionism see J.L. Gaddis's classic work, 'The Emerging Postrevisionist Synthesis on the Origins of the Cold War', *Diplomatic History*, 7:3 (Summer 1983), pp. 171–90. On the pluralism of US diplomatic historiography, see M. Hunt's optimistic prognosis, 'The Long Crisis in U.S. Diplomatic History: Coming to Closure', *Diplomatic History*, 16:1 (Winter 1992), pp. 115–40, and the various essays in M. Hogan and T. Paterson, eds., *Explaining the History of American Foreign Relations* (Cambridge: Cambridge University Press, 1991).
3. See M. Leffler, 'New Approaches, Old Interpretations, and Prospective Reconfigurations', *Diplomatic History*, 19:2 (Spring 1995), pp. 173–96. That post-revisionism could be nothing more than 'orthodoxy plus archives' had already been refuted by Prof. Kimball in his comment on J.L. Gaddis, 'The Emerging Postrevisionist Synthesis', op. cit.
4. On the continuity/discontinuity of the Truman administration's foreign policy, see the differing positions of M. Leffler, *A Preponderance of Power: National Security, the Truman Administration, and the Cold War* (Stanford, CA: Stanford University Press, 1992), and J.L. Gaddis, *Strategies of Containment. A Critical Appraisal of Postwar National Security Policy* (New York: Oxford University Press, 1982).
5. M. Del Pero, 'L'Intelligence Statunitense nel Secondo Dopoguerra', *Passato e Presente*, 40 (Gennaio-Aprile 1997), pp.105–20. For a slightly different position, see R. Jeffreys-Jones, 'The Stirrings of a New Revisionism', in R. Jeffreys-Jones and A. Lownie, eds., *North American Spies. New Revisionist Essays* (Edinburgh: Edinburgh University Press, 1991), pp. 1–30.
6. V. Marchetti and J. Marks, *The CIA and the Cult of Intelligence* (New York: Dell, 1974); P. Agee, *Inside the Company: CIA Diary* (Harmondsworth: Penguin, 1975).
7. This definition is by Clark Clifford; see L.K. Johnson, *America's Secret Power: The CIA in a Democratic Society* (New York: Oxford University Press, 1989). Johnson emphasizes that the expression 'covert operations' is in reality much more complex and elusive. For another definition of covert operations see R. Godson, ed., *Intelligence Requirements for the 1980s: Covert Action* (Washington, DC: National Strategy Information Center: Transaction Books, 1981).
8. It is evident that the typological divisions suggested here are based on distinctions much less explicit in reality; the four types of covert operations can often be distinguished in theory only, as they are not mutually exclusive and consequently appear simultaneously (a political covert action often implies an economic one as well, etc.).

9. T.F. Troy, *Donovan and the CIA: A History of the Establishment of the Central Intelligence Agency* (Frederick, MD: University Publications of America, 1981); B.F. Smith, *The Shadow Warriors: O.S.S. and the Origins of the CIA* (New York: Basic Books, 1983). See also the contribution by P. Marquardt-Bigman in this volume.

10. See M. Hunt, *Ideology and United States Foreign Policy* (New Haven, CT: Yale University Press, 1987); T. Smith, *America's Mission* (Princeton, NJ: Princeton University Press, 1994); H.W. Brands, *The Devil We Knew: Americans and the Cold War* (New York: Oxford University Press, 1993); S.J. Withfield, *The Culture of the Cold War* (Baltimore, MD: Johns Hopkins University Press, 1991).

11. See the excellent book by J.L. Harper, *American Visions of Europe. Franklin D. Roosevelt, George F. Kennan, and Dean Acheson* (Cambridge: Cambridge University Press, 1994), pp. 135–232.

12. According to Kennan, Soviet hostility originated not from an objective analysis of the international situation but from insecurity in relation to the western world, which had its origins in tsarist Russia and was exacerbated by the accession to power of a communist regime strongly hostile to the outside world and harshly repressive inside its borders. He believed that the only possible response by the USA was to increase stability and security in the countries most exposed (internally and externally) to the communist menace. The 'long telegram' is reproduced in T.H. Etzold and J.L. Gaddis, eds., *Containment: Documents on American Foreign Policy and Strategy, 1945–1950* (New York: Columbia University Press, 1978), pp. 50–64.

13. Etzold and Gaddis, eds., *Containment*, p. 52.

14. According to Kennan, the creation of an external enemy to replace the defeated internal one served the needs of a regime whose possibilities of survival were based on a rigid and repressive system of control over its population. The article, entitled 'The Sources of Soviet Conduct', was reprinted in G. Kennan, *Memoirs: 1925–1950* (Boston: Atlantic Little, Brown, 1967), pp. 107–28.

15. Ibid., p. 119.

16. Different interpretations of 'containment' are those proposed by J.L. Gaddis, *Strategies of Containment*; M. Leffler, *Preponderance of Power*, and M. Cox, 'Requiem for a Cold War Critic: the Rise and Fall of George Kennan, 1946–1950', *Irish-Slavonic Studies*, 11 (1990), pp. 1–23.

17. See T. Hoopes and D. Brinkley, *Driven Patriot: The Life and Times of James Forrestal* (New York: Knopf, 1992), p. 311.

18. A.B. Darling, *The Central Intelligence Agency as Instrument of Government to 1950* (University Park, PA: Pennsylvania State University Press, 1990). Darling's book was originally published in 1953 as a CIA classified document.

19. J.L. Harper, *L'America e la Ricostruzione dell'Italia, 1945–1948* (Bologna: Il Mulino, 1987), p. 287 – originally published as *America and the Reconstruction of Italy, 1945–1948* (Cambridge: Cambridge University Press, 1986); J.E. Miller, 'Taking Off the Gloves: The United States and the

Italian Elections of 1948', *Diplomatic History*, 7:1 (Winter 1983), pp. 35–56; A. Brogi, *L'Italia e l'Egemonia Americana nel Mediterraneo* (Firenze: La Nuova Italia, 1996), pp. 44–7.

20. G. Formigoni, *La Democrazia Cristiana e l'Alleanza Occidentale* (Bologna: Il Mulino, 1996), pp. 177–9; F. Romero, 'Gli Stati Uniti in Italia: il Piano Marshall e il Patto Atlantico', in F. Barbagallo, ed., *Storia dell'Italia Repubblicana. Vol. I: La Costruzione della Democrazia* (Torino: Einaudi, 1994), pp. 231–89; A. Varsori, 'La Scelta Occidentale dell'Italia (1948–1949)', *Storia delle Relazioni Internazionali*, 1:1 (1985), pp. 95–135.

21. Miller, 'Taking Off the Gloves', p. 52.

22. J.E. Miller, 'Roughhouse Diplomacy: the United States Confronts Italian Communism, 1945-1958', *Storia delle Relazioni Internazionali*, 5:2 (1989), pp. 279–311.

23. See W.M. Leary, *The Central Intelligence Agency: History and Documents* (Tuscaloosa, AL: University of Alabama Press, 1984), pp. 131–3, and J. Ranelagh, *The Agency: the Rise and Decline of the CIA* (New York: Simon and Schuster, 1986), pp. 193–5.

24. NSC-68 is printed in Etzold and Gaddis, eds., *Containment*, pp. 383–442. On NSC-68, see also M. Trachtenberg, *History and Strategy* (Princeton, NJ: Princeton University Press, 1991), pp. 107–12.

25. John Lewis Gaddis's fascinating interpretation of the Cold War presented in *Strategies of Containment* was based on this assumption.

26. Etzold and Gaddis, eds., *Containment*, p. 385.

27. Ibid., p. 389.

28. Ibid., p. 392.

29. According to Gaddis, this realism, which produced doctrinal prescriptions adapted to the means and resources of the USA, can be found only in Kennan's analyses and not in NSC-68. See Gaddis, *Strategies of Containment*, pp. 104–6.

30. J. Prados, *President's Secret Wars: the CIA and Pentagon Covert Operations from World War II Through the Persian Gulf* (Chicago, IL: Elephant Paperbacks, 1996), pp. 30–44.

31. W. Laqueur, *Un Mondo di Segreti. Impieghi e Limiti dello Spionaggio* (Milano: Rizzoli, 1986), p. 408 – originally published as *A World of Secrets: The Uses and Limits of Intelligence* (New York: Basic Books, 1985).

32. Johnson, *America's Secret Power,* p. 100.

33. On the importance of covert operations in Eisenhower's foreign policy, see R. Jeffreys-Jones, *The CIA and American Democracy* (New Haven, CT: Yale University Press, 1987), pp. 81–99; see also S.E. Ambrose and R.H. Immerman, *Ike's Spies: Eisenhower and the Espionage Establishment* (Garden City, NJ: Doubleday, 1981); on American covert operations in Italy see L. Sebesta, *L'Europa indifesa. Sistema di Sicurezza Atlantico e Caso Italiano, 1948–1955* (Firenze: Ponte alle Grazie, 1991), pp. 213–15, and G. De Lutiis, *Storia dei Servizi Segreti in Italia* (Roma: Editori Riuniti, 1991), pp. 40–3.

34. See D.S. Blaufarb, *The Counterinsurgency Era: United States Doctrine and Performance, 1950 to the Present* (New York: Free Press, 1977).

35. The success of the nationalist and Marxist doctrines in 'underdeveloped' countries compelled the USA to elaborate an alternative doctrinal and theoretical model, as represented by Walt Rostow's theory of the 'stages' of economic growth. See W. Rostow, *The Stages of Economic Growth. A Non-Communist Manifesto* (New York: Cambridge University Press, 1962).

36. Gaddis, *Strategies of Containment*. For a different cyclical model of US history see A.M. Schlesinger, Jr.'s classic work, *The Cycles of American History* (Boston, MA: Houghton Mifflin, 1986).

37. See, for instance, M. Leffler, *Preponderance of Power*; S.E. Ambrose, *Rise to Globalism. American Foreign Policy Since 1938* (New York: Penguin, 1993); S. Brown, *The Faces of Power: Constancy and Change in United States Foreign Policy from Truman to Clinton* (New York: Columbia University Press, 1994); T.G. Paterson, *Meeting the Communist Threat: Truman to Reagan* (New York: Oxford University Press, 1988); W. LaFeber, *America, Russia and the Cold War, 1945–1990* (New York: McGraw-Hill, 1991).

38. Iran, of course, provides the most telling example of this, but even the deep hostility toward the US which often typifies public opinion in Europe and Latin America can be attributed to the indiscriminate use of covert operations.

39. Marchetti and Marks, *CIA and Cult of Intelligence*; Agee, *Inside the Company*.

6

The WRINGER Project: German Ex-POWs as Intelligence Sources on the Soviet Union

Horst Boog

The WRINGER project was an intelligence operation of the US Air Force (USAF) in the late 1940s and early 1950s. It was designed to gain information of military value on the Soviet Union through systematic interviewing of German prisoners of war repatriated from there.

The following is mainly based on an article by James Erdmann,[1] a lieutenant colonel in the USAF intelligence establishment and later professor of history at the University of Denver. The piece was published in 1982 with permission of the USAF. In addition, I drew from articles by Robert Jackson[2] on post-war strategic Air Intelligence and Squadron Leader John Crampton[3] on RB-45 operations. Last but not least, my interpretation benefited from personal experience. Unfortunately, the volume on US air intelligence covering the WRINGER project is still classified.[4] Nevertheless, it can be established without doubt that the results of the WRINGER project were invaluable at the time both for the Strategic Air Command (SAC) and for an overall assessment of the Soviet Union. They filled an information gap that could not be bridged by existing means of air reconnaissance.

In August 1949, the Soviets detonated their first nuclear device near Semipalatinsk. The Soviet long-range bomber force was slowly building up a nuclear lift capacity based on the Tupolev Tu-4, a copy of the B-29. Although an attack on the USA by these planes would have been a one-way mission because of their lack of range, it was thought necessary to observe the bomber bases being constructed in the Arctic region of northern Russia as well as the Soviet air defence radar system in the area reaching from Murmansk across the Barents Sea to the island of Severnajy Zemlya. Therefore, it was necessary to direct overflights of northern Russia by Convair RB-36 reconnaissance aircraft. They began in the summer of 1951 from the area of Norfolk, England. The planes had a range of about 15,000 kilometres. To evade Soviet defences and radar detection they flew at an altitude of over 18,000 metres with 800 kilometres per hour. From the beginning, it was clear that this turboprop-assisted conventional aircraft would soon have to be replaced by a modern jet plane better suited for the gathering of strategic air intelligence under the conditions prevailing. Thus, in 1954 and 1955, several flights were undertaken by the Boeing B-47, penetrating the Soviet Union by up to 550 miles by night. Since the aircraft did not operate in high altitudes, these flights were soon stopped by the new Yak-25 fighter of the Red Air Force.

By the end of 1952, the Soviets had tested three atomic bombs and were about to build a new bomber far superior to the Tu-4. It was the Tu-88, later to become the Tu-16 with the NATO designation 'Badger'. In addition, there had been knowledge of Soviet rocket tests since 1947. They had taken place at Kapustin Yar, north of the Caspian Sea. It looked as if Soviet air armament had shifted its emphasis to rockets. In mid-1953, the testing ground was photographed by a Mk2 Canberra flying at an altitude of more than 19,000 metres. It took off from West Germany and landed in Iran, not without having received some hits by Soviet defences. Other Canberras collected electronic intelligence about the new Soviet radar such as the GCI-system 'Token'. From 1954 onwards, the advanced Soviet radar system made radar surveillance flights and undetected entries into Soviet air space impossible. One reaction to the problem was the Lockheed U-2, a plane that flew only about 20 missions, before it was downed near Sverdlovsk on 1 May 1960. Spy satellites eventually replaced the aeroplane in this sector of intelligence.

The Royal Air Force also made some aerial tanker-based flights with RB-45Cs over the Baltic States, to the Moscow region, and over southern Russia in April 1952. The purpose was to gather intelligence data on intercontinental ballistic missile (ICBM) positions and radar defences. Similar reconnaissance operations with even larger range and inflight-refuelling were conducted in April 1954.[5]

It stands to reason that an all-round intelligence picture of the Soviet Union could hardly be constructed in the years between the establishment of the US SAC in 1947 and the advent of the U-2 in 1956. The reconnaissance flights were sporadic and started only in 1951. As a reaction to the blockade of Berlin in 1948/49 and the early closing of the East German borders with barbed wire, mines, and patrols of the *Volkspolizei*, the German prisoners of war (POWs) returning from the Soviet Union – in addition to the refugees from the eastern bloc – were increasingly seen as the only or main source of information on the Soviet Union. Thus, in view of the danger of Soviet expansion into Western Europe and in view of US and NATO preparations for a defensive war in Europe, the WRINGER programme was born. The Soviet Union had not demobilized after the war and was maintaining an army of four to five million men with 27 divisions in the eastern zone of Germany, against which NATO could muster only a few divisions. During the opening days of a war, these divisions were to contain the Red Army with conventional weapons, while the USA would prepare air attacks to wreak such devastation on Soviet society and war-making potential that the Soviet leaders would recoil from total war. SAC was the primary force for any NATO counter-offensive operations. But SAC had no eyes and did not know exactly what to attack. In the preparation of plans to meet this threat, it became obvious that there was neither current order-of-battle information of Soviet forces nor much knowledge of their war potential and its centres. This was also a consequence of Western euphoria after the defeat of Germany and of Soviet secretiveness during the war owing to their distrust of the Western Allies. But if a war should come, US and NATO commanders would have to know which Red Army targets should be destroyed and in what order of priority; whether the forces attacking from the Soviet zone or their support installations and auxiliary forces should be attacked first; which bases and war industries in central Europe and Russia proper supplied the Red combat units with fuel and weapons; and what were the most critical logistic arteries; what were the most vital centres and how were they defended against air attack. The intelligence gap on the Soviet Union proved to be so extreme that spontaneous efforts to collect information were ordered. Headquarters USAF directed USAF Command in Europe to provide details for target maps on 50 Soviet cities. The reaction in the field was consternation.[6] There had been no reconnaissance missions over the Soviet Union since 1944, when the *Luftwaffe* had attempted in vain to attack Soviet electric power installations and other industries in the Gorki, Moscow, and Volga areas.[7] The captured German aerial photographs taken during the war were quite obsolete by now. Moreover, they did not reach further than Kuibyshev, about 800 kilometres southeast of Moscow, leaving the industrial centres of Sverdlovsk, Magnitogorsk, and Nishny Tagil in the Ural mountains uncovered.

Still, it was with these German target mosaics that the WRINGER project was started. Since the Soviets did not allow free travel on land or by air, there was no other way of collecting intelligence information than by asking German ex-prisoners and, at a later time, returning scientists. The POWs had been incarcerated in labour camps all over the Soviet Union and put to work repairing bomb-damaged installations or constructing new factories. Most of them had been clearing away rubble or working in mines, but some had worked inside new factories, and most had been in or near those urban areas which were listed as priority targets in accordance with the original NATO doctrine of massive retaliation. Almost all ex-POWs were skilled in some craft or trade, and many were engineers. Many also were careful observers and had a good memory and sense of orientation. They provided numerous memory sketches of areas and factories beyond previous aerial photographic coverage. Thus, many white spots in the Ural region could be filled in by putting together, like the pieces of a jigsaw puzzle, hundreds of descriptions of the same object by different observers. The pictures created this way were so accurate that they seemed to allow walking safely in darkness through 'Uralmashzavod' in Sverdlovsk or the steel and aircraft plants in Zaporoshje. Most of the best information came from non-officer ranks. By contrast, the generals, returning last, were poor sources because they had not worked in factories and often had not worked at all.

Before implementing the WRINGER idea, the size of the pool of knowledgeable refugees and POWs, their location, the places where they had been in the Soviet Union, and their value as informants had to be ascertained. As to the first point, the Soviets for a long time concealed the true number of POWs in their custody. The figures provided were usually too low and, in 1950, they even claimed that repatriation had been completed. As a result of protests by the Western allies and the West German government, more reliable data came to light. The shocking physical state of many returning POWs as observed in Vienna in 1948, and the fact that many of them, especially the well-fed, were indoctrinated with communist ideas aroused much scepticism about their value as objective sources. However, by far the majority of them, as was soon discovered, rejected the communist system and were contemptuous of the backwardness of life in Russia. They harboured no strong animosity against the West.[8]

The WRINGER project was started by Major Robert F. Work in Austria. He had been an experienced interrogator of *Luftwaffe* personnel during the war. The First Air Intelligence Service Organization at Fürstenfeldbruck refused to assign translators or intelligence assistants to him, because it was committed to sending them to the headquarters of USAF Europe whenever needed there. Major Work and General Charles Cabell, Director of Intelligence of the USAF, had parallel views. Cabell had experienced the negative Soviet attitude toward the USA during the war in Poltava.[9] He was convinced that they respected military power alone, and he therefore supported the programme wholeheartedly. The nickname 'WRINGER' was adopted in the spring of 1949. In June of that year, the US European Command established the 7001st Air Intelligence Service Squadron, operating from Wiesbaden, to 'collect positive Air Intelligence Information from overt sources'.[10] The squadron consisted of 40 officers, 101 airmen, and 103 foreign nationals, mostly Germans. It established USAF historical research teams in Frankfurt, Munich, Stuttgart-Esslingen, Oberursel, and elsewhere. Each team sent small detachments to the German refugee and POW reception centres to screen the incoming returnees. McBee Keysort Cards completed with the most important data on each interviewee were the basis for later invitations to an interview. Interrogation centres compiled parallel biographical files on POWs already in Germany, and the two lists were combined into a register of almost 400,000 names. The German interviewers and specialists usually had a very good command of English – the interviews were in German or in some eastern language, if necessary, but the report had to be written in English. As businessmen abroad, former *Wehrmacht* officers, or engineers still looking for a job in pre-*Wirtschaftswunder* Germany, they also possessed the pertinent technical knowledge. Most of them were university or high-school graduates.

In 1951, the Third and Twelfth Air Forces were established as a consequence of the Berlin crisis and the Korean War. The formation of the atomic-armed Seventeenth Air Force in April 1953 also increased the need for strategic intelligence. This led to the expansion of the 7001st Air Intelligence Service Squadron into the 7050th Air Intelligence Service Wing (AISW)[11] with positions for 115 officers, 265 airmen, 71 Department of the Air Force civilians, and 589 foreign nationals, again mostly Germans. When needed, Air Technical Liaison Officer Teams consisting of technical and scientific specialists were formed to assist interrogators encountering high-level scientific sources. The 7050th AISW extended its activities to the British zone. Cooperation was good with all US parties, military or civilian; with the West German and British governments, and intelligence agencies such as the BSSO (British Intelligence Organization); with the *Verfassungsschutz*, with the West German Border Police established and deployed in accordance with WRINGER information; with the Gehlen Organization and later with the *Bundesnachrichtendienst*. Cooperation with French intelligence apparently did not function well. Reports were also disseminated to Radio Free Europe, and it stands to reason that NATO and the operational commands were provided with information.

WRINGER information was necessary for the development of national estimates and defence measures. It provided NATO commanders with detailed strategic and tactical intelligence about Soviet and satellite political and military strength upon which to base contingency plans to meet the threats of the Cold War. Vital data for carrying out strategic bombing missions were given to SAC. This preparation was necessary in case deterrence should fail. In fact, the majority of the reports were needed for target establishment. This way the WRINGER programme furnished SAC with eyes consisting of urban and industrial area descriptions, targeting diagrams of key military installations, and analyses of air defence systems around vital centres. Also of importance were the physical vulnerability data of certain urban areas, industrial and military sites, defences, bridges, and routes of transportation. WRINGER claimed to have furnished more than 50 per cent of all reports on the Soviet Union and its satellites used by SAC at that time. These reports also served as the basis for training material for the bomber crews, such as radar target simulators and area prediction films. In the case of the third largest Soviet steel-producing city, Magnitogorsk, POW information about a new dam allowed the correction of the bomb-release point, lest a possible attack fail.[12]

Interrogations took place in about 100 refugee camps, where the returnees were screened, and in urban interrogation centres throughout West Germany, where detailed debriefings were done resulting in more or less lengthy reports. The interviewees were reimbursed for travel expenses, received free hotel accommodation, and a per diem payment. After many years in Soviet custody the German ex-POWs were only too willing to accept the invitations to the debriefing centres and tell the interviewers about their experiences in the Soviet Union – where they had worked, what they had done, and what they had seen and heard. It was sometimes difficult for the interviewers to get the right perspective on the generally negative views about life and politics in the Soviet Union, that is, to find out where the strength of the communist system lay that had enabled such a tight grip on the population for so long. To discover these strong points, whether one liked them or not, demanded distance and balanced interpretation on the part of the interviewer, both in political or social reports, and in reports about important individuals. The reports by the POWs were complemented by those refugees who had experienced political coercion and expulsion by the communists, and who freely expressed their abhorrence of communism.

The WRINGER field operations contributed significantly to the improvement of German-American relations after the war. Both the German refugees and ex-POWs, as well as the interviewers/translators, in talking about new Soviet military and industrial power centres, shared NATO's apprehension of the growing threat of Soviet expansionism. The recognition of this threat and the realization that Germany would be defended as NATO's forward area generated confidence in the Western defence organization and justified German participation in the project. The friendly reception of the interviewees by the WRINGER teams may have strengthened Germans' willingness to see their country rearmed and contribute to NATO's defence of the West after 1954.

In the first year and a half of the project, from autumn 1949 to spring 1951, more than half of the ex-POWs contacted accepted the invitations. They provided almost 100,000 reports, half of them – in compliance with the primary WRINGER requirement for city plans – consisting of area descriptions of military and industrial sites and including detailed maps of specific installations, technical drawings of weapons and machinery, copies of official Russian documents, photographs, material samples, and machine parts, altogether a total of 140,000 separate items of intelligence value. Within five years, over 300,000 former *Wehrmacht* prisoners in the Soviet Union voluntarily agreed to be interviewed. They furnished over a million intelligence reports, helping to determine the military capabilities and intentions of the Soviet Union and its resurgent industrial power. WRINGER furnished new or corroborative data about subjects such as the Soviet military use of television, rocket and missile development, technical methods of making blades for the air compressors of jet engines, Soviet hydrogenation technology, the roadbed strength of transportation nets in strategic corridors, German scientific personnel in the Soviet ballistic missile and aircraft programmes, Soviet military and political personalities, conditions of life in Russia, etc. The Soviet Union's vital industrial targets received detailed coverage to only a small degree; ten per cent of its metals industry, eight per cent of Soviet munitions and armaments plants, five per cent of its aircraft plants, and five per cent of its electric power plants were surveyed.[13] However, this USAF-directed programme demonstrated that mass exploitation of human intelligence sources was feasible and indispensable. The US Army's intelligence service established a similar programme.

Interviews were facilitated by reference files that could be established after countless confirmations of data on certain objects and subjects. Of great help for those interviewers who were not engineers were the guides describing the set-up and production processes of the various industries. Actually, the work of the interviewer and military analyst was similar to the work of the historian. The main difference was that the sources of the historian are generally much older.

After several years, the law of diminishing returns made itself felt, and, as of 1953, one could already say that the last 1,000 reports were not as valuable as the first 1,000. Yet, even after repatriation of the last German POWs in 1955, activities continued, focusing on other sources and objectives.

NOTES

1. J. Erdmann, 'The WRINGER in Postwar Germany: Its Impact on United States–German Relations and Defense Policies', in C.L. Egan and A. Scott, eds., *Essays in Twentieth-Century American Diplomatic History, Dedicated to Professor Daniel M. Smith* (Lanham, MD: University Press of America, 1982).

2. 'Strategic Air Intelligence Post-War', in *Air Intelligence. A Symposium*, Bracknell Paper No. 7, 1997, pp. 111–17.
3. 'RB-45 Operations', ibid., pp. 118–25.
4. Conversation with its author Dr Vance O. Mitchell in Colorado Springs, November 1996.
5. On these flights, see the recent TV documentaries 'Das Megatonnenspiel (1949–1963). Strategische Planspiele während des Kalten Krieges', and 'Himmelsspione – US-Aufklärungsflüge über die Sowietunion'.
6. Erdmann, 'The WRINGER in Postwar Germany', p. 165.
7. For details, see R. Muller, *The German Air War in Russia* (Baltimore, MD: Nautical and Aviation Pub. Co. of America, 1992), pp. 149–235.
8. Erdmann, 'The WRINGER in Postwar Germany', pp. 168–71.
9. Ibid., p. 173; G.B. Infield, *The Poltava Affair: A Russian Warning. An American Tragedy* (New York: Macmillan, 1973), pp. 217–30; G.B. Infield and M.S. Bowman, 'Shuttle Raiders to Russia', *Air Force Magazine*, 55:4 (1972), pp. 46–55; E. Hicks, 'Soviet Sojourn: The First Shuttle-Bombing Missions to Russia', *Airpower Historian*, 11 (1964), pp. 1–5; W.F. Craven and J.L. Cate, eds., *The Army Air Forces in World War II*, Vol. 3 (Chicago, IL: University of Chicago Press, 1951), pp. 308–19; M.J. Conversino, 'Operation Frantic', *Air Power History*, 38:1 (Spring 1991), pp. 23–38.
10. Erdmann, 'The WRINGER in Postwar Germany', p. 175; 12th Air Force Regulation #24–26, Headquarters USAFE Organizations, 'Mission of the 7001 Air Intelligence Service Squadron', 3 June 1949.
11. Erdmann, 'The WRINGER in Postwar Germany', p. 181; USAFE General Order #19, 21 March 1951.
12. Erdmann, 'The WRINGER in Postwar Germany', p. 180.
13. Ibid., pp. 178f.

7

US Intelligence, COCOM, and the Trade War During the Cold War, 1947–55: The French Problem

Frank Cain

Unlike most lengthy wars, the conclusion of the Cold War has no identifiably fixed ending point nor, we must remind ourselves, has it a clear date of commencement. The trade war conducted under the US aegis by the West against the East, under the title of the Co-Ordinating Committee for the Control of East–West Trade (COCOM), was an important element in the conduct of this war. Many of the records of this US-inspired body, particularly the intelligence dossiers, have not been released, but there are other records sufficient to allow us to construct the outline of this important Cold War organization. Most countries reluctantly fell in with the USA's demands to adhere to the COCOM regulations. The French demonstrated their reluctance to do so, and much of this chapter focuses on how the French authorities were able to frustrate the large US intelligence bodies in implementing this Cold War trade-war body. Some small insight into the vast scope of the enormous US intelligence apparatus can also be seen in this brief study. The huge US resources of the war years were remobilized in this early stage of the Cold War and much of the wartime intelligence expertise reappeared to fight a new enemy on a global basis.

THE USA REARMAMENT

Late 1947 marks the decision in US governmental ranks for the rebuilding of the country's military forces. Plans then were laid to expand the US army from its existing 542,000 personnel to 790,000 by June 1948. Naval aircraft numbers were to be increased by purchasing another 1,165 aircraft.[1] The following table demonstrates how this rearmament programme compared with previous expansions in the US military.[2]

Shown below are the strengths of the Army, Air Force, Navy and Marine Corps as of 30 June 1937, 30 June 1947, and 31 December 1947. The numbers in parenthesis in the last two rows show the increase in the several forces over 30 June 1937; for example, the strength of the Army, as of 30 June 1947, was 4.25 times that of 30 June 1937.

	Army		Air Force		Navy	
30 June 1937	159,586		19,147		113,369	
30 June 1947	683,837	(4.25)	305,827	(16)	485,534	(4.25)
31 December 1947	559,226	(3.5)	339,246	(17.75)	403,498	(3.5)

	Marines		Naval tonnage (including auxiliaries) – Operating units	
30 June 1937	18,223		2,133,000	
30 June 1947	92,222	(5)	3,137,400	(1.5)
31 December 1947	83,242	(4.5)	3,275,000	(1.5)

	Active Navy ships	Naval combatant ship tonnage		Active Navy combat ships
30 June 1937	1,086	1,096,000		327
30 June 1947	2,032	1,381,000	(1.2)	280
31 December 1947	2,038	1,381,000	(1.3)	281

The USA was deeply concerned, at this time, to assist the Chinese Nationalist forces to stem the southward thrust of the Chinese communist forces by providing large amounts of arms and ammunition. From VJ day in 1945 to the end of 1951, the USA supplied over 1,000 military aircraft, 131 naval vessels, 6,500 tons of ammunition, enough rifles to equip 9 US infantry divisions and 231 million rounds of 0.30 calibre ammunition.[3] The eventual defeat of the Nationalists in this civil war seemed to confirm in the minds of the US planners the necessity for pursuing war by all other means short of military engagement. It also led to greater emphasis on denying the potential enemy access to as much Western trade as possible.

The USA perceived communism as a monolithic force directed from Moscow. The USA failed to see it as an expression of nationalism in some countries or as a post-war settlement of civil tensions in others. In the latter case, civil war emerged in those countries between the often communist-based partisan forces demanding a dominant role in the re-establishment of governments in Europe and the returning authority figures, who had either fled their countries ahead of invading Germans or joined these invaders. The intelligence assessments made of the communist forces in Italy and Greece reflect this misunderstanding. It was the size of the Italian Communist Party and the persistence of the communist guerrillas, fighting in the Macedonian mountains of Greece, which was a particular focus for the US planners. But the US intelligence reports distorted the threat of communism in both countries. In the interpretation of Italian events, the Italian communists were portrayed as being able to defeat the Italian security forces in armed conflict if outside help were not provided. But later the same report had the Yugoslav communist armed forces coming to the aid of the Italian communists to overthrow the Italian state.[4]

The position of the communists in Greece was also misunderstood by the USA as it moved to take over from the UK the responsibility of helping to fight the anti-fascist EAM/ELAS forces. A report from the US Army Group, the American Mission for Aid to Greece, veered between describing this former partisan force as communist and bandit. Confusion prevailed on the bandits' numbers. This intelligence report put their numbers at 19,000 but then added that they had sustained 5,000 casualties. This force was facing the Greek National Army of 120,000 regular troops supported by National Defense Corps battalions numbering 21,000 men. The report described a situation in which there would have been little need for US concern especially when it was added that the bandits had no township to act as a base, no artillery, and no air support.[5]

REBUILDING US INTELLIGENCE

The dismantling of US intelligence bodies ceased in 1946 when the Central Intelligence Group (CIG), which had been part of the Office of Strategic Services (OSS), was re-formed. From a staff of 100 early in 1946, it expanded to 1,816 people by the end of 1946 to become the Central Intelligence Agency (CIA).[6] The passing of the National Security Act in July 1947 was central to this move to confront communism. It provided not only for the founding of the CIA but also for the coordinating of the three military services, including the newly established Air Force, and later a centralized Defense Department in 1949.

Another important intelligence development at this time was the revamping of the wartime signals or COMINT intelligence organization which had effectively helped defeat the Axis powers. At the end of the war it was in the hands of a coalition of the military, the State Department, and the FBI, and it was eventually to become the National Security Agency (NSA), which eavesdropped on worldwide communications traffic. In 1947, moves were in progress to replace this coalition with more direct control of the National Security Council, and by February 1948 James Forrestal, the Secretary of Defense, was aiming to establish the US Communication Intelligence Board to take it over. This was to be done not by issuing an Executive Order, but simply by implementing the terms of the National Security Act, in the way the CIA had been established.[7] Forrestal could have readily predicted the resentment by the military services of this arrangement, and the management of this highly important US intelligence asset was settled by Forrestal's successor, Louis H. Johnson. In May 1949, he established the Armed Forces Security Agency which placed this vast COMINT organization under the control of the military through the Joint Chiefs of Staff.[8]

TRADE WAR (COCOM)

Trade warfare has long played an important if less publicized role in winning wars. The idea of conducting trade warfare during peacetime impressed US officialdom after the discovery that US firms had supplied machine tools and engine parts to build the aircraft used by Japan in the Pacific war. For example, 85 per cent of the machinery purchased by the Mitsubishi aircraft plant in Nagoya between 1936 and 1940 was obtained from US suppliers.[9]

These and other examples were seized upon in US government circles as reasons for launching a programme to curtail Western trade with the Soviet empire, by then regarded as the major enemy of the USA. The USA had never maintained extensive trading links with the Soviet Union or the rest of Eastern Europe or indeed with the preceding tsarist regime. Manganese, gold, and furs had been imported by the USA and paid for by exports of large electrical generators and oil-drilling equipment. Even this small amount of trade ceased late in 1947 when the Department of Commerce had the Decontrol Act amended. The purpose of this act had been designed more to conserve US commodities for domestic usage and to aid particular allies of the USA. Western Europe, however, quickly restored at the end of the war the trading connections that had existed for over two centuries with Eastern Europe. Such trade had consisted mainly of the East exchanging basic commodities such as timber, coarse grains, foodstuffs, and oil for Western machinery, transport equipment, and consumer goods. Trade treaties lasting two to five years were signed by the West with the East from early 1946. The French exchanged machinery and motor cars for coal from Poland, the Dutch exchanged crude rubber and chemicals for tobacco and dried fruit from Bulgaria, the British exchanged machinery and mining equipment for Soviet timber and grain, and the Italians traded lead and blister copper for Yugoslavian timber. All these countries also traded with Romania to obtain its oil. Much of this trade was paid for in British sterling and later French francs, and the East thereby established a surplus balance of trade – mostly in non-dollar currencies.

The US officials, however, viewed this expanding trade (never to be very large) as a serious strategic threat in the developing Cold War. These fears were expressed in various areas of the US administration, as in the following cable from Acheson, the Secretary of State, to the US Paris embassy:

> US view is that the objective of export control program is to promote and protect our mutual security by curbing development of Soviet bloc war potential to extent possible and to extent consistent with building up western strength relative to that of East. Economic health, political stability, and continued close coopera-

tion between Western countries are all recognised as essential elements contributing to Western strength. US view that industrial potential cannot be separated from war potential, and that both are of strategic importance.[10]

It was against the revival of commercial airlines that US officialdom first became concerned in its progress towards a trade embargo against the East. The US officials opposed airlines in Eastern Europe resuming flights to the West not only on grounds of hindering this new transportation trade but also because the US officials were convinced that the Soviet aircrews would conduct espionage and photographic reconnaissance from their passenger aircraft. During 1947 and 1948, the US officials were eager to stop the revival of this trade. The USSR showed a similar caution by banning foreign over-flights of its territory. The British, however, resumed flying into Warsaw and Prague, and the Polish airline LOT and the Czechs flew reciprocal flights to London. US officials quickly moved to stop this development; 'Crews of these satellite aircraft include Russian personnel', they warned, who would thereby be 'gaining experience in flying over territory containing important strategic objectives'.[11] The US unilaterally declared that it would refuse permission for LOT to overfly the US zone in Germany on the Warsaw–Brussels sector of the route to London. The British attempted to persuade a reluctant US that there would be intelligence advantages in having a Western airline flying into Warsaw because it could be used to evacuate friends of the West (a euphemism for intelligence agents). But the US officials dismissed this British ploy as being 'disingenuous', and pointed out that 'under present conditions Warsaw people whom Britain or US might wish to assist could be "gotten in and out in a hurry" via flights commercial carrier'.[12] The British government, however, refused to have the British Empire Airways (BEA) abandon its post-war airline expansion programmes in Eastern Europe. It was an indication of the importance he placed on the intelligence aspects of civil aviation, or 'air transport containment' as he labelled it, that the US ambassador in London, Lewis Douglas, resorted to behind-the-scene tactics to prevent Eastern European aircrews from flying over West Europe. Douglas suggested that an approach 'should be made in the first instance through military channels, possibly combined chiefs. Assuming British concurrence, the problem might then be broached with other governments through Western Union Military Committee or Atlantic Treaty Organization when set up.'[13] Douglas' suggested intervention demonstrated how the senior US officials, in planning their measures to contain the Soviet Union and its satellites, were willing to manipulate those in foreign governments whom they believed to be sympathetic to the US aims.

The Swedes were also suspected by officials of the Economic Cooperation Administration (ECA) of smuggling aircraft parts to the East via Scandinavian Airlines (SAS). The basis of this suspicion rested on the fact that 'investigation through channels available to the Embassy [indicates] Scandinavian Airlines (SAS) has been carrying inordinately large stocks aviation spare parts in Paris'. This referred to US aircraft parts, and US Ambassador Bruce, in Paris, promised 'further investigations being made of these concerns' of SAS diverting parts to the East. The term, 'channels available to the Embassy', would have referred to a variety of intelligence-gathering operations, ranging from communications interception in Paris to a compliant SAS official passing on information.[14]

THE ROLE OF COCOM

The opportunity for the USA to obtain the support of the West European countries for a ban on most of their exports to the East occurred with the adoption in March 1948 of the European Recovery Program, better known as the Marshall Plan. Lengthy lists were drawn up by the National Military Establishment and CIA representatives of a wide range of munition-type material, together with the vast volume of industrial and manufacturing items, which were to be denied export. An amendment to the legislation for the European Recovery Program, the Foreign Assistance Act of 1948, introduced by Senator Karl E. Mundt, prescribed that Marshall aid would be withdrawn from countries using aid-funded material in exports to the East. Officers of the ECA were assigned to enforce these bans, designed as they were for 'building up the defensive strength of the West and reducing the war potential of the East'.[15]

An oversight body was then formed, known as the Consultative Group in COCOM, which consisted of all participating countries. This was to be a secretive body with headquarters in Paris. By compiling intelligence information derived from open and covert sources, COCOM was to monitor those exporters who attempted to evade the restriction on exports described in the US lists. Its charter declared that it was to 'exchange intelligence reports and information as to end destination and that it should study special problems such as leakages due to transshipments'.[16]

The gatherers of this trade intelligence were mainly State Department officials working in the various US embassies and consular offices. They were assisted by the officers of the European Cooperation Administration, who exercised the legal authority to punish countries who evaded the terms of the Mundt amendment to the Foreign Assistance Act. These officials collected trading intelligence (somewhat like their political intelligence) from foreign friends who were merchants or traders. If a case could be established, the US officials would prepare a documented case for presentation to the government of the exporting country, who would be expected to follow-up the matter in accordance with the trade embargo arrangements that had confidentially been established between it and the US government in the form of a secret agreement.

The principal means of intelligence surveillance was represented in a database consisting of trade and economic statistics relating to each COCOM member country. This information source also contained details about production in the USSR of a range of munitions and manufactured items. The armament industries, the export and import industries, and the trans-shipment ports of the various European countries all had information collected about them. Additional information was obtained from US sources such as the US Department of Commerce, the US Munitions Department, and the intelligence branches of the US military services. One valuable report, for example, was provided by the US Navy's intelligence branch about the rubber exports it had monitored that were being shipped from the Malay states via Singapore to the USSR.[17]

The lists of banned exports were prepared in Washington, and variations of them were prepared for each country, determined by what items they mostly traded in. An unpublished agreement was then obtained from each government as a means of enforcing the embargo. By the end of 1948, US officials went beyond the specifics of the double list of prohibitions to include any machine or equipment that contained a technological development such as 'prototype machinery involving new scientific developments or advances and ... certain plant installations where the element of "know how" is a critical consideration'.[18] This additional restriction required surveillance of a higher technical order, as we shall see.

While the British government totally endorsed these US policies, with Sir Stafford Cripps, Foreign Minister in the Attlee government, undertaking to maintain these trade embargoes,[19] the French were markedly reluctant to agree. The US officials learned that the French considered 'that the proposed East–West trade policy was a politico-strategic move unrelated to European recovery', and that the 'United States was attempting to commit France to a policy of virtual economic warfare against the Soviet bloc.'[20] The left-wing political forces were then strong in France, and the officials argued that discussing the banning of trade with the East would 'from the point of view of public relations be embarrassing to the French Government, especially since a large body of French public opinion was opposed to the policy'. The response of the US officials was to resort to covert practices; that is, to agree with the French officials to remain silent on condition that the embargo policy be implemented. The support of the French government's economic and foreign ministers was also enrolled under the same conditions.

The French government insisted that its membership of COCOM not be revealed by demanding that the names of the participating countries not be announced. The existence of COCOM's headquarters in Paris was also to remain a secret because it would also expose France's involvement in the scheme. The French communist paper, *Liberation,* revealed some information about COCOM in its edition of 30 March 1949. It condemned Sir Stafford Cripps, of Britain, and Robert Schuman, of France, for secretly submitting to US pressure to support COCOM in exchange for Marshall Plan aid.[21]

The efficiency of US intelligence collecting in France on Eastern trade matters was demonstrated by its detection of the sale by France of three Junkers 52 aircraft to Bulgaria late in 1948. After calming the excited reaction this news generated in the State Department in Washington, the French explained that the Junkers aircraft had continued to be manufactured during 1947 in France, well after the German occupation had ended, and that the aircraft had been converted to civilian use. No US-provided materials had been used, the French explained, and the Bulgarian contract had been signed in 1947 before the Marshall Plan was established. The benefit of this trade to France was that it was to receive 2,000 tons of lead from Bulgaria.[22] These events demonstrated how efficient were the US investigative agencies. While they could not stop trade with the East, they forced the exporting country to provide an explanation of their trading relationships.

Another episode in intelligence gathering about French trade with the East demonstrated how the eagerness of the US trade investigators to punish the French led them into the serious misjudgement of blaming the French for crimes that they had not committed. A US intelligence report of mid-1950 indicated that a French metals company had traded 2,000 tons of lead to the Soviet Union in return for asbestos. The US demanded reimbursement from the French government for this lead sale, assuming that it had been originally funded by Marshall Plan aid. After protests from the French and an inquiry by the Chief of the Non-Ferrous Metals Branch of the Industry Division of Economic Cooperation Administration, it was established that the lead had been obtained from Tunisian mines and had not been funded by Marshall Plan aid.[23] Trading in lead remained a strong interest of US trade-intelligence experts because lead was used as a shielding agent in the construction of nuclear reactors.

The USA wished to locate the headquarters of COCOM in London, but it claimed to have settled instead on Paris because of that city's more central position. Such an explanation appears to have been a blind, however. It was not the centrality of Paris to European affairs, but rather the necessity to monitor the French deviance from US rules for firmly controlling trade with the East that determined US planning in this issue. French intransigence in refusing to control exports to the East was often observed by US authorities. The French intention to continue trade with China after the war in Korea had broken out in June 1950 was one example. The French, understandably, justified their intentions to fill a Chinese order on the grounds that this sale of steel rods had been arranged before the outbreak of this war, which was not a declared war and looked more like a civil war. With fear of communism accelerating at an increased pace in the USA under the Truman administration, the USA revoked all export licences for trade with China in July 1950. When China entered the war, US officials sought to stop the export of French rails to China in spite of the French government's having authorized the sale. In an intelligence exercise that coordinated the US Treasury, the Department of Commerce, the State Department, and seemingly the CIA, the French government was assailed in a move to stop the shipment of $US4.5 million worth of French steel rails and other steel products to China. In an arrangement with the Bank of Indochina, the Chinese deposited US dollars in the French American Banking Corporation in New York as backing for an irrevocable letter of credit to show firm intent to make this purchase. In what appeared like a well-coordinated intelligence strike, the USA seized these dollars, thus barring payment to the French steel company supplying the rails. The company contemplated suing the New York bank in the French courts. The State Department warned the French government to stop this shipment on 12 December 1950 with little result. In what appeared like an escalation of the intelligence operation, news of the matter was given to the *Washington Star*, which printed a front-page report on 4 January 1951 that the French government had authorized the shipment of 450 miles of rails to be used in linking the rail system of southern China to that of Indochina.[24] The fate of that shipment is unknown, but the incident demonstrates the speed and range of intelligence coordination that could be achieved by US officials when it came to stopping strategic trade to the communist countries.

The *Washington Star*'s report produced an immediate response among Congressmen alarmed at the prospect of their European allies using dollar aid to support the enemies of the USA. Congressmen Connor, Kem, and later Battle led the debate on legislation that would force all recipients of US aid to conform even more vigorously to US demands to reduce trade with the East to a minimum. The outcome was the passing of the Mutual Defense Assistance Control Act, also known as the Battle Act, on 21 August 1951. This legislation made it easier to stop all aid to recalcitrant nations. Reports on violations were to be presented to Congress by the Battle Act Administration, properly known as the Mutual Security Agency. Exceptions were provided for by the president's being authorized to lift restrictions on aid to an offending country if necessary. The surveillance of the West's trade with the East expanded thereafter.

Some US intelligence agents exercised their own initiatives against French corporations they believed to be violating the trade embargo. They approached French firms directly, outside government channels, to seek assurances that these firms would not re-export goods of US origin. When the French government learned of these unofficial interventions, it expressed concern over this unorthodox US behaviour at a COCOM meeting. The main objection of the French government was that the US actions interfered with the completion of French trading agreements.[25]

A new intelligence system was established by the USA to monitor its recalcitrant allies, particularly the French. This consisted of appointing US intelligence officers to the newly established Destination Control Units within the economic sections of US embassies. Such unit agents investigated the export of goods suspected of being diverted to the Soviet bloc via a third country. Intelligence about these transactions was supplied in many cases by the State Department in Washington. The agents working in the Paris unit, for example, investigated 228 such requests over 17 months. Washington possibly obtained its intelligence from agents in the field, informers, or communication intercepts. The unit also received intelligence on another 63 cases from other embassies, probably collected by similar means. The unit agents denied the issuance of export licences in 43 cases because it was believed that the goods, amounting to nearly $500,000 in value, would be diverted to Soviet bloc countries. The French authorities were advised, but they took little action other than withdrawing those export licences already suspended by the US agents.[26] The case in which a Lyon firm was revealed to be dispatching an order for ferro-alloys, ostensibly for Britain but actually for Czechoslovakia, demonstrates how the interconnected US trade-intelligence mechanism functioned. The US embassy in Vienna first detected this order to the Lyon firm emanating from Metalmix in Prague, presumably by signals intelligence. It also detected an instruction from Prague to the Banque Commerciale pour l'Europe du Nord, Paris, to credit the Lyon firm with nearly $35,000 without mentioning what these funds were for. The ferro-alloys reached Prague, and the USA was reluctant to raise the matter at a COCOM meeting because it 'could only serve to demonstrate the techniques used' in detecting this affair. The outcome was that the US agents demanded that French investigators pursue the investigation and prosecute the Lyon firm.[27] Given the French reluctance to implement US trade intelligence requirements that would endanger its expanding export trade, it is unlikely that any such action was taken.

US INTELLIGENCE AND TRADE

By the middle of 1949, the US intelligence estimates were that the trade embargo was having the desirable effect of hampering the USSR's war potential. Captain M.M. Dupre Jr, of the US Navy, the Munitions Board Military Representative in the office of the Special Representative of the European Cooperation Administration in Paris, declared that the trade embargo would deny to the Soviet bloc 'the key tools of research so as to slow down their economic progress to a point where they will be obliged to remain from ten to fifteen years behind that of Western Europe and the United States'.[28]

The progress of the Cold War and the inability of the Economic Cooperation Administration staff to keep abreast of events (the miscalculation of the French–Tunisian lead was an example), as well as the establishment of new bodies to contain communism such as the Atlantic Pact and the Mutual Defence Assistance Pact, led the US State Department to take over the management of COCOM in January 1950. COCOM was no longer an adjunct to West European recovery. It was viewed as an important weapon in the Cold War. The State Department continued to call on assistance from the Department of Defense for technical information, the Department of Commerce, the Atomic Energy Commission, and for intelligence information from the CIA.[29] All reports issued by the State Department to its embassies dealing with COCOM's trade war were also sent to the CIA, and the intelligence branches of the Army, Air Force and Navy.

The means by which surveillance was maintained on violators of the so-called 'United States Export Control Program' was by placing their names and offences on the US 'Special Check List' and also the 'Coordinating Committee Watch List'.[30] Marshall Plan funds were frequently allocated to private firms that were later detected exporting equipment or commodities to the East. US investigators sometimes traced the paper chain, relating to machinery or equipment being exported to the East, back to its source. This revealed that such exports had been manufactured or otherwise financed with Marshall Plan aid. When such corporations were called upon by the US investigators to account for their violations of US law, they offered a variety of excuses and some exhibited indifference when investigators threatened to place their names on a checklist and that no further funding would be granted.

The Germans appeared to be more strict than the French in compiling lists of their firms detected in the export of goods to the East, as the Federal Republic was still beholden to the US High Commission for some of its government. The US officials in Bonn dispatched lists of the names of firms on the 'administrative action list' to Washington for addition to the main list and to the French and British, who would blacklist such German firms appearing on their own procurement programmes in Germany. The State Department in Washington distributed the blacklisted names in a quarterly bulletin to the governments concerned.[31] The German federal government also undertook prosecutions of embargo evaders and then provided lists of the prosecutions they conducted (sometimes leading to jail terms of five months and fines of DM1,000) to the US High Commissioner for Germany. However, they refused to supply the names of the firms concerned.[32]

As a global power, the USA was able to maintain surveillance of Western trade with the East from numerous international points. In 1952, the US government was alarmed to find that Sri Lanka had agreed to a five-year trade treaty with China to exchange 80,000 tons of rubber for Chinese rice. And this was at a time when a UN embargo had been placed on Western trade with China because of the Korean War. Understandably the Sri Lankan government was reluctant to reveal the details of this trade arrangement to the USA. The State Department ordered its embassy in Sri Lanka to press the host government to abandon the trade agreement. The arguments it employed were that Sri Lanka could lose the US dollar income from the rubber sales, that it could become overreliant on China for food supplies, and that the local Communist Party could exploit this new connection with China. To find out more about this trade agreement, the USA was able to tap into the worldwide intelligence sources available to its numerous embassies – that is, its human intelligence sources, or HUMINT, as it was later known. The State Department sent instructions to its embassies in London, Rangoon, Paris, Jakarta, Singapore, and New Delhi, ordering them to collect information on this trade agreement and specifically about the exact terms relating to the prices, deliveries, length of contract and the inclusion of other commodities, such as graphite, which was reputed to have been included in the arrangements.[33]

The US authorities soon established that the Sri Lankan leader, Susanta De Fonseka, had been instrumental in establishing this trade treaty. By then, he had been appointed the Sri Lankan ambassador in Rangoon and the US ambassador in Burma, William J. Sebald, demanded there that he explain his actions. This informal but tough talking with national leaders marked much of the US technique for collecting intelligence or exerting influence on the trade embargo and other matters. De Fonseka was totally unapologetic and bluntly told Sebald that Sri Lanka had been forced into the arms of the Chinese by US 'obstinacy and short-sightedness [in] refusing to enter into "reasonable" rubber agreement in view essentially [that] Ceylon finds steady market [for] its principal export commodity.'[34] The US could then take little action against Sri Lanka for its disregard of the US trade embargo against China because it was not then in receipt of any US trade. The State Department's notoriously long memory, however, would one day catch up with the recalcitrant Sri Lanka.

THE USA'S TRADE SURVEILLANCE OF ITS ALLIES

Not satisfied with spying on the trading patterns of its allies, the USA wished to investigate the munitions and technical developments in the Western European countries. In July 1949, a technical mission was sent by the USA to examine the military technology developments in Britain, France, and the Netherlands. The expertise of the mission drawn from the Defense Establishment lay in matters of diesel engines, atomic energy, precision instruments, chemical equipment, and metal-working machinery. The British experts were eager not to reveal the presence of the mission to those outside a small circle in the Ministry of Defence because competition existed between Britain and the USA for the markets in defence sales.[35] While news of the visit of the US mission did not leak out, the British officials took issue with the Americans over maintaining sales of British metal-manufacturing machinery. British officials maintained that simply because munitions manufacturing might be one among the many end-uses of this machinery, its export to the East need not be banned. The same argument, they said, applied to many other export items then embargoed. The US officials remained convinced that the Eastern bloc armament industry would always benefit from any imports of metal-working machinery, but, to placate its allies, the US Munitions Board asked the Secretary of Defense, Louis Johnson, on 11 August 1949, as a matter of urgency, to have an evaluation made by the CIA 'of the effectiveness of export controls in minimizing the transfer of war potential materials and facilities to Eastern Europe'. The request was passed to the CIA by Johnson's office five weeks later.[36] Because no relaxation of trade in machinery occurred thereafter, the CIA seemed not to have recommended any changes arising from its investigations.

SURVEILLANCE OF FRENCH TRADE

The US intelligence officials regretted that they could not establish with the French the same harmonious relationship they maintained with their British intelligence and trade counterparts. The British trade intelligence agencies and officials in the Board of Trade and the Federation of British Industries happily cooperated with US intelligence.[37] The French left and others, as well as the French media, perceived the use of the Battle Act by the USA as a measure to dominate European trade, keeping France short of US dollars and compelling four devaluations of the French franc.[38] A lobby group was established in France in the early 1950s (CONFRACI) to press for greater trade with the Soviet bloc and also with Communist China, particularly after the signing of the Korean armistice. Part of the French press condemned this British subservience to US trade embargo demands and claimed that it had led to the British losing a £40 million sale to USSR of copper cables.[39] But this French obstructionism in providing trade intelligence to the US was offset by the Belgian assistance to US intelligence at this time. The US consul general in Antwerp had local maritime officials provide him with copies of the manifests of the ships sailing to Soviet or Chinese ports. This allowed US intelligence to monitor more closely trade to the East from countries, such as Switzerland, that used a third-country port to ship exports to the USSR, or other countries such as Sweden, Finland, Italy, and Lebanon which functioned as transit points for concealing exports to the East. The US consul general's achievement in this intelligence coup led to his being complimented by Secretary of State Dulles himself.[40]

The State Department, while appearing to be the principal player in these trade-embargoing procedures, shared in the controlling and intelligence arrangements with other US agencies through a wide-ranging committee system. Under its Economic Defense Program, the State Department established a series of working groups that were subordinate to the Economic Defense Intelligence Committee. These working groups drew on support from the US intelligence agencies. There was also a technical assistance scheme that conducted exchange visits with foreign officials in customs departments and elsewhere. For some years, France was reluctant to exchange its trade officials with the USA. This committee also had a series of subgroups reporting to it, including one called Capacities of Member Agencies that surveyed the intelligence agencies of the cooperating countries. Another group of intelligence-monitoring committees was established under the Mutual Defense Assistance Act (the Battle Act of 1951) with the title of Mutual Defense Assistance Control. It contained a panel of advisers and a joint operations committee. It oversaw special operations and surveillance of foreign students in US universities, international meetings of foreign scientists, and correspondence between US and foreign scientists.[41]

In spite of these energetic intelligence-gathering and assessment bodies, US officialdom remained unable to achieve the full cooperation of the French in its embargo policies. The result was that the USA had to resort to heavy-handed intelligence techniques whereby bunkering facilities were denied to French trading vessels sailing to the Far East. In October 1953, the *Falaise* was carrying a French and German steel cargo plus Swiss electrical equipment to China. The Swiss cargo was loaded immediately before sailing and thereby came under suspicion by US intelligence officials. The vessel was refused bunkering by the British Shell Company at Djibouti because British Shell claimed that steel appeared on 'the British Simplified Version of China embargo items.' This bunkering refusal was in response to the Swiss electrical cargo, but Shell made no mention of it. The French seemed to know the reason for this obstruction. After obtaining bunkering from another French vessel, the *Falaise* sailed for Saigon where the French promptly unloaded the Swiss cargo and British Shell thereupon provided bunkering for its continuing voyage to China. A second French vessel, *Les Glières,* also carrying Swiss electrical cargo to China, likewise discharged its Swiss cargo at Saigon, before carrying its steel cargo on to China. In the understated terms that were often resorted to by US intelligence agents when concealing the successful outcome of their intelligence operations, the official record of these events characterized them as representing a typical Franco-British trading tiff. In other records, the real explanation was disguised in terms of officialese. There it was explained that 'the discrepancy between the unilaterally administered bunker controls of the US and UK and the multilaterally agreed levels of control in CHINCOM' was the cause. CHINCOM was the counterpart of COCOM, but applied more restrictive conditions to trade with China. M. Charpentier, the French official in charge of Economic Affairs in the French Foreign Office, through whom the US State Department operated, was greatly annoyed by the actions of British

Shell, as it operated in what were then two French territories, but he could do little about it. The lesson driven home by these British actions (no US collusion could be demonstrated) was that there was more than one way to skin the uncooperative French trading cat. The Swiss were also taught the object lesson that its wartime neutrality was to be no protection for its commercial activities during the era of the Cold War. The continued sale of Swiss technology to both the West and the East was placed in jeopardy, as was the sale of French (and German) steel to China.

US trade intelligence activities expanded rather than decreased in the succeeding decades as Western technology developed into new areas of communications technology, computers, and medical technology, all of which had to be policed and watched to prevent exports going eastwards. The French plea for greater economic freedom to trade with the East came to be supported by the British, particularly the Wilson-led Labour government. West Germany also insisted on broader trading with East Germany. COCOM continued to enjoy a long life, operating out of its secret headquarters in Paris well after the Soviet Union had collapsed. In October 1993, it allowed its participating countries to establish their own policies regarding the export of high-performing computers to the East.[42] COCOM later recycled itself into an organization concerned to observe, with a view to controlling, weapons of mass destruction. With the Cold War fast entering an era, which in historical terms may be viewed as a forgotten epoch, it is hoped that the US archival material relating to these events will soon be released so that a firm judgement can be made of the extent to which the COCOM restrictions contributed to the collapse of the USSR.

NOTES

1. Fact Sheet of Ready Reference. Office of the Secretary of Defense, 27 September 1948, D70-1-42. Records of the Office of the Secretary of Defense, RG 330, National Archives and Records Agency, Washington, DC (hereafter NARA).
2. Office of the Secretary of Defense, Memorandum for Mr D.N. Leith, 27 September 1948, in ibid.
3. Report prepared by Foster Adams for Senator Styles Bridges, 16 May 1952. Records of the Secretary of Defense, RG 330, NARA.
4. 'Intelligence Division Special Briefing Memorandum for the Chief of Staff.

Estimate of Italian Situation', 4 December 1947, P & O 350.05 TS (Section IIA) records of the Army Staff, RG 319, NARA.

5. Report by Maj. Gen. Livesay commanding the US Army Group, American Mission for Aid to Greece, in the Greek Military Situation, 26 December 1947, CD 6-1-50, Records of the Secretary of Defense, RG 330, NARA.

6. Testimony regarding civilian director of the Central Intelligence Agency, 22 October 1947, CD12-1-7. Records of the Secretary of Defense, RG 330, NARA.

7. Memorandum by James Forrestal to the Secretaries, Army, Navy and Air Force, 13 February 1948 CD2-1-17, Records of the Secretary of Defence, RG 330, NARA.

8. James Bamford, *Puzzle Palace* (London: Sidgwick and Jackson, 1982), p. 47.

9. See report by the Economic Warfare Section of the Department of Justice War Division, 'Purchase of American Machine Tools by Mitsubishi Enterprises', 11 June 1943, Records of the New York Secret Intelligence Branch S1-OP-56, RG266, NARA.

10. State Department cable no. 900 from Acheson to Paris, 27 August 1950, Records of the Agency for International Development, Mission to France, RG 286, NARA.

11. Douglas, London, to Washington, 9 November 1948, Records of the Agency for International Development, RG 286, NARA.

12. Cable, Acheson to London, 4 February 1949, Records of the Agency for International Development, RG 286, NARA.

13. Cable, Douglas to Paris and Washington, 29 April 1949, Records of the Agency for International Development, RG 286, NARA.

14. Bruce to Secretary of State (with copy to CIA), 4 December 1950, Records of the Agency for International Development, RG 286, NARA.

15. Report by Munitions Board National Security Aspects and Export Controls, 1 January 1949, CD 36-1-1, Records of Secretary of Defense, RG 330, NARA.

16. UK Delegation to OEEC Paris to Foreign Office, 22 June 1949, FO 371/77798, Public Record Office, London (hereafter PRO).

17. Report of the Chief of Naval Operations to SECNAV and SECDEF, 15 June 1948, CD 26-1-7, records of the Secretary of Defense, RG 330, NARA.

18. Memorandum from American Embassy, Paris, to Ambassador Harriman 16 October 1948. Records of the Agency for International Development Mission to France, RG286, NARA.

19. Harriman to SECSTATE, Washington, 30 October 1948. Records of the Agency for International Development, Mission to France, RG 286, NARA.

20. Report of the Economic Cooperation Administration Special Mission to France on East-West Trade, 31 December 1948, pp. 24–5. Records of the Agency for International Development Mission to France. RG 286, NARA.

21. ECA Special Mission to France, Bruce Paris to SECSTATE, 31 March 1949. Records of the Agency for International Development Mission to France, RG286, NARA.

22. Herve Alphand, Minister of Foreign Affairs to American Embassy, 5 October

1948. Records of the Agency for International Development Mission to France, RG 286, NARA.

23. French export of lead to Russia, 5 January to 8 June 1950, Economic Cooperation Administration. Records of the Agency for International Development, RG 286, NARA.

24. Robert P. Terrill, Deputy Counselor for Economic Affairs to State Department, enclosing Note to French government, 12 December 1950; Paris Embassy, to State Department for Treasury, ECA and CIA explaining financial problems; State Department to Paris Embassy with *Washington Star* news release, 4 January 1951, Records of the Agency for International Development, RG 286, NARA.

25. Bonsal, Paris Embassy, to State Department, 17 March 1952, Records of the Agency for International Development, RG 286, NARA.

26. US Embassy to State Department, Investigation of East–West Trade Cases, 27 May 1953, Records of the US Foreign Assistance Agency, RG 469, NARA.

27. Harry Conover, First Secretary, Paris Embassy to State Department, Diversion of ferro-alloys by French Firm St. Beron, 25 June 1953, Records of the US Foreign Assistance Agency, RG 469, NARA.

28. Report to the Fiscal and Trade Policy Division of ECA on technical conferences with representatives of the United Kingdom, Netherlands, and France, 19 July thru 6 August 1949, p. 6, Records of Secretary of Defense, RG 330, NARA.

29. Statement of functions, personnel and budget to be transferred from ECA/W to the Department of State, 27 January 1950, Records of the Agency for International Development, RG 286, NARA.

30. Henry Parkmon, Chief of Mission to Ambassador C. Tyler Wood, Deputy US Special Representative, Paris, 21 September 1950. Records of the Agency for International Development, RG 286, NARA.

31. A.F. Kiefer, Chief Eastern Economic Relations Division to Department of State, Washington, DC, 17 March 1954, Records of the Agency for International Development, RG 286, NARA.

32. E.M. Brown, Acting Deputy Chief Eastern Economic Relations Division, 'Statistics on Prosecutions Administrative Action', 8 February 1954, Records of the Agency for International Development, RG 286, NARA.

33. Cable from State Department Washington, DC, to Colombo, 24 October 1952, Records of the Agency for International Development, RG 286, NARA.

34. Cable from Sebald, Rangoon, to Washington, DC, 30 October 1952, Records of the Agency for International Development, RG 286, NARA.

35. Meeting between Representatives of the Government of the USA and Representatives of the Government of the UK, 27 July 1949, FO 371/77802, PRO.

36. Memorandum for the Director, Control Intelligence Agency from Louis Johnson, 21 October 1949, CD 26-1-1, Records of the Secretary of Defense, RG 330, NARA.

37. US Paris Embassy to State Department, Cable No. 6626, 28 April 1952, Records of US Foreign Assistance Agencies, Deputy Director, European Operations Office, French Division, RG469, NARA.
38. US Paris Embassy to Secretary of State, 28 December 1951, Records of the US Foreign Assistance Agencies, Deputy Director, European Operations Office, French Division, RG469, NARA.
39. US Paris Embassy to State Department, 2 September 1953, Records of US Foreign Assistance Agencies, Deputy Director, European Operations Office, French Division, RG469, NARA.
40. Dulles to Consul General, Antwerp, 3 January 1955, Records of the US Foreign Assistance Agencies, Office of the African and European Operations, RG469, NARA.
41. Economic Defence Program Report 29 April 1955, Records of the US Foreign Assistance Agencies, Office of the African and European Operations, RG469, NARA.
42. *Intelligence Newsletter*, 10 February 1994, p. 7.

8

'A New Apparatus is Established in the Eastern Zone' – The Foundation of the East German State Security Service

Monika Tantzscher

> We know the cooperation will continue, just as during the formation of the organs after 1949 when they were set up by order of the Political Bureau of the CPSU[1] and Walter Ulbricht.
> Erich Mielke[2]

The beginning of the Cold War soon after the conclusion of World War II, as well as the gradual separation of the Soviet occupation zone from the three Western zones, brought about a continual extension of security-related and political tasks the Soviet Union was unwilling or unable to perform by itself. Although regulations had been issued by the Allied Control Council after the defeat of Germany, according to which German police forces were to confine their activities to the protection of the population and the maintenance of law and order, Soviet authorities soon took steps aimed at setting up a secret police. The Control Council's Act No. 31 prohibited a political police force in all occupation zones, and the occupation authorities themselves were to assume responsibility for state security and both internal and external defence. However, by officially ordering the Germans to assist in executing the Control Council's edicts, the Allies implicitly assigned tasks to them normally carried out by a secret police.

From the very beginning, the police apparatus established in the Soviet occupation zone exhibited characteristic features of a secret police force. The police units in charge of denazification, which received their orders from the Soviet occupation authorities, were soon also used to persecute political opponents in the name of 'anti-fascism'. Under the cloak of 'denazification', the police and the judiciary were modelled after their Soviet counterparts to ensure that they would willingly cooperate with the communists in their quest for power.

This chapter deals with the intensive, top-secret activities conducted in 1949 to set up the organization that in February 1950 became the Ministry for State Security of the newly founded German Democratic Republic (GDR). The opening of the now defunct republic's archives to researchers has made it possible to shed new light on this interesting period of contemporary history. Files stored in these archives now provide additional background information on decisions taken at the highest level in Moscow. Moreover, new material is available on the various restructuring activities undertaken within the police organs in the Soviet occupation zone, and on the careers of many functionaries who were to play an important role in the Ministry of State Security.

In December 1948, a delegation of the Socialist Unity Party consisting of Wilhelm Pieck, Otto Grotewohl, Walter Ulbricht, and Fred Oelssner went to Moscow for consultations with the leadership of the CPSU. They met with Stalin on 19 December. In his outline of the meeting, Wilhelm Pieck noted that the *Kriminalpolizei* (agency responsible for criminal investigations) was to be purged and better trained, while in place of K-5 (political police force) a 'Central Department for the Protection of the Economy and the Democratic Order' was to be established under the direct control of the Soviet occupation zone as well as of the president of the German Interior Administration and provincial chiefs of police. An officer in charge of defence against sabotage was to be appointed in every factory. The staff of the new office was to consist of so-called proven functionaries who hitherto had worked for the *Kriminalpolizei* and of party functionaries, who were to undergo special training for this purpose. Training facilities were to be established at the upper police academy.[3]

On 28 December 1948, the Politburo of the CPSU approved the request by Socialist Unity Party envoys to strengthen 'state security'.[4] Colonel General Koval'chuk, the commissioner of the Soviet Ministry for State Security[5] (MGB) in the Soviet occupation zone, and his minister Abakumov, who had long opposed increasing the authority of German security units, were forced to abandon their opposition.[6] The restructuring of the *Kriminalpolizei* was scheduled to take effect on 1 March 1949.[7] It had previously consisted of commissariats and departments, followed by the sections K-1 to K-7 based on types of crime. Now the departments A, B, C, E and F and a field office were to be assigned to both Department K of the German Interior Administration and the provincial headquarters of the People's Police. Every police station was to receive the commissariats B, C, E, and F and a field office. Department A was to deal with statistics, reporting, and training; Department B with economic crimes; and Department C with all non-economic offences. It was the job of one of its sections, Task Force C 10, to 'combat anti-democratic activity'.[8] Department E was responsible for identifications and technical equipment, and Department F for investigations.

That area of responsibility formerly assigned to the Political Police, K-5,[9] continued to exist as a field covered by Task Force D, though it was no longer under the direction of the *Kriminalpolizei*. The various commissariats, departments, and sections of K-5 had arisen after 1945 out of a special division of the *Kriminalpolizei* in charge of political affairs (*Kriminal-Sonderstellen für politische Angelegenheiten*). It had at first been responsible primarily for the execution of orders issued by the Soviet military administration, as well as for the persecution of war criminals, Nazi activists and members of the Nazi hierarchy. The latter included members of the *Reichssicherheitshauptamt*, the *Sicherheitsdienst* (SD), the Gestapo, and agents of the Gestapo. In addition, K-5 had been responsible for selecting personnel with suitable political credentials for the newly created administrative apparatus. As an executive body of the Soviet occupation forces, K-5 cooperated closely with the operational groups of the Soviet security service, the *kommandanturas* (local headquarters of the Soviet occupation forces), and Soviet prosecutors. The Soviet military administration supervised K-5's activities through direct contacts with the heads of police agencies and through a system of instructors. K-5 was systematically established in the *Länder* (states) following Order No. 201 of 16 August 1947 on denazification, which provided for the transfer of both executive and judicial functions to the German police agencies. Erich Mielke, the German Interior Administration functionary entrusted with enforcing Order No. 201, played a vital role in this process. He instructed the states' interior ministers and chiefs of police on the

115

denazification measures to be taken and ensured that regular reports were submitted to the Soviet military administration in Berlin-Karlshorst. At a meeting between the German Interior Administration and the provincial heads of K-5's departments and commissariats in October 1947, Mielke pointed out that the police had been assigned the execution of tasks which had previously been the responsibility of the occupational forces. 'The course of denazification to date,' he stated, 'has shown that we as German agencies have not done our job well. It is time that we dispense with empty words once and for all. Order 201 has raised the issue of the struggle for power.'[10] When the Saxon Minister of the Interior, Kurt Fischer, who had worked for the Soviet military secret service during his exile in the Soviet Union, was named president of the German Interior Administration in July 1948, Erich Mielke advanced to the position of first vice-president. In addition, Mielke, who had been responsible for matters related to police personnel and training since the establishment of the German Interior Administration in 1946, was put in charge of the Central Secretariat of the Socialist Unity Party's organs of *Politkultur* (political culture), which had been set up in July 1948 to monitor the political orientation of the police agencies. In the police hierarchy, the *Politkultur* officers always occupied the position of first deputy to the head of the particular organizational unit, which in effect meant the power of the communist party (that is, the Socialist Unity Party) had merged with the power of the government. In the meantime, Mielke's area of responsibility, personnel policy, had been extended from the police to the central administrations, the provincial governments, and the German Economic Commission (*Deutsche Wirtschaftskommission*), founded in February 1948.

On 6 May 1949, an order was issued to the provincial sections of K-5 instructing them that they were no longer to accept orders from the police and criminal investigation authorities. K-5's departments and commissariats were now directly responsible to the K-5 department of the German Interior Administration.[11] As had previously been the case, all findings related to security matters were to be passed on to the administration's vice-president, Erich Mielke.[12] Personnel planning for the provincial offices of the *Kriminalpolizei* established that one-third of the total staff were to be made available to Department D as the nucleus of the future State Security Service.[13] In Berlin and the provincial capitals, Wilhelm Zaisser, who was to become the first Minister for State Security, selected administrative staff for the security service.[14]

On 2 April 1949, Colonel General Koval'chuk reported to Stalin that in all district administrations of the newly founded German State Security Service, MGB groups had been formed to guide and control the German security services, and that an additional 115 MGB officers were to be assigned to the Soviet zone of occupation for this purpose.[15]

A confidential dossier prepared by the Hessian Ministry of the Interior on the establishment of the security service in the Soviet occupation zone reveals the various names used for the newly established local offices, listing such terms as *Abteilung D* (Department D) of the *Kriminalpolizei*, *Neue Dienststelle* (New Agency), *Exekutivbüro* (Executive Office), or – based on the Soviet model – *Operative Gruppe* (Operational Group). The dossier also noted that the East German authorities were dissatisfied with the work of K-5 and had taken steps to establish an independent security apparatus with its own offices, mostly in confiscated villas near the NKVD[16] or in houses vacated by the NKVD. These buildings were equipped with special security and surveillance systems, while the basement rooms were converted into prison cells.[17]

These restructuring activities are confirmed by personnel directives issued during the period after July 1949 by the German Administration of the Interior and the Central Administration of the German People's Police (*Hauptverwaltung der Deutschen Volkspolizei*), which had been formed after the founding of the GDR in October 1949. Starting in July, police officers – in particular those from the security-related branches of K-5, Border Police, and *Politkultur* – were assigned to the heads of provincial police authorities 'to fulfil special tasks'.[18] Chief Inspector Richard Staimer was responsible for setting up the security service in the state of Brandenburg. In Mecklenburg-West Pomerania, the provincial chief of police and later head of the State Security Administration of Greater Berlin, Karl Kleinjung, was entrusted with this task. His deputy was Josef Kiefel, later the head of Central Department II (counter-intelligence) of the Ministry for State Security. In Thuringia, the president of the German Interior Administration appointed Chief Inspector Leander Kröber as officer-in-charge; his assistants included the superintendent of the People's Police, Rudolf Gutsche.[19] On one day alone, 10 August 1949, about 170 police officers were assigned to Department D of the *Kriminalpolizei* in various states, among them officers who were later to assume leading positions within the Ministry for State Security, such as the deputy ministers Bruno Beater and Fritz Schröder, along with Josef Kiefel, Alfred Scholz, and Herman Gartmann, future members of the Collegium[20] of the Ministry for State Security. All of these functionaries had a similar background. While some had fought in the Red Army or against Franco's forces in Spain, others had been Soviet partisans, or worked as propagandists in the National Committee for a Free Germany[21] or as instructors in Soviet prisoner-of-war camps. Another source of officers for the new security services were the communist resistance fighters who had been liberated from Nazi concentration camps and prisons in 1945. Among them was the former head of the German Interior Administration's K-5 department, Erich Jamin, who was transferred on 1 November 1949 to Mielke's 'Department K D'. Jamin was to assume important functions in the Ministry for State Security until 1965.[22]

These activities did not go unnoticed in the West. Radio station RIAS, headquartered in West Berlin, reported on 6 August 1949 that a new apparatus resembling the former *Sicherheitshauptamt* was being established in the eastern zone. This new body was to be given particularly extensive powers.[23]

In the same broadcast, the radio station mentioned a report from the German Interior Administration regarding the 'people's growing resistance to the terror system in the Soviet zone', allegedly resulting in a wave of arrests by K-5 and the NKVD. There were claims, for example, that around 2,500 arrests had been listed in K-5's monthly report for July 1949.[24]

A meeting of the Politburo of the Socialist Unity Party took place on 10 September 1949.[25] At this meeting, Wilhelm Pieck, reporting on the 'preparation of measures to be taken by the state', also raised the question of national security. The minutes of his report fully correspond with the aforementioned outline of the meeting with Stalin, which had taken place on 19 December 1948.[26]

After the founding of the GDR on 7 October 1949, three administrative agencies were established under the Ministry of the Interior: the Central Administration German People's Police (*Hauptverwaltung Deutsche Volkspolizei*), the Central Training Administration (*Hauptverwaltung Ausbildung*), and the Central Administration for the Protection of the Economy (*Hauptverwaltung zum Schutz der Volkswirtschaft*).

Kurt Fischer was named chief of the People's Police, while Alfred Schönherr, vice-president of the People's Police, was simultaneously put in charge of the *Kriminalpolizei*. Other high-ranking functionaries who doubled as vice-presidents of the People's Police included Heinz Hoffmann, the head of the Administration *Politkultur*; Erich Mielke, the head of the Central Administration for the Protection of the Economy; Wilhelm Zaisser, the head of the Central Training Administration; and Willi Seifert.

The principal departments within the Central Administration People's Police were Political/Cultural Affairs, Personnel, Civil Police, *Kriminalpolizei*, Administrative Police, Fire Department, Transport Police, Directorate, and Detentions. It also incorporated the Vehicle Inspection and Border Police Departments.

Within the *Kriminalpolizei*, Department C assumed those duties formerly performed by K-5. Erich Mielke continued to deal with security matters as vice-president of the German Interior Administration.[27] The lists drawn up in connection with the transfer of officers from the People's Police to Department D were now addressed directly to him.[28] Official documents from the Ministry for State Security confirm the decisive role played by Mielke in pushing for the organization of a state security service prior to its official foundation:

> During that time, the various roles of the State Security Service in combating crimes against the state were initially fulfilled by the Central Administration for the Protection of the Economy. The head of this administration was Comrade Inspector General Mielke, who had already begun forming the Central Administration in the course of 1949 by order of the Political Bureau of the Socialist Unity Party.[29]

According to Zaisser, this central administration had a staff of about 30, including the technical personnel.[30] This means that measures were taken to establish the central administration during the same time Department D of the *Kriminalpolizei*, which also answered to Mielke, was engaged in its day-to-day activities.[31]

At the time the GDR was founded, the establishment of a so-called Sectional Service in Civil Police precincts was also considered. The Sectional Service had been mentioned as early as 1946 in connection with the creation of a 'system of confidants' (*Vertrauensmänner*) by the vice-president of the German Interior Administration, Willi Seifert.[32] It was designed to provide the police with information intended to help them 'more easily identify the enemies of the new democratic order, the lawbreakers, criminal elements and those persons whose activities were directed at harming the economy in the Soviet zone of Germany'.[33] For this purpose, individual police officers were to be provided who were well trained and politically reliable, and who had, in particular, close contacts with the *Kriminalpolizei* and Administrative Police. They were authorized to 'wear civilian clothes in special cases'.[34] Their observations were to be recorded in special journals. Reports from *Hausbevollmächtigte* and *Straßenbevollmächtigte* (informants responsible for gathering intelligence on the occupants of houses and occurrences in the streets) and from other persons were to be noted in a confidential file in which the informants were to be registered under a special number. Once a sufficient amount of information had been gathered on a particular citizen, an index card was to be issued.[35]

A manuscript of unknown origin found in the archives of the Ministry for State Security sheds some light on the personnel aspects of the creation of the State Security Service. It describes the reorganization efforts undertaken with a view to establish a separate ministry and provides details on the persons involved in these efforts as well as on the prospective candidates for the office of the Minister of State Security.

They included, apart from Zaisser, the former Lieutenant General Rudolf Bamler, who had been the chief of Military Intelligence III (counter-espionage) under Admiral Canaris from June 1938 until February 1939 and had been taken prisoner by the Russians on 1 July 1944 as commander of the 12th Infantry Division near Minsk; former Major Bernhard Bechler, forced to surrender to the Russians in a bullet-riddled house in Stalingrad in January 1943; former Lieutenant Helmut Borfuka, taken prisoner near Stalingrad on 18 January 1943; and Hermann Gartmann, inmate of a concentration camp and a former functionary of the Communist Party of Germany, as well as a number of other former members of the German army and communist functionaries.[36]

A second group of candidates is said to have included the future ministers for state security Erich Mielke and Ernst Wollweber. In the 1930s, Wollweber had gained specific experience in setting up an illicit apparatus for carrying out acts of sabotage against ships around the world. The manuscript just quoted indicates that a special commission was established at the beginning of January whose German members included Walter Ulbricht, Otto Buchwitz, and Hans Jendretzky, communist resistance fighters and former prisoners, as well as Bernhard Koenen and Anton Ackermann,[37] political émigrés who had returned to Germany on the heels of the Red Army. The Soviet representatives in the commission included Colonel Tuchanov, Lieutenant Colonel Lyssajak of the Ministry for State Security, Major General Kotikov, and Colonel Tulpanov. On 28 January 1950, the commission decided in favour of Wilhelm Zaisser.

Four days earlier, on 24 January 1950, the Politburo of the Socialist Unity Party had agreed that the next session of government should address the reports on arson and sabotage submitted by the Commission for State Control, the *Kriminalpolizei*, and the Central Administration for the Protection of the Economy. The Minister of the Interior was instructed to file a petition to have the Central Administration for the Protection of the Economy converted into a Ministry for State Security. It was also decided at this meeting by the Politburo that 'an SED (Sozialistische Einheitspartei Deutschlands – the Socialist Unity Party) speaker' was to declare during the next budgetary debate in the *Volkskammer* (East German Parliament) 'that we are willing to defend the German Democratic Republic and regret that the People's Police is not sufficiently equipped'.[38]

At the thirteenth meeting of the Provisional Government of the GDR on 26 January 1950, the chairman of the Central Commission for State Control, Fritz Lange; the head of the Central Administration for the Protection of the Economy, Erich Mielke; and the chief of the People's Police, August Mayer, reported on the alleged intensification of activities by enemy agents, spies, and saboteurs. At the end of this report, Fritz Lange pronounced: 'I hereby openly declare that there is hardly another country which is still as poorly protected and as endangered as our German Democratic Republic.'[39] Mielke added that the constitution of the GDR had to be vigorously enforced by the creation of suitable agencies leading the 'struggle against agents and saboteurs, and by introducing appropriate criminal laws which will enable the judicial authorities to bring to justice those perpetrators arrested and convicted with the help of these agencies.'[40]

The 'Resolution on the Defence Against Acts of Sabotage' passed at this meeting demanded, among other things, that 'not a single action taken by the enemy, no act of propaganda shall be ignored', and that the reporting system for cases of sabotage, espionage, etc., was to be organized in a manner ensuring that 'comprehensive information will be obtained at all times with regard to hostile propaganda from external enemies and the activity of agents inside this country'.[41]

A draft of the 'Act on the Creation of the Ministry for State Security' was submitted at the same meeting. Section 1 of this act stipulated:

> The Central Administration for the Protection of the Economy, which has hitherto been under the Ministry of the Interior, shall be converted into an independent Ministry for State Security. The Act of 7 October 1949 on the Provisional Government of the German Democratic Republic shall be amended accordingly.

At the legislative session on 26 January 1950, Mielke, as Inspector General of the Central Administration for the Protection of the Economy, submitted a report on alleged acts of sabotage in the explosives works at Gnaschwitz and Schönebeck, as well as on agents and spies of the US and British secret services. The newspaper *Tägliche Rundschau* published the report that same day with the headline 'Gangsters, Robbers and Murderers'. Three days later, the Socialist Unity Party's official newspaper, *Neues Deutschland*, published a speech by Fritz Lange, Chairman of the Central Commission for State Control, on acts of sabotage, together with a report by Chief Inspector August Mayer 'on the activity of agents in rural areas'. In this report, Mayer elaborated on the 'adverse conditions' prevailing in the GDR compared with the Soviet Union, Poland, Hungary, Bulgaria, and Czechoslovakia. The reasons for this situation, according to Mayer, were the division of Germany and the situation in West Berlin as a 'base of US imperialism': 'From here they incite people to commit acts of sabotage and murders. Schumann, Kaiser, Reuter, Schwennicke, Neumann and the likes have radio stations, printing presses and means of transportation at their disposal and do not hesitate ... to incite the people of the German Democratic Republic to commit criminal acts against the state, against the life and property of the citizens.' No leniency should be shown to such elements, he continued, and 'measures [must be taken] which thwart their plans right from the outset. Hence, the diverse measures adopted by the government of the German Democratic Republic to strengthen the security services and improve internal vigilance are an absolutely necessary and welcome development.' He then announced that 'we will also introduce a bill in the *Volkskammer* on the creation of a Ministry for State Security'.

On 28 January 1950, radio station RIAS reported:

> In connection with the creation of a special state security ministry designed to fortify the defence against alleged acts of sabotage, *Neue Zeit* has revealed the Minister of Justice for the eastern zone is preparing a bill providing for the death penalty for all so-called economic criminals and enemies of the people.[42]

According to an RIAS transmission on 28 January 1950, representatives of the Western Allies in Berlin viewed the creation of an East German security ministry as 'clear proof of the increasing internal insecurity of the regime in the Eastern zone'. This could only be viewed as an attempt 'to use alleged sabotage as a thin disguise for the real reasons behind the poor supply situation'. Another observer came to the conclusion that the Ministry of the Interior had obviously been unable to cope with its multitude of tasks, making it necessary to convert the former Central Administration for the Protection of the Economy into a Ministry for State Security.[43]

On 30/31 January 1950, the third meeting of the Central Commission for State Control took place. There Fritz Selbmann, Minister of Industry, pointed out that the dissolution of the Soviet internment camps was a clear expression of the restoration of German sovereignty,[44] and that, in view of this the issue of independent state security services had now also reached a decisive stage.[45]

At the fourteenth session of the Provisional Government of the GDR on 2 February 1959, Fritz Selbmann submitted a 'Report on the investigation of monopolistic-capitalist intrigues in the VEBs [nationalized companies]'. A draft resolution adopted at the meeting mandated that the material contained in the report be submitted to the Central Commission for State Control, where it was to be evaluated and decisions on 'necessary measures' were to be taken. At a meeting of the Politburo of the Socialist Unity Party five days later, Wilhelm Zaisser was appointed Minister and Erich Mielke Permanent Secretary of the Ministry for State Security. At the same meeting, the Politburo decided to co-opt Zaisser onto the party executive and nominate him as candidate for the Politburo.[46]

The Ministry for State Security was founded on 8 February 1950. At the sixteenth session of the Provisional Government of the GDR on 16 February 1950, Deputy Prime Minister Walter Ulbricht officially appointed Wilhelm Zaisser and Erich Mielke to their respective positions in the newly created ministry. The former tax office building in Berlin-Lichtenberg, the district in which Erich Mielke's career as head of this police precinct had begun in June 1945, became the headquarters of the Ministry for State Security. Mielke was given a staff of about 1,150. Four decades later, the 'shield and sword of the party', as Mielke liked to call the State Security Service, the *Stasi*, had grown into a monstrous apparatus of espionage and repression with 91,000 full-time employees and 173,000 'unofficial' members. It is certainly one of the wonders of recent history that this apparatus simply vanished without notable resistance in the course of the peaceful revolution that swept through East Germany in the spring of 1990.

NOTES

1. Communist Party of the Soviet Union.
2. *'Notiz über die Gespräche zwischen dem Vorsitzenden des KfS der UdSSR, Genossen Generaloberst Fedortschuk, und dem Minister für Staatssicherheit der DDR, Genossen Armeegeneral Mielke am 9./10. September 1982'*; Federal Commissioner for the Documents of the State Security Service of the former GDR (BStU), Zentralarchiv (ZA), Abteilung X, Bündel 62/2, p. 2.
3. Pieck: *'Antwort auf die Fragen zur Besprechung am 19.12.1949'* in R. Badstübner and W. Loth, eds., *Wilhelm Pieck – Aufzeichnungen zur Deutschlandpolitik 1945–1953* (Berlin: Akademie Verlag, 1994) p. 252.
4. J. Foitzik, 'Organisationseinheiten und Kompetenzstruktur des Sicherheitsapparates der Sowjetischen Militäradministration in Deutschland (SMAD)', p. 13 (unpublished manuscript).
5. Ministerstvo Gosudarstwennoj Besopasnosti.
6. J. Foitzik, *Organisationseinheiten und Kompetenzstruktur*, footnote 4.
7. *Jahresbericht der Hauptabteilung K der Hauptverwaltung Deutsche Volkspolizei für das Jahr 1949*; Bundesarchiv Potsdam (BA-P), Ministry of the Interior (MdI) 11/699, pp. 1–13.
8. Bestand HVDVP 11/636, p. 39, Bundesarchiv, Abteilungen Potsdam (BA-P).
9. Whereas the former *Kriminalpolizei* had distinguished between ten types of criminal offences based on the penal code, this number was reduced to five in the Soviet zone. The designation K-5 was retained in most cases after the restructuring in the spring of 1949.
10. *Diskussionsprotokoll zum Befehl 201*, Abteilung K, Referat K 5, *Bericht über*

die Arbeitstagung K-5 vom 7. und 8.10.1947; BStU-ZA, AS 442/66, pp. 176–92; here 185.

11. *An das Dez. K 5 Brandenburg, Mecklenburg, Sachsen, Sachsen-Anhalt, Thüringen. Betr.: Änderung des Verhältnisses des Sachgebietes K 5 innerhalb der Polizeibehörden. 6. Mai 1949* (at that time, Reimann, Wunderlich, Markert, Kiefel, and Feilen headed the respective K-5 sections in these states); BStU-ZA, AS 364/66, p. 151.

12. Among other things, Mielke was thus informed on a regular basis about Western newspaper articles and radio broadcasts dealing with the Soviet occupation zone, such as articles on the Task Force against Inhumanity (*Kampfgruppe gegen Unmenschlichkeit*), the Eastern Bureau (*Ostbüro*) of the SPD, and the conditions prevailing in Soviet special camps as well as the repressive policies of the NKVD or K-5. He then had taken appropriate measures. See clippings from the press (*Presseausschnitte*); BStU, ZA, AS 19/54.

13. *Niederschrift über die Dienststellenleiterversammlung der thüringischen Kriminalpolizei vom 22. Mai 1949 in der Landeskriminalpolizeiabteilung in Weimar;* BA-P, MdI, Bestand Nr. 7, DVdI, BD. 359, pp. 115/116. See also *Landesbehörde der Volkspolizei, Abt. K, Niederschrift über die Dienststellenleitertagung der Thüringer Kriminalpolizei am 26.9.1949,* pp. 163–7.

14. B. Sagolla: *Die rote Gestapo. Der Staatssicherheitsdienst in der Sowjetzone* (Berlin: Kampfgruppe gegen Unmenschlichkeit, 1952), p. 10. According to minute no. 18 of the Politiburo meeting on 26 April 1949, Zaisser, until then Minister of the Interior in Saxony, was put in charge of the riot police (*Polizei-Bereitschaften*); Bestand SED, ZK, Beschlüsse Politbüro IV 2/2/18, Stiftung Archiv der Parteien und Massenorganisationen der DDR im Bundesarchiv (SAPMO-BA).

15. J. Foitzik, *Organisationseinheiten und Kompetenzstruktur*, see footnote 4, p. 14.

16. People's Commissariat of Internal Affairs.

17. Hessian Minister of the Interior, Department I P: *Innerpolitische Information Nr. 103 a (Abschrift) vom 1. November 1950;* Bestand Wilhelm Zaisser. *Betr.: Staatssicherheitsdienst der Sowjetzonen-Republik,* Archiv der sozialen Demokratie der Friedrich-Ebert-Stiftung.

18. *Personalbefehle 1949;* Federal Ministry of the Interior, Schriftgutverwaltung Außenstelle Berlin.

19. Kröber went on to become the head of the State Security Department in Thuringia, with Rudolf Gutsche as his deputy. He later became head of Department VIII (observation) in the Ministry for State Security.

20. An advisory body to the minister, which included the heads of the most important departments and of the party.

21. Organization made up of German communists and prisoners of war. It had been established in connection with the VII Central Administration of the Red Army for the purpose of demoralizing the German troops.

22. BStU-ZA, Ministry for State Security KS I 2/84, ff.

23. *Mitschriften von RIAS-Meldungen 1949*; BStU-ZA, Sekretariat des Ministers (SdM) 339, p. 2.
24. Ibid., p. 6.
25. *Protokoll Nr. 43 der Sitzung des Politbüros am 10. September 1949.* DY 30/IV 2/2/43, SAPMO-BA.
26. See footnote 2.
27. *Übermittlung einer westlichen Presseveröffentlichung zum Thema 'Spitzel im Dienst der NKWD' durch Generalinspekteur Hoffmann vom 22. Oktober 1949 an Generalinspekteur Mielke*; BStU-ZA, AS 19/54, p. 81.
28. *Personalbefehle 1949*; Federal Ministry of the Interior, Schriftgutverwaltung.
29. VVS JHS 001 – 30/80, p. 181.
30. W. Otto, 'Zur Biographie von Erich Mielke. Legende und Wirklichkeit', *Heft Nr. 23 zur DDR-Geschichte*, Berlin: 1994, p. 13.
31. P. Siebenmorgen, *Staatssicherheit der DDR. Der Western im Fadenkreuz der Stasi* (Bonn: Bouvier, 1993), p. 5: 'The equality of the two pillars is also reflected later on in the structure of the Ministry for State Security: K-5 as the basis for the organs of political counterintelligence; the HVzSV for economic counterintelligence.'
32. *Protokoll über die Konferenz der Präsidenten der Deutschen Verwaltung des Innern mit den Chefs der Polizei der Länder und Provinzen in der sowjetischen Besatzungszone und den Vertretern der SMAD am 30. Oktober 1946*; BStU-ZA, AS 229/66 p. 134.
33. *Instruktion für den Sektionsdienst bei den Revieren der Schutzpolizei*, addressed to the president of the DVdI, Fischer, on 4 October 1949; BA-P, DVdI, Abt. Sekretariat, Bestands-Nr. 7, Bd. 49, pp. 36–41.
34. Ibid., pp. 38/39.
35. The Sectional Services continued to exist after the creation of the Ministry for State Security. Their lack of efficiency is criticized in an inspection report by Central Department S in the Ministry of the Interior (13 April 1950); ibid., pp. 53–4.
36. *Das nachrichtendienstliche Analphabetentum*; BStU-ZA, SdsM 1397, p. 70.
37. Anton Ackermann was later named to set up and head the GDR's foreign intelligence service.
38. *Protokoll Nr. 68 der Sitzung des Politbüros am 24. Januar 1950, Pt. 3*; SAPMO-BA Bestand IV 2/2/68.
39. *Stenographische Niederschrift aus der Ministerratssitzung am Donnerstag, dem 26. Januar 1950*; BA-P, Bestand Deutsche Demokratische Republik, Protokolle der Sitzungen C 20/I, Bd. 11, p. 23.
40. Ibid., pp. 49–50.
41. Ibid., Anlage 4, p. 2.
42. *Mitschriften Rias-Sendungen*; BStU-ZA, SdM 339, p. 54.
43. Ibid., p. 71.
44. *Besprechung Semjonow, Pieck, Ulbricht am 10.1.1950 über die Realisierung des Beschlusses der sowjetischen Regierung über die Auflösung der sowjetischen Internierungslager in der SBZ/DDR (ZPA NL 36/736, pp. 24–6)*, in Badstübner/Loth, *Wilhelm Pieck*, p. 322: 'Matter of internees, resolution of

the government of the SU 1) 15,038 people shall be released from camps and prisons, of whom 5,404 have been convicted and 9,634 have not; 2) handed over to German authorities (interior minist.) to continue their sentences in German prisons: 10,513 convicted persons, another 3,432 persons (handed over) for conviction, 3) 649 persons who have participated in the active struggle against the SU will remain in Soviet custody.'

45. *Staatliche Kontrolle-Volkskontrolle*. Schriftenreihe der Deutschen Demokratischen Republik, Heft 2; BStU-ZA, SdM 381, p. 12.
46. *Protokoll Nr. 70 der Sitzung des Politbüros am 7. Februar 1950*; Bestand SED, Zentralkomitee – Beschlüsse Politbüro – IV 2/2/70, SAPMO-BA.

9

US Intelligence and the GDR: The Early Years

Christian Ostermann

Even though the German Democratic Republic (GDR) vanished from the political landscape in 1990, and even though its archives are now largely accessible to researchers, much of its history is still hidden in far-off archives, those in Moscow and Washington. This chapter will attempt to develop some initial thoughts on US intelligence and the GDR, in particular the CIA's views and involvement. Much of this effort, particularly with regard to the CIA's covert operations in East Germany, is only scratching the surface due to the CIA's (and the other intelligence agencies') refusal to declassify documents that disclose 'sources and methods'. I will approach the subject by trying to answer two questions: What were the main characteristics of the CIA analysis of the GDR between 1949 and 1955? What do we know about the CIA's clandestine subversive operations against the GDR?

While public and scholarly curiosity – and Cold War propaganda – have focused on the clandestine subversive operations, it is often overlooked that, at the outset, the CIA's main mission was to provide strategic intelligence on the Soviet Union, which, by 1947, was widely considered the only power with a capacity to threaten US national security interests on a global scale. A persistent argument in most memoirs by former intelligence officers, as well as journalistic and scholarly treatments, is the scarcity of information on the USSR available in the early years of the Cold War. It was this void that the CIA was to fill, an ominous, daunting task which, however, in Evan Thomas's words, those 'very best men' took on eagerly and seriously.

The Soviet Union was a 'closed society', and information on Soviet military strength, nuclear capabilities, and political cohesion was hard to come by. Therefore, many within the US intelligence community saw the approach to the Soviet target as a 'series of concentric circles'.[1] The inner circle, the Soviet Union itself, was difficult to penetrate, as the often abortive airdrops of agents close to military targets within the USSR in the early years revealed.

Much greater opportunities were offered by the second circle, the countries surrounding the Soviet Union, its European satellites, in particular those which the Red Army had occupied. Within the northern tier of satellite states – Poland, East Germany, and Czechoslovakia – targets deemed crucial for early warnings of a Soviet ground advance into Western Europe, the Soviet Occupation Zone played perhaps the most important role. The massive influx of refugees from the eastern territories, the relative openness of the zone, its commercial and human ties to the Western zones, and the widespread disaffection from the Russian occupiers, as well as daily collaboration and confrontation with Soviet officials and local communist party leaders, provided manifold opportunities for intelligence gathering. Anti-communist groups such as the Fighting Group Against Inhumanity, the Investigative Committee of Free Jurists (UfJ), and the eastern bureaus of the West German political parties, and the US Radio in the American Sector (RIAS), constituted other sources of information. Soviet military and civilian defectors and refugees added to an increasingly sharper picture of Soviet intentions and military capabilities. Perhaps the most spectacular success in intelligence gathering was the 'Berlin tunnel' operation, the CIA's tapping of three GDR underground telephone cables in the Soviet sector, allowing the agency for about 18 months to listen in on some 1,200 Soviet and East German communication channels.[2] Jointly occupied Berlin, as a CIA report had put it as early as 1948, provided 'a center of an intelligence net covering the city itself, the Soviet Zone of Germany, the eastern satellites and the Soviet Union.'[3]

Given their efforts to gauge Soviet intentions and capabilities in the growing confrontation with Moscow, Washington intelligence analysts and policy makers demanded that the 'Berlin Operation Base' of the War Department's Strategic Services Unit provide strategic, long-term intelligence on the Soviet Union. Largely dependent on the US Army for its autonomy, logistics and cover, indeed supervised by USFET (United States Forces, European

Theater)'s G-2 (Intelligence), the Berlin intelligence mission initially focused on military targets, in particular the Soviet Army's order of battle. Agents of the Berlin Operation Base provided an enormous amount of detailed information on Soviet airfields, barracks, and ammunition dumps, as well as troop movements and manoeuvres, information that was much appreciated both in the US military government headquarters in Frankfurt and in Washington. While 'early intelligence warning' remained an important objective – by November 1951, Frank Wisner, CIA Deputy Director for Plans, could pride himself that Soviet troop movements were 'normally known within three days'[4] – monitoring current developments in the Soviet Occupation Zone (SBZ) increasingly became the Berlin base's primary task.[5]

Intelligence on the SBZ was crucial to assessing Soviet policy in Germany. What were Soviet intentions with regard to the SBZ, to the Western zones, to Germany as a whole? Since the forced merger of the Social Democratic Party (SPD) and the Communist Party in April 1946, US intelligence had emphasized the weak internal condition of the communist 'Socialist Unity Party' (SED), the Soviets' main vehicle for the transformation of the SBZ. Far from an effective fighting force, the SED, to US observers in Berlin, seemed split into former social democrats and communists, and unease seemed to persist even among communists over the leading role which the Muscovites, headed by Walter Ulbricht, had gained within the party. Intelligence reports from Berlin repeatedly noted that the Soviet Military Administration seemed 'in a state of flux' with regard to the pace of socialization in the Eastern Zone, and, after the debacle which the SED suffered in the local and state elections in autumn 1946, appeared less committed to the SED than ever.[6] Concurrently, the Soviet Military Administration was apparently striving for a rapprochement with the noncommunist parties, the Christian Democrats (CDU) and the Liberal Democrats (LDPD), which had exhibited such surprising strength in the autumn elections. There was even talk that the Soviets might permit the readmission to politics of the SPD in the Soviet Zone. To US intelligence, the Soviets had shifted towards what was called a 'new policy' – an easing of the socialization policy and a rapprochement with the noncommunist parties at the expense of the SED. By March 1947, shortly before the Council of Foreign Ministers' (CFM) conference in Moscow, OMGUS intelligence analysts speculated that in return for economic concessions, 'the Soviets seemed prepared to open up their own zone to the West and to put the "iron curtain" back behind the Oder-Neiße line, notwithstanding the fact that they apparently want to keep as large a share in the industry of the Eastern Zone as may be permitted by the Western allies.'[7]

In the aftermath of the inconclusive Moscow CFM meeting, however, intelligence reporting from OMGUS grew increasingly wary of Soviet intentions and was now much more in line with the view which the Central Intelligence Group (CIG) and later the CIA had been holding. As early as July 1946, the weekly intelligence summary for the president warned that '[p]osing as the champions of German nationalism and rehabilitation', the Soviets would 'attempt to discredit the policy of the Western powers and facilitate communist penetration of their zones.'[8] Later that month, the CIG stated that the Soviet objective was 'presumably such a centralized "anti-Fascist" republic with a coalition government of the eastern European type, but actually under strong communist influence and bound to the Soviet Union by ties of political and economic dependency'.[9] Arguing that the Soviet position on German unification had to be viewed 'in the light of developments in the Soviet Zone', the CIG argued in its 2 August 1946 weekly summary that the Soviets' 'control over Eastern Germany is now secure and that they are in a position to launch a vigorous campaign to communize the Western Zone as soon as the zonal barriers would be removed'.[10] By December 1947, after the failure of yet another CFM session in London, the CIA predicted the 'accelerated consolidation of eastern Germany'. The USSR would 'attempt to incorporate thoroughly the economic system of its Zone into the Soviet economy and to orient the political system still more closely to the Soviet ideology'.[11]

The Soviet blockade of Berlin seemed to bear out these predictions. As the CIA informed President Harry Truman in March 1948, the Western Allied presence in Berlin prevented the Soviets from effectively consolidating communist rule in the Soviet Zone: it 'hinders ruthless and forcible communization of all [of] eastern Germany, helps to sustain noncommunist opposition and demonstrates that the US does not intend to abandon or partition the country'.[12] One month later, after the Soviet walkout from the Allied Control Council and increasing interference in the communications between Berlin and Western Germany, the CIA was certain that the Soviet Union aimed at forcing the Western powers to leave Berlin, placing the SBZ under the 'permanent control of a well-organized German group, loyal to the USSR and supported by police state methods', and extending Soviet influence into West Germany.[13] Unlike OMGUS, which had warned Washington in early March that war might be imminent, the CIA argued more cautiously and ambiguously that, 'while the risk of war may be involved', the Soviet programme 'possibly can be effected without military violence'.[14]

CIA analysts became increasingly convinced that Stalin sought to expand Soviet influence in West Germany *not* by communist subversion or quadripartite negotiations, but by setting up a provisional all-German government based in the SBZ: 'The CIA has believed and continues to believe that the USSR might encourage the People's Congress to organize a future "national" administration and establish a de facto Government for the Eastern Zone while propagandistically claiming to speak for all the country.'[15] The intelligence agency concluded that, while Soviet control over all of Germany remained the maximum objective, the Kremlin had 'decided that a "neutral" Germany, prevented from making a firm alignment with the West, was a more feasible goal for the immediate future'.[16] With its ambiguous assessment, the CIA might not have been far off the mark. Recent studies on the Soviet occupation zone in Germany have revealed that Stalin's policy was deeply divided and inherently contradictory. Soviet policy options in post-war Germany – the Sovietization of the Eastern occupation zone, the creation of a unified, socialist Germany, or the establishment of a demilitarized 'neutral' Germany – remained essentially unresolved during the early years of occupation.[17]

After the establishment of the GDR in October 1949, the CIA continued to argue that Soviet policy was ambivalent. According to early CIA estimates, the Soviet objective in Germany was to make the GDR a 'reliable and effective instrument' of Soviet policy – a reflection of 'the Kremlin's growing optimism regarding its improved world power position and its increased confidence in gaining eventual control over all of Germany on Soviet terms'.[18] By September 1950, the CIA's Office of Research and Evaluation assessed that the USSR would 'accelerate its efforts to transform the GDR into a People's Democracy' and to integrate it into the Soviet orbit as an 'ostensibly equal member'. At the same time, the Soviet Union remained committed to its long-range objective of bringing 'all of Germany under Soviet domination', and it would use the GDR as the principal means for penetrating West Germany. Calling any hopes for a Soviet acceptance of a neutral, unified Germany a 'delusion', the CIA tended to reinforce the negative American attitude towards four-power negotiations on Germany.[19]

CIA analysts also predicted that, in its effort to make the GDR a thoroughly reliable Soviet instrument, the USSR would 'push the GDR further on the path toward the single-party state' by strengthening the Socialist Unity Party, by the increased use of mass organizations, and by the elimination of potential or active resistance. Impressed by the Free German Youth's *Deutschlandtreffen*, a massive gathering of youth, numbering 500,000, mainly from East Germany, in Berlin in May 1950, intelligence officers believed that it would be the 'rising percentage of vigorous and enthusiastic younger communists' in the ranks of the SED that would make the party a more effective organization. At the same time, the continued expansion of East German security forces, in particular those of the Ministry for State Security, would enable the SED to cope with 'any internal security threat', an exaggerated assessment of the regime's true control capabilities. Even though CIA analysts acknowledged that widespread passive dissatisfaction with the SED regime existed, 'no serious threat or open opposition' was 'likely'. In fact, periodic improvements in prices and the supply of foods and consumer goods would gradually reduce the existing dissatisfaction.[20]

Concurrent with this assessment of the GDR, CIA analysts found themselves increasingly impressed with the strategic, economic, and political importance which Moscow apparently ascribed to its East German client state. Interest in keeping the GDR in the socialist camp was so strong, the CIA stated, in the National Intelligence Estimate (NIE-4) of February 1951, that even the threat of West German rearmament, which surfaced in late 1950, would not cause Stalin to abandon his control over the GDR.[21] A year later, with the negotiations on the European Defense Community and the Bonn Treaty in the works, NIE-50 unequivocally negated any chance that Stalin would strike a deal: 'We do not believe that the Kremlin will give up or weaken its control over East Germany either as part of its strategy for attaining control over a unified Germany or as part of its efforts to prevent the integration of West Germany with the West.'[22] Interestingly, US Air Force intelligence analysts apparently opposed such a rigid view, arguing that 'we should recognize that the Soviet Union may not look upon the advantages of poised military threat or control exactly as we do at any one time'. According to them, 'the possibility should not be excluded that "the Soviet Union may see its way clear to stalemate or destroy the effectiveness of NATO through such devices as withdrawal of forces or the insistence upon a neutral demilitarized state".'[23] Thus, one can find the origins of the 'missed opportunity' debate in the early arguments within the intelligence community.[24]

NIE-4 continued the positive assessment of GDR strength by holding out the possibility of a direct attack by GDR paramilitary forces on West Berlin: GDR forces would 'in the near future, if not at present, have the strength to overwhelm the garrisons of the Western Powers in West Berlin'.[25] By February 1952, the CIA analysts had become less sanguine about East German military strength: the paramilitary forces were 'limited by inadequate equipment, insufficient training, and low morale'. Nevertheless, the SED would be able to consolidate its control. While aware that the vast majority of East Germans remained opposed to the regime, the CIA had no evidence of organized opposition and predicted that this would not develop in 1952. By downsizing and shedding some of its unreliable elements, the SED would instead become an even more reliable and effective party, and could be expected to increase its popular appeal, especially among the youth.[26]

In essence, this assessment continued into 1953. Neither the worsening crisis in the GDR as a result of the massive collectivization, nationalization, and militarization campaign in the wake of the Ulbricht's proclaiming the 'construction of socialism' in July 1952, nor the increasing signs of unrest, nor Stalin's death in March 1953 and the peace campaign inaugurated by his successors had much impact on the CIA's assessment of the GDR and Soviet policy in Germany. In May 1953, just as the new Soviet leaders were debating the future of the GDR, NIE-81 denied any chance of the Soviets giving up or weakening their control over East Germany. Somewhat contradictorily, the intelligence estimate argued that the Kremlin would remain, so long as it retained the GDR, in a position to use East Germany as a lever in negotiations with the West and to prevent German unification on terms unfavourable to Soviet goals. The Soviet Union would not abandon a 'valuable base for either offensive or defensive military operations' and an economically and technologically important asset. It was thus unlikely that Stalin's successors would surrender 'the great advantages' which the Soviet Union derived from its control over the GDR in return for the establishment of a united and neutral Germany.' If anything, Moscow would seek to increase East Germany's economic and military power. Significantly, CIA analysts even suggested that the Kremlin might remove some of its overt control mechanisms, even some of its military forces. In fact, they thought it conceivable that 'at some stage the Soviet leaders might withdraw all Soviet forces from German'.[27]

Such confidence in the stability of the Ulbricht regime, shared as we now know by key Germany specialists within the Soviet Foreign Ministry,[28] was, of course, called into question by the popular uprising in East Germany of 16–17 June 1953, only a few days after NIE-81 had been completed.[29] The CIA found it difficult to assess the extent and significance of the 17 June disorders.[30] In their initial assessment, CIA analysts focused on the somewhat unexpected intensity of popular resentment against the regime and the even more surprising degree to which East Germans were willing to engage in active resistance against the regime despite an extended period of communist control. Moreover, the fact that Soviet tanks were used to quell the widespread riots and demonstrations indicated to CIA analysts the Soviet distrust of the GDR police, and military and security forces. The disorders had probably convinced the USSR, they argued, that Soviet control over the satellite state could be ensured only by continued Soviet troop presence in the area.[31]

In fact, many within the CIA speculated that the SED regime had lost its standing with the Soviet leadership and that Ulbricht's fate – after all, he had been the advocate of the ill-fated policy of the 'forced construction of Socialism' – was doomed. 'We believe,' the Special Estimate SE-47 of July 1953 stated, 'that within the next several months the Soviet authorities will probably reconstitute the East German government and purge the East German Communist Party (SED).' Since few political leaders in East Germany were left who were not well-known communist collaborators, the estimate predicted that the Soviets would build a new East German government around a purged SED which would continue the soft-line 'New Course' policy which Moscow had forced upon the SED in early June.[32] The latter point was right on the mark (Moscow would indeed continue the New Course policy for a few months), but, otherwise, the Special Estimate reflected how little the CIA knew of what was actually happening inside the GDR. Apparently, the CIA was not aware of the near-ouster of Ulbricht in the days following the uprising, nor did it seem to have realized that by mid-July Ulbricht had turned the tables on his opponents within the politburo led by Rudolf Herrnstadt and Wilhelm Zaisser.[33]

The unexpected outburst of popular resentment against the German communist regime during the 17 June uprising highlighted the problem of resistance potential behind the Iron Curtain and spawned a growing number of vulnerability studies by the US intelligence community. Between June 1953 and January 1956, at least 20 studies were completed on Eastern European resistance and vulnerabilities, and much of this effort was channelled into NIEs. New working groups within the intelligence and policy-making communities were created to concentrate and coordinate the Eisenhower administration's efforts on this issue. Thus, for example, an inter-agency 'Working Group on USSR and Satellites' was specifically formed in July 1953 to study Eastern European vulnerabilities. Later that year, a special interagency intelligence committee – the Resistance Intelligence Committee – was created and given the task of producing so-called 'Resistance Intelligence Reports'. The CIA, of course, contributed to and participated in these efforts.[34]

Interestingly, virtually all of these vulnerability studies, as they appeared in 1954 and 1955, culminating in NIE 10-55 on 'Anti-Communist Resistance Potential in the Sino-Soviet Bloc', confirmed that dissatisfaction and dissidence were widespread behind the Iron Curtain. Yet, at the same time, the intelligence community consistently concluded that there was little likelihood that Eastern European unrest would undermine Soviet or communist control.[35] As NIE 10-55 of April 1955 concluded, 'even in countries where dissidence is strongest, such as East Germany, we see no prospect of resistance activities developing on a scale sufficient to threaten the stability of the regimes'.[36]

This gloomy, pessimistic view of resistance potential behind the Iron Curtain was, however, not shared by all within the intelligence establishment. In contrast to the CIA analysts who contributed to the NIEs and various Resistance Intelligence Reports, many within the CIA's Directorate of Operations, those individuals who actually planned and conducted clandestine operations, believed that Soviet control of East Germany and other satellites was inherently shaky. Hence these countries offered fertile ground for clandestine subversive operations in an effort to undermine the communist party and Soviet position and encourage and strengthen the forces of anti-communist resistance, to mount that 'counter-offensive' which became the other side of the coin of 'containment'.

Given the problematic documentary record on clandestine operations, it is still difficult to assess this aspect of the CIA's involvement in East Germany in the early 1950s. Since the late Truman administration, various US government agencies had been engaged in 'psychological warfare' activities in Germany aimed at reducing Soviet power and hastening the collapse of the East German regime. The US High Commission in Germany (HICOG) under John J. McCloy reinforced its efforts by establishing an 'Eastern Affairs Division' within HICOG's Berlin Element in early 1950, and, later that year, a 'Political and Economic Projects Committee', which focused almost exclusively on the GDR. In December 1950, a secret report by State Department consultants Wallace Carroll and Hans Speier had called for the implementation of a whole series of overt and covert tactical projects directed against the GDR, ranging from military demonstrations, propaganda infiltration, and sabotage, to abductions and assassinations. Based on classified vulnerability studies of the East German regime, the report proposed economic warfare in the form of trade restrictions, and by depriving the GDR economy of key personnel. Most importantly, the report suggested the US-sponsored creation of a 'unified, strong, growing resistance movement within the Soviet zone, which has a name, is secure and disciplined, acts according to plan, and awaits its time'.[37]

Based on the Carroll–Speier report and other blueprints for fighting the Cold War in Germany, the Psychological Strategy Board (PSB), an interagency committee staffed by the State Department, the CIA, and other government offices, had, by October 1952, drawn up and adopted a comprehensive psychological warfare plan for Germany (PSB D-21) outlining propaganda efforts directed against the East German communists. PSB D-21 called for a concerted and stepped-up effort to expose oppressive conditions in the GDR and to encourage disaffection and defection. The plan envisioned psychological, political, and economic harassment of the GDR as well as 'controlled preparation for more active resistance'.[38]

The CIA's efforts, expanded drastically after the outbreak of the Korean War in June 1950, covered a spectrum of covert operations. The CIA's Office of Policy Coordination (OPC) thus supported the establishment of anti-communist radio stations such as Radio Free Europe and Radio Liberty, headquartered in Munich. Perhaps the most important element was the secret funding of anti-communist groups operating from Berlin or inside East Germany, such as the Fighting Group Against Inhumanity and the eastern bureaus of the West German political parties. As a 'principal project' of the OPC station in Berlin, the CIA began to subsidize the *Kampfgruppe* headed by Rainer Hildebrandt in 1949, and by 1950, the agency was underwriting approximately half of its budget. The next year, when Ernst Tillich, the group's business manager, took over the leadership from the apparently more cautious and independent Hildebrandt, the CIA successfully 'encouraged' the group to step up its subversive activities in the GDR, such as the dropping of leaflets and the falsification of official GDR documents.[39] The OPC also provided support for the setting up of the Congress of Cultural Freedom, an anti-communist organization, which held its first session in Berlin in June 1950.

The OPC played an even more decisive role in the establishment of the UfJ,[40] an anti-communist group which ostensibly provided legal aid and other services to Soviet zone residents, as well as refugees, and created a network of East German legal professionals who reported on illegal acts by the SED regime. As the collective memoirs of the CIA's former Berlin Operation Base chief David Murphy and the KGB's Germany specialist Sergei Kondrashev reveal, CIA agent Henry Hecksher not only recruited the UfJ's leader Horst Erdmann but also initially acted as the group's fund-raiser. Hecksher apparently refrained from imposing intelligence requirements on the UfJ and was satisfied that it was enough to 'hand Erdmann an occasional assignment or debrief him along lines of interest to us'. In view of the UfJ's growing influence within the GDR, CIA headquarters decided in 1952 – over the objections of Hecksher, as it seems – to use the group to establish covert stay-behind assets in East Germany, and at a later stage set up a paramilitary stay-behind programme. This programme, however, was quickly uncovered by the KGB.[41]

Documents in the Eisenhower Library also reveal that the CIA provided assistance to Bishop Otto Dibelius, head of the United German Protestant Church in Berlin, who, because of his steadfast advocacy of religious freedom in East Germany, had come under attack by the SED regime. When the regime set out in early 1953 to destroy the influence of the church on youth by striking at the *Junge Gemeinde*, the Protestant church youth movement, setting off a virtual war with the church, a *Kirchenkampf*, the new CIA Director Allen Dulles channelled some $50,000 to the beleaguered bishop.

The CIA probably also underwrote the publication of anti-communist literature and its covert distribution throughout the GDR.[42]

Defections of prominent satellite regime officials were another means that served both intelligence and psychological warfare purposes. As early as 1948, US intelligence agencies had tried to induce Otto Grotewohl, then co-leader of the newly founded SED and later GDR Minister President, to seek asylum in the West. A former social democrat, Grotewohl had thrown his lot in with the communists in 1946, when, for reasons that have remained unclear, he decided to support the merger of the Social Democratic and Communist Parties in the Soviet Zone. In the months before the October 1950 elections in the GDR, proposals again surfaced to undermine the SED's electoral campaign propaganda by convincing prominent GDR personalities, such as Grotewohl or Otto Nuschke, the collaborationist chairman of the East CDU, to defect to the West, though some CIA officials apparently opposed an open-ended invitation to collaborationist GDR politicians.[43] Though the defection of key personalities was the preferred choice, US intelligence agencies also considered the covert encouragement of mass defections by East German male youth when, in the autumn of 1952, recruitment for an East German army seemed imminent. It is likely that the CIA was among those 'interested agencies', as a recently declassified top-secret State Department aerogramme puts it, which, in 1956, 'agreed on exploring the practicability of operations aimed at weakening the economic structure of the Soviet Zone through the attraction of critically needed groups of technicians and scientists'.[44] Preparatory papers assigned to US intelligence agencies operating out of Berlin the task of establishing contacts with the targeted officials and scientists by 'strictly covert media'.[45]

Perhaps the most controversial case of the CIA's covert operations against East Germany was the question of the agency's involvement in the June 1953 uprising. Soon after the uprising, East German press organs reported that 'certain American agencies had participated directly' in the 'fascist coup'. 'Informed sources', the *Tägliche Rundschau* claimed, had confirmed that the provocations against the GDR government had been planned as early as Berlin Mayor Ernst Reuter's visit to Washington three months earlier. A mission to Berlin led by General Tracy Vorhees had allegedly served as further preparation for 'Day X'. GDR newspapers also pointed to the arrival of the sister of CIA chief Dulles, Eleanor Dulles, in Berlin just six days before the uprising. The characterization of the popular riots as a US imperialist-inspired coup provided a convenient pretext for the SED regime's crackdown on dissidents after the uprising, and it became the official historical interpretation of the events in the GDR which still lingers on as a popular myth.[46]

The available evidence is still scanty, but the documents we have suggest that the US government, including the CIA, was surprised by the demonstration and reacted with caution. To be true, all spring, RIAS had led a relentless campaign against the 28 May norm increase that seems to have been the focal point of the workers' anger. But even the radio station's staff were initially rather surprised when on 16 June, a delegation of East Berlin workers demanded that the station issue a call for a general strike the next day. Probably without much coordination with Bonn and Washington, RIAS director Gordon Ewing decided on a more cautious line of 'factual reporting' rather than incitement, though several of the RIAS political commentaries went beyond mere reporting. Similarly cautious seems to have been the CIA's initial response. Initially, Henry Hecksher, apparently cabled Washington for permission to hand out pistols to the rioters, who were already pelting the advancing Soviet tanks with rubble and cobblestones. Quoting John Bross, the then head of the Eastern European Division, Deputy Director of Central Intelligence (DCI) for Operations Wisner responded: 'Give support and offer asylum. But don't issue guns. With twenty-two Russian divisions in East Germany it was the same as murder.'[47] Other former CIA officials have, however, raised serious doubts as to whether such a cable was ever sent.

A CIA current intelligence report of 17 June reflected the uncertainty with which the agency initially assessed the crisis (and may have underlain that caution). Among other things, the report held it likely that the demonstrations were 'planned to enable the [GDR] government to yield on the question [of work norms] without losing face'. While the report frankly stated that, in the early afternoon of 17 June, 'American observers mingled freely' with groups of demonstrators, the report noted at the same time that 'the only known formal encouragement from West Germans' was the early morning RIAS broadcasts during which a West Berlin trade union leader called on the East Berlin population to support the workers' demonstrations.[48]

The cautious, hesitant, and indeed somewhat perplexed reaction to the uprising in East Germany and concurrent signs of unrest in Plzeň (Czechoslovakia) also marked the National Security Council's discussion on the day after the uprising. DCI Dulles

> described in as much detail as possible the uprising in Berlin and East Germany, where, he pointed out, the Soviet relaxation program had likewise backfired. Mr. Dulles said that the United States had nothing whatsoever to do with inciting these riots, and that our reaction thus far had been to confine ourselves, in broadcasts which were not attributable, to expressions of sympathy and admiration, with an admixture of references to the great traditions of 1848. In summary, Mr. Dulles described what had happened as evidence of the boundless discontent and dissension behind the Iron Curtain, and added that it posed a very tough problem for the United States to know how to handle. President Eisenhower's Special Assistant for Psychological Warfare, a former World War II psy war veteran, C.D. Jackson, then pointed out that the '64-dollar question' was precisely how far the United States was prepared to go 'if this thing really gets cracking'.
>
> The President asked whether Mr. Jackson meant that we should intervene to prevent slaughter by the Soviet forces. Mr. Jackson replied, not only that, but it was quite possible that some of the satellite regimes were now prepared to follow the road that Tito had taken. Indeed, he added, this could be the bell pealing the disintegration of the Soviet empire. Do we stand idly by, or do we help the disintegration? And how much responsibility are we willing to take for the results of helping?
>
> The President's first response was to say that this decision depended on how widespread the uprising became. Would the riots spread to China, or even possibly to the USSR itself? If this should happen, we would probably never have a better chance to act, and we would be well advised, for example, to supply arms. The question of whether we should slip arms to the East Berliners, said Mr. Jackson, was one of the first of his questions. The President answered that if to do so was just inviting a slaughter of these people, you certainly didn't supply the arms. If, on the contrary, there was a real chance of success, you might well do so. Our problem was to weigh the prospects of success. In his opinion, the President added, the revolts would have to be more serious and more widespread than at this moment before they promised real

141

success and indicated the desirability of our intervening. Mr. Jackson agreed with the President's point, but added the question, do we help to make this movement more serious and more wide-spread? The President stated his view that it was not quite the time yet. He felt that it was very important that the unrest spread to China, because while the USSR would have no great difficulty in crushing uprisings in Europe alone, they should find it tough to deal with trouble both in Europe and in the Far East.

Allen Dulles then 'observed that great caution must be used in any distribution of arms to the participants in these uprisings. It would be foolish and dangerous to distribute arms in countries where there were Soviet armed forces. On the other hand, Czechoslovakia was free of such forces, and the time might indeed be ripe to ship arms there and even to undertake to subvert the Czech National Army.'[49] Uncertain of his policy options, Eisenhower finally asked the PSB to devise a short-term plan on how to deal with the East German riots.

Led by C.D. Jackson, who, as he put it in his diary, 'decided [to] work in partnership with Allen D.' on the issue, the PSB drew up an 'Interim US Plan for Exploitation of Unrest in Satellite Europe' (PSB D-45), which, in revised form, was adopted by the National Security Council (NSC) on 25 June as NSC directive 158 and approved by Eisenhower on 26 June. PSB D-45 viewed the East German uprising in the context of existing signs of unrest in Czechoslovakia, Poland, Romania, and Albania. While resentment over excessive production quotas, food shortages, and poor living standards had triggered the revolts, these grievances were, in the analysis of PSB D-45, 'overshadowed by the clearly expressed political objectives of the German rebels'. More than anything, the uprising seemed to be 'a kind of spontaneous direct-action plebiscite in which the East German masses voted with their fists for free elections, the reunification of Germany and the withdrawal of Soviet occupation forces'. The PSB expected that local strikes, demonstrations, or other manifestations of continuing resistance could easily be renewed, and concluded that, with popular resentment of the Soviets 'near the boiling point', the uprising in the GDR created *the greatest opportunity for initiating effective policies to help roll back Soviet power that has yet come to light*.[50]

The recently declassified directive NSC 158 and its summary show the degree to which the PSB would rely on covertly stimulating acts and attitudes of resistance short of mass rebellion. NSC 158 called for the establishment of secure resistance nuclei capable of further large-scale expansion, the intensification of defection programmes, aimed at satellite police leaders and military personnel, the launching of black radio intruder operations to encourage defection, the formation of a Volunteer Freedom Corps which would recruit Eastern European émigrés, and encouragement of the elimination of key puppet officials, as well as the consideration of large-scale systematic balloon propaganda operations to the satellites.[51]

Despite Jackson's emphasis on 'the importance of vigorous implementation of PSB D-45 and its amended summary',[52] few of the measures, as far as one can make out from the declassified documents, were actually carried out. Sharp criticism of aggressive psychological warfare soon mounted within the administration which, in the course of its secret 'Operation Solarium' policy reassessment later that summer, decided against an extreme roll-back policy. The US allies, moreover, were also vehemently opposed to some of the more extreme measures envisioned in NSC 158. The British and French governments, afraid of setting precedents for criticism of 'internal affairs' of 'colonial empires', considered a propaganda offensive in the United Nations anathema. West Germany's federal chancellor, Konrad Adenauer, facing elections in the autumn, effectively blocked any immediate action on the Volunteer Freedom Corps which was to be based in Germany. Allied scepticism therefore severely limited the possibilities for large covert operations.[53]

Ironically, the most important actions taken in response to the East German uprising by the Eisenhower administration were therefore a proposal for a new foreign ministers' conference on Germany and a large-scale food programme – measures which temporarily put the Soviets and the East German regime on the defensive, especially since the CIA had predicted at the time the food programme was installed 'that the workers are planning another blow-up',[54] but they hardly lived up to the expectations many East Germans and East Europeans had with regard to a roll-back. Ultimately, interest in the destabilization of East Germany was secondary to the Eisenhower administration's German policy. Notwithstanding calls for a more aggressive policy, including admonitions by hardliners, such as DCI Allen Dulles, not to engage in a 'do-nothing policy',[55] or by officials on the interagency Operations Coordinating Board, which replaced the PSB in 1954, who argued for 'a concentration of political, economic and psychological means ... with East Germany as target',[56] US policy in the end took a 'softer approach' that would not pose a risk to the administration's overall policy on Germany. As State Department officer John Ausland put it, 'if there is any conflict between our policy of reducing Soviet power in Soviet Occupied Germany (as well as the other satellites) and our policy of integrating the Federal Republic with the West, our policy of integration should be given priority'.[57]

NOTES

1. H. Rositzke, *The CIA's Secret Operations. Espionage, Counterespionage, and Covert Action* (New York: Reader's Digest Press, 1977), p. 39.
2. The most recent account of the tunnel operation is given in D.E. Murphy, S.A. Kondrashev, and G. Bailey, *Battleground Berlin* (New Haven, CT: Yale University Press, 1997), pp. 205–37, 423–8. See also Murphy's and Kondrachev's accounts in this volume.
3. CIA, ORE 41-48 'Effect of Soviet Restrictions on the US Position in Berlin', M. Warner, ed., *The CIA under Harry Truman* (Washington, DC: CIA, 1994), pp. 207–12.
4. [Office of the DCI], 'Staff Conference', 21 November 1951, in ibid., p. 457.
5. Murphy et al., *Battleground Berlin*, pp. 3–18.
6. G-2 Observer's Memorandum No. 212, 31 May 1946, OMGUS, Record Group [RG] 488, National Archives, College Park, MD [NA].
7. OMGUS Office of the Director of Intelligence, Weekly Intelligence Report No. 43, 8 March 1947, OMGUS, RG 488, NA.
8. W.J. Kuhns, ed., *Assessing the Soviet Threat. The Early Cold War Years* (Washington, DC: CIA, 1997), p. 53.
9. CIG, ORE 1, 'Soviet Foreign and Military Policy', 23 July 1946, ibid., p. 61.
10. CIG, Weekly Summary, 2 August 1946, ibid., p. 67.
11. Memorandum for the President, 22 December 1947, ibid., p. 182.
12. R.H. Hillenkoetter, 'Memorandum for the President', ibid., pp. 180–3.
13. ORE 29-48, 'Possible Program of Future Soviet Moves in Germany', 28 April 1948, ibid., pp. 198–9.
14. Ibid. The CIA's reporting during the Berlin Crisis of 1948/49 corresponded with the generally cautious assessments of the Soviet threat. As W. Kuhns has most recently stated, the 'most consistent – and perhaps most important – theme of CIG/CIA analysis during this period, however, was that Soviet moves, no matter how menacing they might appear in isolation, were unlikely to lead to an attack against the West', Kuhns, *Assessing the Soviet Threat*, p.15.
15. Ibid.
16. CIA, Weekly Summary, 22 April 1949, Kuhns, *Assessing the Soviet Threat*,

pp. 303–4.

17. N.M. Naimark, *The Russians in Germany. A History of the Soviet Zone of Occupation* (Cambridge, MA: Harvard University Press, 1995).
18. CIA, Weekly Summary, 17 March 1950, Kuhns, *Assessing the Soviet Threat*, p. 363.
19. CIA, ORE 34-50 'Probable Developments in Eastern Germany by the End of 1951', 28 September 1950, National Security Archive (NSA), The Soviet Estimate Collection. On the CFM issue, see H. Rupieper, *Der besetzte Verbündete* (Opladen: Westdeutscher Verlag, 1991), p. 196.
20. Ibid.
21. CIA, NIE-4 'Soviet Courses of Action with Respect to Germany', 1 February 1951, NSA, The Soviet Estimate Collection.
22. CIA, NIE-50 'Probable Developments in Eastern Germany Through 1952', 12 February 1952, ibid.
23. Ibid., footnote, page 2.
24. On the debate about 'missed opportunities', see R. van Dijk, *The 1952 Stalin Note Debate: Myth or Missed Opportunity for German Unification? Cold War International History Project Working Paper No. 14* (Washington, DC: Woodrow Wilson Center, 1996).
25. CIA, NIE-50 'Probable Developments in Eastern Germany Through 1952', 12 February 1952, NSA, the Soviet Estimate Collection.
26. Ibid.
27. CIA, NIE-81 'Probable Soviet Courses of Action with Respect to Germany, Through Mid-1954', 22 May 1953, ibid.
28. See C.F. Ostermann, '"This is Not a Politburo, But a Madhouse", The Post-Stalin Succession Struggle, Soviet Deutschlandpolitik and the SED. New Evidence from Russian, German and Hungarian Archives', *Cold War International History Project Bulletin* 10 (March 1998), pp. 61–110.
29. The best study of the 1953 uprising is I.-S. Kowalczuk, A. Mitter and S. Wolle, eds., *Der Tag X. 17. Juni 1953* (Berlin: Chr. Links Verlag, 1995).
30. Compare also D. Murphy's contribution in this volume.
31. ICA, SE-47, 'Probable Effect of Recent Developments in Eastern Germany on Soviet Policy with Respect to Germany', July 1953, National Security Archive, the Soviet Estimate Collection.
32. Ibid.
33. N. Stulz-Herrnstadt, *Das Herrnstadt-Dokument. Das Politbüro der SED und die Geschichte des 17. Juni 1953* (Reinbek bei Hamburg: Rowohlt, 1990).
34. J. Marchio, 'Resistance Potential and Rollback: US Intelligence and the Eisenhower Administration's Policies Toward Eastern Europe, 1953–1956', *Intelligence and National Security* 10:2 (April 1995), pp. 219–41.
35. Ibid., p. 222.
36. Ibid. See also Soviet Estimate Collection, National Security Archive, Washington, DC.
37. W. Carroll and H. Speier, 'Psychological Warfare in Germany. A Report to the United States High Commissioner for Germany and the Department of State', 1 December 1950, NA, RG 466, box 3:352 (FOIA release to author).

For a critical review of covert operations under the late Truman administration, see B. Heuser, 'Subversive Operationen im Dienste der 'Roll-back'-Politik 1948–1953', *Vierteljahrshefte für Zeitgeschichte* 37:2 (1989), pp. 280–97.
38. Ibid.
39. Murphy et al., *Battleground Berlin*, pp. 107–8.
40. F. Hagemann, *Der Untersuchungsausschuß Freiheitlicher Juristen 1949–1969* (Frankfurt: Peter Lang, 1994), pp. 36–8, 62–3.
41. Murphy et al., *Battleground Berlin*, pp. 113–26.
42. Eisenhower to Myron C. Taylor, 25 April 1953, Dwight D. Eisenhower Library (DDEL), White House Central Files (Confidential File), 1953–1961, Subject Series, Box 83.
43. John B. Holt to George A Morgan, Memorandum 'Invitations or Encouragement to Leading Noncommunists in the Soviet Zone to Desert or Escape to the West', NA, RG 466, HICOG Berlin records, Box 3.
44. Department of State to American Embassy Bonn, CA 9430 'Defection of Key Technicians from the Soviet Zone of Germany', 28 May 1956, NA, RG 59, 762B.00/5-2856.
45. US Mission, Berlin, to Department of State, 27 July 1956, NA, RG 59, 762B.00/7-2756.
46. See also the articles by M. Tantzscher and S.A. Kondrachev in this volume.
47. B. Hersh, *The Old Boys* (New York: Charles Scribner's Sons, 1992) p. 377.
48. CIA, Office of Current Intelligence, 17 June 1943, DDEL, C.D. Jackson Papers, Box 3.
49. Memorandum, 'Discussion at the 150th Meeting of the National Security Council, Thursday, 18 June 1953', 19 June 1953, NSA, Soviet Flashpoints Collection.
50. Diary, 18 June 1953, DDEL, C.D. Jackson Papers, 1934–1967, Box 56.
51. NSC 158 is published: see C.F. Ostermann, 'Implementing 'Roll-back': NSC 158', *Newsletter of the Society of Historians of American Foreign Relations* 26:3 (September 1996), pp. 1–7.
52. PSB, 'Memorandum of Informal PSB Meeting, July 1, 1953', 1 July 1953, NSA, Soviet Flashpoints Collection.
53. See C.F. Ostermann, '"Keeping the Pot Simmering" The United States and the East German Uprising of 1953', *German Studies Review* 19:1 (March 1996), pp. 74–80.
54. 'Telephone Conversation with Allen W. Dulles'. 10 July 1953, DDEL, John Foster Dulles Papers, Telephone Call Series, Box 1.
55. Department of State, ed., *Foreign Relations of the United States 1955–57* (Washington, DC: GPO, 1992), VIII, p. 158.
56. Department of State, ed., *Foreign Relations of the United States 1952–54* (Washington, DC: GPO, 1986), VIII, p. 143.
57. Memorandum, John C. Ausland to Brewster Morris, 17 October 1953, Department of State, ed., *Foreign Relations of the United States 1952–54* (Washington, DC: GPO, 1986), VII, 2, p. 1666.

10

The CIA's Berlin Operations Base and the Summer of 1953

David E. Murphy

The Soviets and many in the leadership of the SED (Sozialistische Einheitspartei Deutschlands – the Socialist Unity Party) recognized that the demonstrations of 16–17 June 1953 had their origins in the legitimate grievances of East Berlin construction workers. It was also evident in both Karlshorst and Moscow that the Ulbricht regime had lost control of the situation and would have to be rescued by the Soviet Army. Nevertheless, within hours after the outbreak of the disorders in East Berlin, these truths were ignored and the blame for instigating and supporting the riots was placed on the USA, including the CIA.

The rhetoric of the Eisenhower election campaign in 1952, promising to 'roll back' the Iron Curtain, might have been sufficient to persuade the Soviets that such charges would be believed. Moreover, in October 1952, the US Psychological Strategy Board (PSB) had issued a plan which envisioned psychological, political and economic harassment of the German Democratic Republic (GDR) as well as 'controlled preparation for more active resistance'.[1] Unfortunately, while the CIA was represented on the PSB, there was a considerable gap between the plans adopted by that body and the CIA's covert action capabilities in areas under Soviet control. Furthermore, according to Wayne G. Jackson, Director of Central Intelligence (DCI), Bedell Smith's special assistant for PSB matters in late 1952, the clandestine services were most reluctant to expose to outsiders their plans and programmes.[2] It is one thing to formulate grandiose plans to destabilize a Soviet client state, but it is quite another to execute them.

Could the CIA operations base in West Berlin indeed have provoked a crisis of this magnitude in East Berlin? In fact, did it? To answer that question it is necessary to examine the CIA's Berlin Operations Base (BOB), study its origins in 1945 and its transition from the Office of Strategic Services (OSS) to the CIA, describe the organization and functions of the base in the period just before the 17 June uprising, and see how the base learned about these events and what its response was.[3]

The image in the Western media of the CIA as an omnipotent force with tremendous resources bears no resemblance to the small group of OSS personnel that arrived in West Berlin on 4 July 1945. The senior OSS officer in Berlin was Allen Dulles, who had been designated chief of the OSS German mission. For his headquarters he selected a site on Foehrenweg in Dahlem, the former headquarters of Field Marshal Keitel, designed by Albert Speer and built in 1936. Because General Lucius Clay made his headquarters in Berlin, the site of the Allied Control Council, it was assumed by OSS that its mission headquarters would also be located there. This never happened.

In September 1945, President Truman ordered the OSS abolished as of 1 October and its intelligence collection and counter-intelligence functions transferred to the War Department as the Special Services Unit (SSU). On 1 October, Dulles left Berlin and was replaced by Dick Helms, who did his best to keep the Berlin detachment alive. At that time, the intelligence branch had nine officers, and the X-2 or counter-intelligence element, five. Helms departed just before Christmas 1945 and was replaced by Dana Durand, a charter member of the OSS's X-2. Peter Sichel was deputy base chief and head of the intelligence branch, later becoming base chief. The Berlin base would become the BOB of the German station under the new CIA's Office of Special Operations (OSO). The station headquarters, initially in Heidelberg, was later moved to Karlsruhe. All OSO elements in Germany were under Department of the Army cover.

By 1950, the new CIA Office of Policy Coordination (OPC), responsible for covert action, had established an OPC German station in Frankfurt and its own base in Berlin. It would function independently of the OSO base on Foehrenweg. To emphasize its independence, it selected offices at Tempelhof airfield under Department of the Air Force cover. Gradually the OPC unit began to provide funding for groups such as the *Untersuchungsausschuss frei-heitlicher Juristen* (UfJ; Investigative Committee of the Free Jurists), the *Kampfgruppe gegen Unmenschlichkeit* (KgU; Fighting Group Against Inhumanity), and the Eastern bureaus of the SPD and CDU. Contact with some of these organizations had already existed on the part of the OSO Berlin base and Region VIII of the US Army's Counter-Intelligence Corps (CIC). Both the OSO and the CIC had tried with limited success to tap the intelligence potential of these groups. They resisted control by their benefactors, however, and when the OPC subsidies began, these organizations were given considerable, and in some cases total, freedom of action.

In January 1951, the OPC and the OSO at CIA headquarters were placed under a Directorate for Plans. Later in 1951, Lieutenant General K. Truscott was sent to Germany as CIA senior representative or chief of mission, charged with supervising both OSO and OPC activities. It would not be until August 1952, however, that the two offices were integrated into a single clandestine services organization at CIA headquarters. Integration in the field took longer. Whereas the Berlin units of the OSO and the OPC were placed under command of the chief of the OSO base, because of lack of space at the Foehrenweg, the two units remained separated by a 30-minute drive from Tempelhof to Foehrenweg in Dahlem. The distance factor, plus the resentment of the OPC 'cold warriors' at having been 'taken over' by the OSO, did not make for efficient command relationships. It would not be until August 1954 that the former OPC group could be brought together with the Berlin base at its new, much larger, offices in the former US Headquarters Compound on Clayallee.

In December 1952, Bill Harvey arrived as base chief. Harvey spoke no German and had never been overseas before. There was only one reason for his assignment: the Berlin Tunnel. During the spring of 1953, test recordings by BOB agents of Soviet telephone cables in East Berlin had demonstrated the potential value of the lines to be tapped; by early June, Harvey was hurrying to prepare a detailed tunnel proposal for General Truscott and DCI Dulles. Harvey's deputy was Henry Hecksher, who had served in Berlin since OSS days. When Peter Sichel became base chief in 1949, Henry was made deputy. Before Harvey's arrival, he had hoped to become chief, but this was not to be.

In the weeks before the June events, BOB's covert action branch, the former OPC unit, was still in Tempelhof. In addition to a chief

149

and a deputy chief, it had two officers charged with propaganda operations. One of their responsibilities was overseeing the KgU, which included refereeing the constant infighting between the founder of the group, Rainer Hildebrandt, and his successor, Ernst Tillich. More important, the group had not recovered from the effects of a Soviet KGB penetration of the KgU and the arrest of numerous collaborators in East Germany. The UfJ had managed to develop extensive contacts with members of the legal profession in East Germany and thus became an important target of Soviet and East German state security operations. The kidnapping of Dr Walter Linse in July 1952 resulted in mass arrests and show trials throughout East Germany; Linse's interrogation in the Soviet prison in Karlshorst lasted until June 1953, when Linse was tried by a military court of the Group of Soviet Forces in Germany and sent to the Gulag. Coping with the impact of Linse's arrest on the UfJ was a major preoccupation of the covert action branch as of June 1953.

In addition to the two officers responsible for propaganda, there were three paramilitary specialists who had been sent to Berlin to handle a 'stay behind' network to be recruited from adherents of the UfJ in East Germany. This scheme was adopted despite vigorous dissent by Henry Hecksher, who well understood the limitations of the UfJ in the field of unconventional warfare. Unfortunately, the entire scheme had been described to the Soviets by Linse while under interrogation, thus causing the arrest of scores of individuals during 1953. The Berlin OPC paramilitary officers were fully occupied by these unfortunate circumstances throughout the summer of 1953.

The fallout from these flaws in the covert action projects was also felt in the former OSO element of BOB at Foehrenweg. In June 1953, it consisted of a counter-intelligence branch, Soviet and East German intelligence operations branches, and smaller Czech and Polish branches as well as two reports officers and administration. The reports officers were responsible for reviewing raw reports obtained by case officers from agents to determine whether they contained intelligence information worthy of formal dissemination. More than other officers, the reports people were expected to stay abreast of current developments in Berlin and alert operations personnel to their significance.

Base chief Harvey made BOB's counter-intelligence (CI) branch responsible for conducting investigations of the large-scale arrests in the covert action projects. One of the two largest branches at BOB (the other was the Soviet branch), the CI branch ran double-agent cases and an important, tightly compartmented penetration of the newly created East German foreign political intelligence service, which would one day become Markus Wolf's phenomenally successful *Hauptverwaltung Aufklärung* (HVA). The CI branch also handled the so-called support agents who served as couriers, letter mailers, and surveillance agents in East Berlin and throughout the GDR. The new responsibilities, interviewing the relatives of arrestees and those members of the nets who escaped with their lives, and analysing the results, placed an extraordinary burden on the branch. An added difficulty was the fact that the CI branch chief was also handling special duties connected with the tunnel in 'his spare time', tasks which he could discuss only with Bill Harvey.

The Soviet branch operations were directed at the recruitment or defection of Soviet personnel stationed in Germany. The German branch was primarily concerned with handling penetrations of the Administration of Soviet Property in Germany (USIG) in Berlin Weissensee and enterprises throughout the GDR which contributed to the Soviet nuclear programme, such as the uranium mining and processing facilities known as Wismut. While the Polish branch occupied itself with debriefing the occasional Polish refugee who made it through to West Berlin, BOB's Czech branch ran agents among truckers and canal boatsmen carrying cargoes to Prague. To put these organizational factors in perspective, then, in June 1953, only a handful of BOB's personnel were involved in covert action, and those who were so engaged faced major problems brought about by tough, effective Soviet countermeasures.

Many BOB officers, including, of course, the report officers, were aware of and had reported on the increasing tensions in East Berlin and throughout the GDR, which led to the introduction of the so-called New Course earlier in June. Nevertheless, when they arrived at their billets from the BOB offices on Tuesday evening, 16 June, and settled down for drinks and dinner, they were wholly unprepared for the news broadcasts describing the extensive demonstrations that day by dissatisfied workers and the timid, confused response of the SED. No BOB reports disseminated earlier that day had predicted these activities, and to BOB officers it seemed wholly out of character for East Germans, any Germans, to have challenged authority in this way. As the evening drew to a close, no special alerts were issued by either BOB or Berlin Command; no one had any inkling of the dramatic events to come.

151

Next morning, as BOB officers arrived at the office on Foehren-weg at the usual 0830 or 0900, the atmosphere was calm, and most personnel proceeded to follow whatever agendas they had planned for the day – agent meetings, refugee debriefings, or attacking the usual backlog of reports, or financial accountings. Soon, though, word of the dramatic events unfolding in East Berlin began to get through. One officer recalls hearing on his car radio of the appearance of tanks on Potsdamer Platz, whereupon he drove to the vicinity and confirmed that indeed there was shooting from machine guns on the tanks, whose turrets were clearly visible over the heads of the crowds which had gathered. Two other officers also visited the Potsdamer Platz area and reported firing from the tanks and also ambulances from West Berlin, under police car escort, taking wounded East Berliners to hospitals in the Western sectors.

Back at BOB on Foehrenweg, excitement grew; those officers who had not yet visited the sector borders sat transfixed by news reports on their radios. One of BOB's two reports officers had started his day by making a sign for his office reading 'East Berlin Demonstration Desk'. He could not savour his exercise in gallows humour for long, however, because Bill Harvey sent him to the 'war room' at Berlin Command to serve as a liaison officer between BOB and military intelligence. This move was prompted by growing concern for the level of Soviet Army intervention. Would the armoured units converging on East Berlin remain within the Soviet Sector or might they enter West Berlin? As for Harvey himself, he seemed tied down for most of the day attending conferences with the US Commander Berlin, his staff, and that of the State Department's Berlin mission. Occasionally, orders from the 'chief' would filter through to the base, such as that requiring all officers to call into the BOB switchboard every hour with an update on their location and to report any new information. Later that day, BOB personnel were told to stay away from the sector borders but this was after most had already satisfied their curiosity.

BOB's second reports officer spent his day preparing situation reports for CIA headquarters which incorporated anything the base could glean from any source, including eyewitness accounts by case officers. He recalled that these 'sitreps' were 'slugged' or designated for DCI Allen Dulles and had to be no longer than a page because they were shown to President Eisenhower. Occasionally, Bill Harvey would dictate his own assessments of the situation, reflecting his own surprise at the developments and his admiration for the courage shown by the East Berliners.

This reporting was not, however, based on carefully organized assignments of case officers to designated, critical areas along the sector borders. It developed rather from the desire of individual officers to see for themselves what was happening. After their forays to Potsdamer Platz, many continued on to the vicinity of the Brandenburg Gate in the British Sector. They reported that on the Soviet side, an artillery battery served by troops in full combat gear was drawn up along Unter den Linden with their guns pointed towards the West. Large crowds had gathered and since they were not allowed to approach the gate, they took out their resentment on the British military police who had been assigned to protect the Soviet War Memorial located just beyond the gate in the British Sector.

Ironically, just a short distance away from the border, along the Kurfürstendamm, then West Berlin's most elegant thoroughfare, there was no sign of the excitement. One BOB couple, tired of being caught up in the milling crowds of West Berliners shaking their fists at Soviet tank crews (from a safe distance), stopped at the Cafe Kranzler for a quiet coffee. Not far away, in front of a theatre connected with the ongoing Berlin film festival, was a huge crowd of young Berliners surrounding the US actor, Gary Cooper. Desperate for his autograph, they seemed oblivious to the sound of gunfire a mile or so away.

Not everyone in BOB was playing 'war correspondent'. The chief of the Czech branch was furious when one of his officers disappeared on 'border reconnaissance' just as a major operational development was reaching a climax (after weeks of concentrated effort, this was to be the day when a barge operator-agent would smuggle into Czechoslovakia several radio sets sealed in concrete gravestones). Other officers were frustrated by their inability to contact agent sources. At first, many agents were frightened by the violent clashes. Later, the sector border closure made it impossible for them to attend meetings in West Berlin. This meant that BOB was unable to exploit its sources in the East German railway system or in the Administration of Soviet Property in Germany (USIG). A report, obtained later from one of these sources, would have been extremely valuable had BOB been able to publish it on 17 or 18 June. The agent, who spoke Russian, described in detail the Soviet Army's deployment in

East Berlin, the behaviour of the troops, and the negative impact this had on the population, most of whom were not directly involved in the workers' actions or the riots which followed. The thirst for information was so great that consideration was given to trying to activate remnants of the UfJ's paramilitary structure in East Germany. Luckily, this suggestion was tried out on one of the CI branch officers who was investigating the many arrests that had already taken place. The idea was rejected.

A great deal of the information on Soviet Army and East German paramilitary movements within Berlin itself came from the West Berlin police, who somehow managed to maintain contacts with opposite numbers in the East. Because of the importance of these police reports, the regular BOB liaison officer was assisted by deputy base chief, Henry Hecksher, who, having served in Berlin since the winter of 1945–46, had excellent contacts in the police. The later assertion that he had asked CIA headquarters for permission to arm the rioters cannot be verified, and few CIA retirees give it any credence. By the time BOB had come to realize the extent of the uprising in East Berlin, it had also become clear from the presence of massive Soviet firepower that any resistance would have been hopeless.

For many of the BOB women, Wednesday, 17 June, was the day of a long planned bridal shower for one of their number whose marriage would occur within a week or so. The shower went forward that evening as scheduled. Meanwhile, at BOB headquarters, Harvey had called a meeting to review the day's events. It was at this meeting that arguments arose as to the meaning of the uprising. One officer opined that the Soviets and East German communists had actually staged the affair to demonstrate how democratic they were. BOB officer David Chavchavadze, who had been one of the first to witness the clash between demonstrators and tanks on Potsdamer Platz, disagreed, saying that 'no communist leader would stage a labor strike against himself', to which Harvey commented, 'Right on, Dave'. Others chimed in with their own experiences and comments, Harvey sent over to the Officers Club in the Harnack House for sandwiches, and, on that note, 17 June 1953 ended for the CIA's BOB.

The rest of the German Mission was equally surprised by the events in the East. General Truscott, his deputy, Mike Burke, and his aide, Tom Polgar, had spent 17 June in the Nuremberg area with CIA and Army intelligence representatives discussing cross-border operations into Czechoslovakia from Bavaria. They returned by train late in the day and when the train stopped in Stuttgart, their first aware-ness of the events came from the headlines of the newspapers being sold on the station platform. As for the report of a cable sent by Hecksher asking for permission to arm the rioters, Gordon Stewart, deputy to Truscott for OSO operations, who was acting mission chief in the absence of Truscott and Burke, denied that such a message was ever sent. Polgar added, that had such a message been sent, Truscott would have moved quickly to relieve Harvey.

The German Desk of the CIA's Eastern European (EE) Division, which was responsible for Germany, was also taken completely by surprise. This was confirmed by Peter Sichel, division chief of opera-tions, who had been chief of BOB until 1952. Incidentally, Sichel also denied that a message asking for arms had been sent from BOB by Hecksher. Frank Wisner, formerly head of the OPC and now Deputy Director for Plans, the combined clandestine services, sent a memo-randum on 18 June to the Chief, EE Division, after having participated in 'high-level considerations of the developments of the last 48 hours in Germany'. This was a reference to a meeting of the National Security Council (NSC), which took place earlier on 18 June, at which Allen Dulles reported that 'the United States had nothing whatsoever to do with inciting these riots and our reaction so far has been to confine ourselves … to expressions of sympathy and admiration'. In his memorandum to EE Division, Wisner noted: 'We seem to have hit pretty close to the right line in our own effort of yesterday and last night', emphasizing that we 'should do nothing at this time to incite East Germans to further actions which will jeop-ardize their lives'. There was no reference to arming the rioters in Dulles's statement before the NSC or in Wisner's memorandum, although, certainly, Wisner and many of his colleagues were frus-trated by their inability to influence the East German events (it would be three years before the Hungarian revolt, which would produce similar reactions).

This frustration was not confined to the CIA but was felt else-where within the Eisenhower administration and in Bonn itself. Western passivity in the face of the uprising and the swift Soviet response was coming under criticism. It was, apparently, to counter this reaction that on 29 June the PSB drew up an 'Interim Plan for Exploitation of Unrest in Satellite Europe'. Many of the measures were wholly unrealistic and never adopted with the exception of one, a 'large scale food program for East Germany, approved by PSB on 1

July 1953'.[4] Ironically, at the very moment when the PSB was striving to snatch victory from defeat with regard to the East German situation, it was about to disappear. Even before his inauguration, Eisenhower instituted a review of the PSB's activities by a committee chaired by William H. Jackson (a former Deputy Director of Central Intelligence, not to be confused with that staunch 'cold warrior', C.D. Jackson). On 30 June 1953, the 'Jackson Committee' found that the PSB had overreached itself in trying to develop a separate 'strategic concept for psychological operations', and recommended its abolition. By September 1953, it had been replaced by the Operations Coordinating Board.[5]

Nevertheless, the food programme, the PSB's last major effort, did go forward during the summer of 1953 and was a resounding success, if success is measured by the alarmed reaction of the East German SED and the Soviets to the destabilizing effect of the programme. Christian Ostermann has made extensive use of SED archives to describe measures resorted to by the SED in its efforts to minimize the extent and impact of the food distribution. Indeed, *Battleground Berlin*, written by journalist G. Bailey, former KGB officer S. Kondrashev, and D. Murphy, parallels these descriptions in presenting the analysis of the situation by the Soviet state security apparat in Karlshorst under General Yevgeny Pitovranov. The latter believed that 'the American food program posed a serious threat to security and stability in the GDR', and undertook several steps to cope with the problem. Most important was the need to reinforce the GDR's own security forces, badly shaken by the events of the preceding June.

It is the ultimate irony, therefore, that when this programme was proposed, the BOB strongly objected. In an 11 August 1953 memorandum to the Director, Central Intelligence, the Chief, EE Division, reflected the BOB's views in arguing that the programme would be 'contrary to the best interests of the United States'. Specifically addressing the plan to establish food depots along the interzonal and sector borders, the EE Division noted that since the interzonal borders were more difficult to cross, those seeking food parcels would do so in Berlin, thus providing the Russians 'with a pretext for sealing the Sector border as well as the zonal boundary. This would, of course, greatly hamper our operations both in Berlin and in East Germany.' This was a parochial view, perhaps, particularly when one considers that the operations in question were primarily related to intelligence and counter-intelligence and not to covert action.

Of course, the food programme did go forward. It was concentrated along the East Berlin sector border, and while the Soviets and East German authorities tried various stratagems to lessen the programme's impact, at no time did they actually seal the border, nor did they employ physical force to prevent people from reaching the food depots on the Western side. It would be exactly eight years later, on 12–13 August 1961, that the borders would in fact be sealed tight.

In retrospect, therefore, the experience of the summer of 1953 highlights the gap that existed in the US government between high-level psychological warfare plans and the field units responsible for their execution. The CIA Berlin base could never have been capable of executing the bold proposals advanced by the PSB in October 1952 nor could it have fomented the uprisings on 17 June 1953. The real reason for the success of the food programme was Soviet concern that, given the demoralized state of the SED and GDR security forces, any attempt to employ brute force to prevent food distribution might have courted disaster. This is why over the next three years the Soviets concentrated on rebuilding GDR state security, with the result that when the Polish riots of October 1956 and Hungarian rising of November 1956 occurred, the East German population remained calm. Nonetheless, this blind faith on the part of succeeding US administrations that somehow the CIA could create, sustain, and direct resistance forces in East Germany at levels capable of influencing Soviet behaviour in successive Berlin crises seemed as unshakeable as it was unwarranted. For example, despite repeated statements challenging this view by CIA Soviet and German specialists, President John Kennedy and his brother Robert could never rid themselves of the idea.

To some extent, this naive belief may have been based on the views advanced by Soviet and East German propaganda to the effect that subversive forces directed by the CIA were responsible for the 17 June uprisings as well as virtually every other internal security problem faced by the GDR. Often repeated in the Western media, these inflated versions of CIA prowess may have convinced many in the US national security bureaucracy and led to the unrealistic planning of the kind which characterized that of the PSB in 1952–53.

NOTES

1. C. Ostermann, '"Keeping the Pot Simmering": The United States and the East German Uprising of 1953', *German Studies Review*, 19:1 (February 1996), p. 61.

2. W.G. Jackson, *Allen Welsh Dulles as Director of Central Intelligence, 26 February 1953 – 29 November 1961*, Vol. III, Covert Activities, Historical Staff, Central Intelligence Agency, 1973.

3. Except where otherwise stated, the material in this section is taken in part from D.E. Murphy, S. Kondrashev and G. Bailey, *Battleground Berlin: CIA vs. KGB in the Cold War* (New York: Yale University Press, 1997), and from interviews with CIA retirees present in Berlin on 17 June 1953 conducted by D. Murphy. The latter served on a liaison team with the Red Army on the zonal demarcation line during 1945, and with the CIA in Germany from January 1951 to June 1961.

4. Ostermann, op. cit.

5. Jackson, op. cit.

11

The Early History of the Gehlen Organization and Its Influence on the Development of a National Security System in the Federal Republic of Germany

James H. Critchfield

The acceptance of West Germany as a member of NATO and the formation of the Warsaw Pact, both in May 1955, completed the creation of a geopolitically divided world, a development Reinhard Gehlen had foreseen by the autumn of 1943 when he was chief of the German intelligence organization *Fremde Heere Ost* (Foreign Armies East). In the security of his walks in the Mauerwald in East Prussia, Gehlen had discussed these thoughts on the future with his deputy, Gerhard Wessel. Gehlen had weighed the implications of Roosevelt's and Churchill's agreement on 'unconditional surrender' at Casablanca in January 1943, the major military reversals on the eastern front, including Stalingrad, and the inevitable consequences of the total mobilization and determination of the USA to defeat both Japan and Germany. Most thinking officers had come to believe that the war could not be won. But Gehlen had gone beyond that point. The two individuals closest to Gehlen in 1943, Gerhard Wessel and Heinz Herre, have credited Gehlen alone with the foresight of predicting the reversal of the Soviet alliance with the West. He had the concomitant idea that *Fremde Heere Ost* would be of real value to a Western alliance and to a future German government entering this alliance against the threat posed by the Soviet Union.

In May 1955, 12 years had passed and Gehlen's vision of 1943 seemed likely to become reality. The final step, the legalization of his organization and the founding of a German intelligence service, seemed imminent. The 'appropriate circumstances', to which Adenauer repeatedly referred but which he never defined, while committing himself to the establishment of a national intelligence service appeared to have come about. My own mission in post-war Germany was about to end; it had turned out to be more complicated than I had been led to believe when the CIA assumed responsibility on 1 July 1949.

The summer of 1948 was a time of considerable tension due to the Soviet blockade of Berlin, which was the Soviet reaction to the determination of the USA and Britain to push ahead with the formation of a separate West German economy and government. There was a high level of active interchange between the Evaluation Staff in the city of Pullach, the American military intelligence service, G-2, in Heidelberg, and the Army Air Force intelligence organization, the A-2, in Wiesbaden. Concerning the future of Operation Rusty, the army's name for the Gehlen Organization, the Pentagon presumably was getting mixed signals from Germany. Gehlen had been complaining bitterly about the lack of support. But at the same time, because of the threatening posture and strength of Soviet forces in East Germany, tensions were rising and production from Rusty was critical. No intelligence immediately available to General Curtis LeMay in Wiesbaden and General Bill Hall in Berlin was quite as useful as the raw intercepts out of Gehlen's station at Schloss Kransberg monitoring Soviet military voice communications. This station provided immediately available intelligence on whether the Soviet MIG 17s were up or down and what fields they were flying from. General Clay's famous message in March 1948 warning of a possible Soviet attack had shocked Washington; in midsummer 1948, Clay was involved in a daily exchange with Washington over the question whether the USA should abandon its position in Berlin, leaving the city to the Russians. General Clay, supported by Foreign Minister Ernest Bevin in London, was insisting on a firm stance emphasizing that the Russians were bluffing. Almost everyone in the Pentagon and State Department seemed inclined to withdraw US dependents and to bow to Soviet demands in Berlin. Only President Harry Truman, Ernest Bevin, and General Clay were solidly opposed to considerating a Western withdrawal from Berlin; Truman was unwavering: 'We stay in Berlin.' Clay describes General LeMay, the US community in Berlin, and the German people of Berlin as all staunchly on his side. It was in this remarkable atmosphere in the autumn of 1948 that I arrived in Pullach.[1]

I had been sent to Pullach by the CIA to take a look at Operation Rusty. I was to ascertain whether the CIA should assume responsibility for all or any part of it and whether there were parts which could be distributed to other elements of the US intelligence community in Germany. I was to recommend whether the operation as a whole should be continued or dismantled. I was given no hint of agency preference for any of these solutions. In the only discussion I had with senior CIA officers in Germany, I had detected a negative consensus. But the station chief, Gordon Stewart, clearly was open-minded. He was by training a student of German history and had spent the war in the OSS's Research and Analysis branch.

There was no mention by anyone of any existing commitments by US military sponsors to Gehlen and no hint of a 'gentlemen's agreement' between the G-2, General Sibert, and Reinhard Gehlen. I was somewhat surprised at the lack of material provided by the CIA and received nothing useful from the Army. Shortly before Christmas 1948, I wrote a 1900-word cable report addressed in my mind to Dick Helms in Washington and Gordon Stewart in Germany. I knew they were interested and thoroughly familiar with the circumstances in Germany and the country's recent history. I was new to the CIA and had no idea of who in Washington might be involved in the Rusty affair. I think it was in this cable that I adopted the name of 'the Gehlen Organization' and dropped the use of 'Rusty'.

Gehlen was desperate to be associated with the new CIA; it was my impression that even if the CIA assumed responsibility, his expectations would prove unrealistic. During the five or six weeks after my arrival, it became evident to me that the US government had only one choice – to keep the organization alive, to avoid anything that would disturb the intelligence coverage on Soviet forces on East Germany, and to defer any other judgement until we knew a great deal more. It had become clear that all the Army was doing was to provide a facility, military cover, and various kinds of support, including financing, that had, following the currency reform, become quite inadequate. Assuming that the CIA was prepared to assign to it a staff of intelligence specialists, it seemed logical that the CIA should take over a project that had clearly gone beyond the point of no return. The problem in the future would be to establish an interface between the Gehlen Organization and whatever might develop in Germany as a government, which might at some point transform it into a German service. In the circumstances of late 1948, that seemed to be a remote possibility. It became clear to me that Gehlen saw himself as the German head of a German intelligence organization. Up to a point, I thought this a necessity if we were ever to arrive at the stage where its legalization as a German service became conceivable. For Gehlen, it was important to promulgate this image with his associates, and later with the German government; his credibility depended on it.

In Pullach in 1949, there were two developments that, from a CIA viewpoint, set the stage for 1950, the year of decisions. The first was the CIA's assuming responsibility on 1 July 1949; the second was the CIA's recognition that it had not one but two operations in Pullach – Gehlen in intelligence and Heusinger in remilitarization. They had joined forces in 1948. Gehlen had been out of contact with Adolf Heusinger during the three years after 20 July 1944. But at a discreet meeting in Marburg in September 1947, Gehlen offered Heusinger a position in his organization. In February 1948, Heusinger arrived in Pullach bringing with him a tightly structured think-tank and contingency planning entity made up of only three former generals – Adolf Heusinger, Hans Speidel, and Herman Foertsch. In sporadic contact during the first two years after the war, these three had been systematically observing the geopolitics and military balances in western Eurasia reaching from the Atlantic to the Urals; their purpose was to think through and develop plans on how a new German government could participate in the collective defence of Western Europe against the threat of Soviet communist aggression from the East.

Shortly after the CIA assumed responsibility in Pullach, Adolf Heusinger, in several evening conversations, described to me in considerable detail the history, purpose, and current status of his efforts. I early concluded that I was dealing with an intellectually very formidable trio. Dr Hans Speidel was a part-time professor at Tübingen University and was connected with the Gehlen Organization solely by his connections with Foertsch and Heusinger. Foertsch stayed in an operational villa in Nymphenburg; Heusinger lived and worked in the compound at Pullach.

There is no doubt that the CIA's attitude toward the Gehlen Organization changed within two years of my late 1948 report. The German Federal Republic was established in Bonn and the communists started a conventional and full-scale war in Korea. After Gehlen had established a firm connection with Chancellor Adenauer and both Gehlen and the CIA were separately in touch with Dr Globke, Adenauer's principal aide in national security matters, we all accepted the 'held in trust' idea and looked upon Gehlen's position as significantly altered from what it had been when I met him in 1948.

As a whole, 1950 was a year of important decisions in the saga of the Gehlen Organization. But through the first half of the year, Reinhard Gehlen was under intense strain – unresolved financial difficulties, problems in agreeing with the CIA on policy, the temptation to get into internal West German security issues, differences with Heusinger on style and strategy, and management problems piling up in Pullach. The British added to these with a number of moves in Bonn hostile to both Gehlen and Heusinger. Between early January and early April, Gehlen appeared to be balanced on the edge of a precipice, and he was threatening to give up and close down the operation. His inner circle was somewhat alarmed. Heusinger had a serious one-to-one talk with him in early April. Although I did not take seriously Gehlen's threat to resign, I eased off on pressures from the US side where it was possible. We got through the spring of 1950. Then, with the war in Korea, the whole international political environment changed.

The North Korean attack on South Korea on 25 June 1950 was an event that marked the beginning of a new era in world history. The Korean attack was probably the event that put Germany on the path to a close relationship with the USA and membership in NATO and the Western community of nations. It set in motion the consolidation of the strength of the non-communist world that in the end defeated international communism, secured the West a victory in the Cold War, and led to the collapse of the Soviet Empire, thus making the reunification of Germany possible. It also marked the beginning of changed attitudes on the part of both the CIA and the Gehlen Organization, a development which got us through the six years until the founding of the *Bundesnachrichtendienst* (BND; the German intelligence organization). It is in this context that 1950 as a year of decisions was so significant.

The initiatives and decisions taken in 1950 provoked five years of intense struggle between the Soviet Union and the West over whether and how Germany was to be integrated into Western Europe and NATO, and how and whether the Gehlen Organization would be transformed into a German intelligence service. The struggle over the

Western European and NATO question was carried out mainly at the official diplomatic level; but it was accompanied by an intelligence war, in which the Soviet aim was to neutralize Germany and block its entry into NATO and, at the level of intelligence, to destroy, if possible, the Gehlen Organization or, at a minimum to block its legalization as the BND. What became virtually an intelligence war centred in Germany was well under way by 1953 and continued for much of the decade that followed.

After 5 May 1955, Gehlen had been assured by Dr Globke that Adenauer intended to create a German intelligence service. Gehlen had satisfied himself that all other NATO services were supportive. The opposition party, the SPD, had, from Gehlen's first contacts with Dr Kurt Schumacher in September 1950, remained positive. Not everyone in Bonn was supportive, but five years of effort had produced a wide range of satisfactory relationships with the Chancellory, the Foreign Office, and the Interior Ministry.

On the surface, Gehlen had every reason to be optimistic. The objective that had gradually taken such explicit form over more than a decade was about to be achieved. But with my 20/20 hindsight on the history of the Gehlen Organization, I am persuaded that Gehlen was not a man without anxieties as he looked forward to the final steps required to achieve his long-held goal. I believe that the unresolved problem of communist penetrations into important positions of his organization was probably the deepest of Gehlen's concerns. This had been a preoccupation of all of us in Pullach since the Soviet-engineered show trials and the propaganda war that had started in 1953 and extended into late July 1954. At that time, the head of the *Bundesamt für Verfassungsschutz* (BfV; the German counter-intelligence service), Otto John, had disappeared into East Germany and later made an appearance at a press conference in East Berlin.[2] There were, we would learn in 1961, at least two BND members, Heinz Felfe and Hans Clemens, actively reporting to the KGB in that summer of 1955. They had been working for the Soviets since 1951. Gehlen had looked at Felfe with some suspicion in the summer of 1954; we do not know the extent to which this concern had abated just a year later. I have often wondered what reasoning led the KGB not to sacrifice Felfe and Clemens during 1955 in a final try to destroy Gehlen. A well-timed KGB spy scandal might have changed the early history of the BND. Perhaps Felfe was considered too valuable a resource to be dropped with uncertain results. Adenauer and his cabinet had demonstrated a very thick skin in all but ignoring the spy trials and propaganda operation launched by the Soviets and East Germans in 1953. On 12 July 1954, Adenauer obtained a unanimous vote of support for his plan to take over the Gehlen Organization in the appropriate circumstances.

Gehlen was also concerned, and justifiably so, about the position of the US Army G-2. Gehlen had been made fully aware of G-2's effort of late 1954 to draw Speidel and Heusinger into a conspiracy to sabotage Gehlen's plans and aspirations. General Trudeau, the chief of G-2, made a last-minute direct private approach to Adenauer in Washington in June 1955. He attempted to persuade Adenauer to abandon his plan to create a centralized civilian general intelligence service with Gehlen at its head. Gehlen had also been disturbed by evidence that the Counter-Intelligence Corps (CIC) was maintaining unauthorized contacts with his own counter-intelligence organization and was having these investigated. The early summer of 1955 was still a time of stress and some uncertainty for Reinhard Gehlen.

The understanding reached in 1948 by Heusinger and Gehlen to cooperate had become more important to both after the Korean attack in June 1950. Chancellor Adenauer, on his own initiative, reached out and established contact with both. By the end of the year, he had taken over the Heusinger effort, separating it from the intelligence side of the Gehlen Organization. In 1956, Gehlen had finally achieved his objective of the formation of the BND. Gehlen and Heusinger joined forces in early 1948 – a significant event in the evolution of the national security system in which Adolf Heusinger became the founding father of the armed force of the Federal Republic of Germany, the *Bundeswehr*, and Reinhard Gehlen the founder and first president of the BND.

Inevitably, persons exposed to this 'Pullach story' ask fairly logical questions about relevant US policies: Was the initial creation of the *Fremde Heere Ost* operation at Oberursel a result of a secret US policy to fill the void of US intelligence on the Soviet Armed Forces at the end of World War II? Was the relocation to Pullach, the move of Heusinger from his position with Halder in Neustadt to join Gehlen's operation in Pullach part of a US secret plan to influence the development of German armed forces, a role for Germany in NATO, and a centralized German intelligence service?

I would very much like to state that these developments were the consequence of very secret and sophisticated planning generated at or even before the end of the war. I wish I could say that Eric Waldman's secret meeting with Heusinger and Gehlen in a medical facility in Marburg in September 1947 and my sudden move from mainstream army intelligence to Pullach in 1948 were links in an imaginatively contrived operation. Unfortunately, we Americans were at that point in history wholly uncapable of such creative planning. It did not happen that way.

Now I think it equally logical to ask how much of all this was a secret plan generated someplace along the way from the Mauerwald to Pullach. And I would not find it difficult to construct a reasonably plausible scenario of policy planning on the German side. I think that to some modest degree, this happened. But it was piecemeal, and not a grand conspiracy.

NOTES

1. See also M.E. Reese, *General Reinhard Gehlen: The CIA Connection* (Fairfax, VA: George Mason University Press, 1990). Pullach, the small Bavarian city where the American intelligence organizations were located after 1945 and where the German post-war intelligence service *Bundesnachrichtendienst* (BND) was established, is often used synonymously with the BND.
2. See also S.A. Kondrachev's contribution in this volume.

12

The KGB and Germany: Some Thoughts by a Participant in the Events

Sergei A. Kondrachev

Before entering into the main subject of this chapter, I wish to say that we, the veterans of the Soviet and Russian secret services, more than anybody else feel the whole depth of the tragedy the peoples of our country have lived through before the war and in the first post-war years. I say before the war, but if we go into the history of our country, we also register a wide use of punitive practices by secret services in the Russian Empire as far back as Ivan the Terrible. However, historical precedent cannot serve as justification for later abuses and there is no limit to our condemnation of punitive practices where security services were involved by decision of supreme authority. In all, nearly 24,000 officers and functionaries of special services were the victims of their own government, most of them losing their lives.

The situation in the Soviet Union before the war caused many foreign and especially German diplomats and intelligence officers to misjudge developments and conclude that the Soviet Union could not withstand an attack of the German army and would collapse within a few weeks. In the Russian archives are copies of the reports written by able German diplomats such as the minister counsellor of the German Embassy in Moscow, Gustav Hilger, who drew the attention of the German general staff to the weakness of Soviet agriculture and industry. This was certainly true in substance, but not concerning the possible consequences. The war efforts displayed by my compatriots demonstrated the ability of the people to mobilize their inborn forces when the very existence of the country was at stake. We entered the last war in a very complicated psychological situation, following the purges in the party and the show trials of the late 1930s. We ended the war united as one nation as never before in our history. Yet, the seeds of the Cold War were sown in the course of World War II.

At the Tehran Conference in 1943, the Big Three agreed on contacts between their secret services with a view towards their co-operation in the war effort. I cannot say that the cooperation between the intelligence services of the Soviet Union, the USA and Great Britain developed to the expectations of the participants and their leaders.[1]

To be objective, I must say that the US side took the initiative in the cooperation between the intelligence services. The talks were held in late 1943 in Moscow with the participation of Molotov on the Soviet side and Ambassador Harriman on the US side. The discussions involved methods for the overthrow of governments in some German-occupied countries by the combined efforts of US and Soviet agents. The concrete proposals were initiated by the US side. In my opinion, at that stage, both sides thought there were real prospects for this operation. At the same time, it was clear that entering into negotiations with such political forces and groups as were capable of staging a putsch would entail rewarding them by granting them a role in the future state.

The US side thought that these political groups should be promised milder conditions of surrender after a successful overthrow of the governments allied to the Nazis. Molotov replied that the Soviet Union could not deviate from the requirements of unconditional surrender. Due to the seriousness of the problem, he consulted Stalin and was confirmed in his position.

There were several points of view in this situation. First, if we granted milder conditions of surrender in case of a successful overthrow of the government in one of the countries under Nazi occupation, that would have meant that the main political forces would have remained in place and that those left-wing forces who fought the Nazis would have had no chance to strengthen their influence. Second, it was obvious at that time, but never openly expressed, that should the Soviet leadership refuse to enter into discussions about the suggested operation it would lead to a continuation of the war and further loss of lives on both sides. Certainly, we must not forget that with the enormous death toll already sustained in the

Soviet military and civilian population it was hard to imagine that anybody would propose to stop the advance and rely on combined operative methods. There is a third consideration that should not be forgotten in the historical analysis. Near the end of the war, both the Western Allies and the Soviet Union had contacts with political leaders in the occupied countries who could not be regarded as agents but were ready for a very close, secret political cooperation, which they regarded as beneficial to the future of their countries. It is difficult to say whose political positions in the occupied countries were better, those of the Western Allies or those of the Soviet Union. There is a fourth factor that played no lesser role. The advancing Soviet armies were met by a jubilant population, a fact which meant more political influence with every mile.

The cooperation which was decided upon between the secret services of Great Britain, the Soviet Union, and the USA produced an exchange of information, the importance of which should not be exaggerated. The information received from the OSS was reported to Stalin, Molotov, and Beria. There was a parallel channel of information from our sources in the British secret service. Today, after the death of Otto John, I wish to say, as a tribute to this brave man, that in July 1944 we had received his report of 6 December 1943, passed on to the British secret service and containing information on the plans of the opposition to eliminate Hitler and conclude a peace treaty with the Allies. Remembering Otto John, I wish to say that he displayed courage twice – first, when he came to us as a kind of protest against former Nazis getting important positions in the West German government, and, second, when he chose to return to the German Federal Republic, demonstrating that for him allegiance to his fatherland was more important than political friendship or enmity.

After the Tehran conference, the participants were actively seeking solutions to the problem of the future role of Germany in Europe and in the world. Our foreign intelligence was able to procure the most important documents of the British government and Foreign Office related to British plans for Germany. Out of many interesting considerations contained in the documents written by Foreign Minister Sir Anthony Eden, I will mention only three. In his letter to the British representative to the Provisional Government of France, Duff Cooper, Sir Anthony named the prevention of any form of Russian-German rapprochement as one of the tasks of British foreign policy.

There are two further important ideas in Sir Anthony's writings. The first was that the Germans should themselves determine their future political system, and the second that it was impossible to divide Germany, lest the future peace be undermined. The full text of these British documents was reported to Stalin and Molotov.

I would say that Soviet foreign intelligence supplied Stalin and other leaders with abundant information on the divergence of views on the future of Germany among the Allies. Nevertheless, it seems that the political leader who profited most from such divergent views was Chancellor Adenauer.

I cannot abstain from mentioning another important document, which I have published in March 1997 in form of an article, and which presents considerable interest for the analysis of the last weeks and months of Hitler and his surroundings; that is, the personal notes on the events by Walter Schellenberg, written in Sweden within three weeks after his effort to negotiate a separate peace treaty with the Western Allies on the order of *Großadmiral* Doenitz in the last hours of the Third Reich. Fully conscious of an uncertain future, depending on the mercy of the victors, Schellenberg wrote a most revealing document. He gave the transcript of discussions with Himmler of how to get rid of Hitler, who had become the main stumbling block in the way of saving Germany as a state. It is clear from his document, called by historians 'the Trosa memorandum' (after the name of the Swedish town where Schellenberg stayed from 3 May until some time in June 1945), that Schellenberg had hoped for help from the Allied secret services. He did not deny his contacts with the British secret service.

The last stages of the war led to the formulation of Soviet policy regarding the future of Germany. Thanks to the leading role of the Soviets in the unconditional surrender of the Third Reich and because of Hitler's death, it became possible to build a democratic Germany. The basic ideas of the Soviet leaders were directed towards building a new political system attractive to Germans in East and West alike. Soviet security forces were acting according to this principle in trying to eliminate all resistance to this principal object.

Very soon the high command of the Soviet occupation forces realized that the new German authorities created with Soviet help did not enjoy the support and respect of the population. Even the formation of the Socialist Unity Party did not engender public backing. Nor was Soviet economic and social policy in Germany received positively in the German population.

The late 1940s witnessed one of the most complicated periods in the history of Soviet foreign intelligence. An initiative by Molotov in a short note to Stalin started the merger of the Soviet Union's political, military, and diplomatic intelligence services. His ideas were very sound: to eliminate the discrepancies in intelligence reporting and to combine the views of the Foreign Office, the Ministry of Defence, and the Ministry of State Security into one common assessment of the international situation. The Committee of Information (CI) was formed with very broad powers. It took away from the chiefs of the three most important agencies the prerogative of reporting directly to the boss, as we called Stalin. The CI did not last long. In 1949, the Red Army's general staff intelligence directorate, the GRU, withdrew, leaving a small CI, which in turn vanished quickly. It was difficult to merge the information and views of the three agencies in Moscow, but it was even more problematic to combine their efforts and responsibilities abroad.

In the early 1950s, the future of East Germany was becoming a great concern for the Soviet leadership. On 2 November 1951, the chief of foreign intelligence, S.R. Savtchenko, reported to Stalin, Molotov, and other Soviet leaders the statement of Duncan Sandys, the son-in-law of Sir Winston Churchill and minister of supplies in the British government. According to the information received from friendly Polish intelligence, Duncan Sandys had said that in 1952 several terrorist acts had to be expected against politicians of the German Democratic Republic (GDR). These acts would be carried out by German military organizations. Sandys also stated that the communist power in East Germany would be seriously undermined. He even predicted workers' uprisings in 1953. When the predictions of Sandys, supported by information from other sources, started to come true, they contributed to the further escalation of the Cold War.

The situation in East Germany was becoming more tense and complicated every day. In the course of the Cold War, foreign intelligence officers on several occasions felt that their information about the worsening situation was disregarded by the government and party leadership. The national interests of the country, particularly in that period, were secondary to the leaders in their struggle for power.

As was customary in that period, analytical documents by the Central Committee of the Communist Party and by the Foreign Office about the events of 17 June 1953 stated that the demonstrations by large masses of workers in Berlin and other cities were

171

unexpected and were caused by the subversive activities of Western intelligence services and mass media. In reality, the picture was much more complicated. In the second half of 1952, the Socialist Unity Party, on the initiative of Walter Ulbricht, took the decision 'to speed up the building of socialism' in the GDR. Consequently, shortages of basic consumer goods arose. The fuel for heating and electricity became scarce. The situation worsened with the attempt by the East German Socialist Unity Party, SED, to eliminate the bourgeoisie classes in the cities and in the countryside. Long before 17 June, strikes and outbursts of protest against the increased norms of productivity introduced by Walter Ulbricht were observed in different parts of the GDR.

Under direct Soviet influence, the measures to speed up the development of socialism were slowed down, but it was too late to stop the uprising. This revolt by the broad masses of the population nearly swept away the political system of the GDR. It was upheld only by the force of Soviet tanks. Our intelligence apparatus in Berlin was receiving information on the rapid worsening of the situation, but its director realized that neither the representatives of the Soviet Communist Party in Berlin, primarily responsible for the situation, nor the SED leaders reacted to the warnings.

Throughout our history, we had many occasions when, despite foreign intelligence reports, the leaders of the government and of the party did nothing to avert impending troubles. As in many similar instances, the prestige of foreign intelligence was saved by producing an extensive and deep analysis of events prepared by a prominent Western diplomat for the foreign office of his country. The Foreign Intelligence directorate was lucky to get such information at this very crucial moment.

Ambassador A.S. Paniushkin, Chief of Soviet Foreign Intelligence, forwarded the report by this foreign diplomat in Germany to Gromyko. In the accompanying letter, Paniushkin wrote:

> In this report ——— dealt with following questions: June events in East Berlin and GDR and comments on them in West Germany, views of Adenauer regarding convening of four-power conference, the case of Beria and Soviet foreign policy, 'New Course' in the GDR, results of the activity on the first West German *Bundestag* and perspectives on coming elections in West Germany.

In the next paragraph, Paniushkin introduced a quotation from the report of this highly positioned Western diplomat.

> ——— asserts, that June events in West Berlin and in the GDR, had, on the one hand, 'spontaneous, unorganized, anarchist character', on the other hand were prepared and directed from the West. He pointed out, in particular, that 'the flame was fanned, slogans and directives to the insurgents were given not only by the radio station RIAS Berlin', but also by the leader of trade unions in West Berlin, Scharnovsky, and by the West Berlin based 'Investigative Committee of Free Jurists', by the 'Fighting Group against Inhumanity', by the editorial boards of the newspapers *Der Telegraph* and *Der Tagesspiegel*, which by the words of ———, were 'serving as cover' for subversive activity against the GDR ... 'The Social Democrats went even further and demanded that their merits in organizing the uprising be recognized since the most ardent participants were the workers of East Germany'.

In addition to the information from this foreign source, I wish to introduce a very short quotation from an hour-by-hour observation report of 17 June 1953: 'Three times in the course of the day of June 17 this year, 9 American planes dropped leaflets by the "Fighting Group Against Inhumanity" calling on the population of Berlin to rise against Soviet occupying power.'

Despite the fact that we were conscious of extensive activities by the US and other intelligence services, and especially by the CIA's Berlin Operation Base, who were trying to influence public opinion in the GDR,[2] we reached the conclusion that the main reason for the uprising was the large degree of discontent among the German population with the politics of the Ulbricht administration.

One of the most important tasks and requirements confronting Soviet intelligence was the obligation not to miss any signs indicating the preparation by the NATO powers for military conflict with our country. The information we received contained extensive coverage of NATO contingency military planning. It is difficult to assess the depth and broadness of such information from the material published so far. Information of that character, especially when originating from very important sources, in many cases was reported only to one person, or to two or three of the highest leaders, and usually collected and returned to the chairman of the KGB the same day.

Such sensitive intelligence was not used for propaganda purposes for fear of compromising its source. Protection of the sources of important information had priority over other considerations. In rare cases, when military information was vital for foreign policy decisions, it could be made public after thorough analysis. We know the story of the Berlin Wall. The necessity to introduce some system of rigid control on the line separating East and West Berlin was studied very thoroughly at the highest levels between leaders of the Soviet Union and of the East European states. The increasing number of people fleeing across the demarcation line to the West and differences in prices for consumer goods were of prime importance for the decision-making process. The consequences of rigid controls were also assessed. The exchange of views between leaders of the East European states took place on 3 to 5 August 1961.

During some of the meetings, no statements were taken down. But those which were, were explicit enough. N.S. Khruschev, in his long statement, often talked without a prepared text. As an illustration, I may quote one passage from his speech touching his meeting and talk with the former High Commissioner for Germany, John McCloy, after and in connection with Kennedy's statement on television about the situation in Germany. 'We talked quite a bit there. I said to him he should tell President Kennedy that he could start the war, but that I thought if he started it, he would become the last president of the United States, because after the war the people would scarcely be willing to be reconciled with those who unleashed wars in which millions died.' I know that McCloy transmitted this message accurately.

The Soviet leadership had serious grounds for supporting Ulbricht's initiative to construct the wall in Berlin. On 12 August 1961, the Präsidium of the Central Committee of the Communist Party adopted the decision to make public several authentic documents of CENTO, the Central Treaty Organization (the former Baghdad Treaty), including the 'Choice of targets for strikes with atomic weapons on the territories of the Soviet Union, China, Iran, and Afghanistan'. In the statement of the Soviet Telegraph Agency (TASS), public attention was directed towards suspicious military activities in the countries adjacent to the Soviet Union's borders, especially in Iran and Turkey. It was pointed out that at the meeting of CENTO the representatives of the USA, Great Britain, Turkey, Iran, and Pakistan decided to broaden their military preparations in the Middle East by way of building new military bases, unifying systems of arms, and creating a united general staff. The decision to publish these documents was based on two considerations. The first was to support the GDR, as suggested by Ulbricht; the second was to respond to the military buildup of the military alliance directed by the USA and Great Britain on our southern border.

Thirty-five years ago, the Soviet Union together with the GDR responded to the dangers looming in Germany and on our southern border by forceful action. A similar situation is now at the centre of public interest in Russia and the other former republics of the Soviet Union and in Europe in general; I mean the expansion of NATO to the East. I believe that by common effort we will be able to reconstruct the events of the past tragic period of our common history.

NOTES

1. S.A. Kondrachev, 'Zapiska Waltera Schellenberga ('Memorandum Trosa')', *Otyetchestvennuye Archivuy*, 2 (1997), pp. 58–78.
2. For the role of the CIA, compare the chapter by C. Ostermann in this volume.

13

Canada and the Intelligence Revolution

Wesley K. Wark

The *fin de siècle* of the 1990s was a period of uncertain transition for intelligence communities. They found themselves caught between a familiar, Cold War past and an uncertain future. It was a peculiarity of the debate over intelligence in the 1990s that as the future grew ever murkier, the past came to take on a degree of nostalgia. Intelligence community veterans came close to lamenting the disappearance of the Soviet target, in retrospect discussed as a highly predictable and near transparent object for intelligence collection and assessment.

There were commendable efforts launched during the decade of the 1990s to come to terms with the changes that had beset the world of intelligence since the collapse of the Soviet Union. These included the 1996 report of the Aspin-Brown Commission, established by Congress to review the entire mandate of the US intelligence community. Aspin-Brown was the largest and most significant public investigation of its kind since the end of the Cold War.[1] A near equal in heft and significance was the study prepared by the Permanent Select Committee on Intelligence of the US House of Representatives, *IC21: Intelligence Community in the Twenty-First Century*.[2] The US think-tank lobby weighed in with two reports. One, from the Council on Foreign Relations, *Making Intelligence Smarter*, gained some press notoriety for having advocated the unfettered use of journalists and 'other private citizens to conduct intelligence in denied areas. The other think-tank product, *The Report of the Twentieth Century Fund*

Task Force on the Future of US Intelligence, provided its own critique of an ill-focussed intelligence community, backed by impressive analytical papers from Allan Goodman, Gregory Treverton, and Philip Zelikow.[3] Scholarly treatments also addressed the issues posed by the future of intelligence.[4] The cumulative effect of this outpouring of blue ribbon and academic studies is still difficult to discern. What is notable in many of the studies of the 1990s is an absence of broad historical context, the inability, or lack of desire, to root prediction of the future in some kind of historical vision of the past.

SOFT POWER, THE INFORMATION AGE, AND THE INTELLIGENCE REVOLUTION

Thinking of changes to intelligence communities and their functions is a sterile exercise unless embedded in some serious reflection about the new shape of the international system and about consequent shifts in the definition of national interest and national security. One of the most provocative theses about the future shape of statecraft that emerged during the 1990s concerned the advent of 'soft power' and the implications of the new information age. Joseph Nye and Admiral William Owens led the way in an article published in *Foreign Affairs* in 1996 entitled on 'America's Information Edge'.[5] Nye, a former chairman of the National Intelligence Council and now dean of the Kennedy School of Government at Harvard, and Owens, a former vice-chairman of the Joint Chiefs of Staff, are a formidable duo. Using Nye's definition of soft power, which emphasizes the deployment of information resources and technology to shape the international system to an American model, and to ward off threats to US/global interests, the authors argue that the twenty-first century will be 'the period of America's greatest pre-eminence'. 'Information,' according to Nye and Owens, 'is the new coin of the international realm, and the United States is better positioned than any other country to multiply the potency of its hard and soft power resources through information.'

Nye and Owens are undoubtedly on to something. But new ideas carry their own baggage of hyperbole. The topicality of the information age has been burnished to a red-hot glow by consumption of personal computers, by the internet, by e-mail, and other fast communication technologies, and by popular hype. There are undoubtedly revolutionary changes underway in how people access and use information, and communicate knowledge. But states have been engaged in an on-going information revolution since at least the dawn of this century; one of its most significant manifestations has been the little understood or discussed 'intelligence revolution'.[6]

> The 'information revolution' can seem so new only because of the invisibility that cloaks the longer-run 'intelligence revolution'.

To complicate matters the twentieth century intelligence revolution fits no easy metaphor of change: it is not even clear whether revolution is quite the right concept, denoting as it does short, sharp, recognizable change. For this revolution proceeded *sub rosa*, in fits and starts, sometimes bounding forward linearly, sometimes conjuring cyclical patterns. It seems to have some global attributes, but is clearly shaped by national histories and political structures. Like the information revolution, it threatens to disappear in its own cloud of smoke the moment one seeks a stable definition. But the intelligence revolution does, in retrospect, seem to have had some identifiable motors of change which had an almost universal impact. At the very least, they help us understand the sheer quantity of change that affected intelligence communities during the course of the twentieth century.

THE MOTORS OF THE INTELLIGENCE REVOLUTION

Technology

Information technology and its dynamic of change occupy a central place as a mover and shaper of intelligence practice and intelligence communities. The dawn of the modern age of intelligence was made possible by such nineteenth century inventions as the telephone, the telegraph, the radio, and the camera. These devices cumulatively brought the speed, volume, and reach of information flows to a point where the timeliness, ease, ubiquity, and indeed the vulnerability of communications created unprecedented opportunities for governments to learn rapidly of developments within and without their policies and to fear what others might learn in turn. The mobilization and professionalization of intelligence communities through three successive international crises: World War I, World War II and, hard on its heels, the Cold War, created international and domestic surveillance regimes with potential powers beyond the wildest imaginations of dystopian writers such as George Orwell or theorists such as Michel Foucault.

Changes in information technology have transformed intelligence practice by moving intelligence out of a centuries-old stasis, involving dependence on the human agent, the mail, the Gutenberg press. Advances in information technology have moved intelligence services towards real-time intelligence, and the ability to consume an unprecedented volume of knowledge. The engine of technological change comes with some inevitable costs. Simply put, it is extremely expensive to stay current with the latest technological platforms for intelligence collection and information processing. Nor does their possession automatically enhance intelligence capabilities. The reason has to do with the art of tasking and more broadly what Michael Handel calls the 'politics of intelligence'.[7] Contemporary intelligence services with access to high technology face the daunting problem of information-overload. The only solution rests with precision tasking, which in turn depends on the maintenance of finely and constantly tuned links between the producers and the consumers of intelligence in government. Such links at least on the historical evidence, are very difficult to sustain, especially so in authoritarian societies, or in countries practising a cult of leadership, as the Axis powers (and the Soviet Union) discovered to their cost during World War II.

Globalization

The years since 1914 have witnessed a revolution in the global practice and global reach of intelligence services, one that mirrors the end of the European dominance of the international system, the increasing diffusion of international power, the emergence of a world trading system, and indeed the globalization of conflict. Whereas once upon a time the practice of intelligence was the unique preserve of a handful of European powers, it is now a ubiquitous phenomenon of the international system, and not even the preserve of the nation-state. Whereas once upon a time the geographical reach of

179

intelligence services was restricted to Europe, it now of necessity spans the globe. Yet the global exportation of intelligence from its historic European base has not proceeded equitably or smoothly, largely due to the high technological costs, the resource implications, and the complex political conditions necessary for the smooth functioning of intelligence services. It seems likely that current disparities in intelligence capabilities are likely to continue, and perhaps to grow even more stark, raising the prospect of an intelligence hegemony, as the late twentieth century information revolution takes off at its own very uneven rates of diffusion.

Expansionism

Advances in information technology and the globalization of intelligence are closely related to a third feature of the intelligence revolution: the stunning expansion in the size and mandate of intelligence communities. The secret services of pre-1914 Europe all possessed minuscule establishments, often consisting of a handful of agents and a one-man central bureau (as characterized British intelligence). Their geographical beat was Europe and their mandate was almost exclusively the collection of military intelligence. Changes to this intelligence practice came in a profound wave during World War II. Under the pressures of total, transcontinental war, new intelligence communities began to generate a knowledge base far in excess of the older military handbooks, which were the staple of turn-of-the-century intelligence services. The creators of that knowledge base were no longer that cadre of active or retired military and police officers who had peopled the intelligence services from 1914 to 1939. Instead, bureaus such as the Office of Strategic Services's Research and Analysis branch, and the code-breakers of Bletchley Park, or Canada's Examination Unit, became polyglot collections of talent whose closest, peacetime exemplar was the university. What the R & A branch were after were profiles of a nation, the wartime precursor to contemporary all-source intelligence analysis.

The punctuated expansion of intelligence services in the twentieth century has resulted in a massive growth of dedicated personnel working on an ever-expanding range of information collection and analysis tasks. Like the application of technology to intelligence, and the embrace of global collection, the correlates of intelligence establishment growth have been widely different among nation states. As

180

with the technological dimension and the phenomenon of globalization, the expansion of intelligence communities has been accompanied by inevitable growing pains – principally to do with the challenges of recruitment, the constant fine-tuning of skills, and the maintenance of morale in agencies usually divorced by the culture of secrecy from the society in which they function. As Walter Laqueur has reminded us, intelligence, no matter how technologically driven its collection and processing systems might be, is an art, not a science, and its fundamental resource is human talent.[8] The historical record suggests the massive difficulty that intelligence communities have had in creating and sustaining such talent, especially in peacetime, and matching its profile to that of the nation.

Bureaucratic Politics

As the collection capabilities of intelligence services grew ever more sophisticated, as globalization progressed, and as intelligence services expanded in size and scope of operations, their place in the bureaucratic grid also began to change. This process can best be visualized as a form of burrowing from periphery to centre, occasioned by two factors. One was the increasing recognition by governments that high quality intelligence was fundamental to statecraft and national survival, and that organizations on the periphery could scarcely do the job.

As the tasks of intelligence grew more important and as intelligence services moved to the centre of government in an effort to accomplish them, a phenomenon certainly accomplished by mid-century, a second factor came to the fore – bureaucratic politics. Intelligence services, like other government agencies, found themselves engaged in the daily struggle for bureaucratic survival that is life in the official jungle. They had to defend turf, and battle for high political attention. They had to protect budgets. But once intelligence services became important enough and central enough to have to engage in bureaucratic politics, so then did governments have to think seriously about ways to referee disputes and to manage an 'intelligence community' often consisting of competing bureaucracies with quite different professional components (military vs. civilian vs. police agencies). The proper management of an intelligence community requires strong political interest, commitment and oversight. When those ingredients are missing, trouble ensues. The fate of the

Royal Canadian Mounted Police (RCMP) Security Service is a good, made-in-Canada example of such trouble. Without consistent political direction, but under pressure to achieve results, especially in their watch on violent Quebec separatism, the RCMP Security Service drifted into ill-considered and illegal acts in Quebec. The McDonald Commission was blunt about this in its report:

> A point of fundamental importance, of which we became acutely aware as we conducted our inquiry, was the absence of a clear and shared understanding by ministers, government officials and RCMP members of the policy issues relating to police and security operations about which responsible ministers ought to be informed and on which they should be able to give direction.[9]

In the Canadian case, a fundamental restructuring of the security service, a new legal mandate, and an oversight mechanism seem to have been a success in solving the problems of the 1960s and 1970s. But whether it will be adequate to address the problems of the twenty-first century is another matter.

The historical process of the burrowing of intelligence services from periphery to centre solved the problem of irrelevance, but did not automatically bestow its opposite – relevance. Instead it created bureaucratic challenges for which, it seems, there are no formal, finite solutions. The universality of this process suggests that states have much to learn from looking around at the experiences of others. Again, as the McDonald Commission suggested, there might also be wisdom in knowing the lessons of one's own past. In the Canadian case, we have the opportunity of watching and learning from larger intelligence communities struggling with adjustment to the information revolution and the management and dissemination of intelligence. We also have the chance of re-examining organizational solutions which are dated (though not necessarily out of date) and not entirely made-in-Canada.

Popular Culture

Popular culture is rarely mentioned or taken seriously in discussions of intelligence. But popular culture portrayals of espionage were present at the creation, and have been intimately bound up with the intelligence revolution, for good or ill, since 1914. Spy fiction and spy film enjoy a mass audience and communicate to that audience myths of espionage which, depending on their content, serve either to legitimize or de-legitimize its societal function. This is a powerful role, shaping as it does the political climate in which intelligence services must ultimately attempt to operate and setting expectations about intelligence, however fantastic, that cannot help but penetrate even the sober imaginations of politicians and civil servants, not to mention eager young recruits to the espionage world. It is astonishing how many women entered intelligence agencies during World War II worrying about the myth of Mata Hari; and how many of their male counterparts went to the secret wars with visions of John Buchan's Richard Hannay or Somerset Maugham's grimmer cast of characters from the Ashenden stories firmly lodged in their minds. Perhaps we are more sophisticated now; perhaps not.

Spy fiction and film have not, by and large, taken their story lines from the driving power of technological change, nor from the globalization, the expansion, nor the bureaucratization of intelligence. Instead they have created their own competing visions and imbued them with a cyclical dynamic all their own. Two formulas dominate the genre. One stresses intelligence services and their agents as redemptive forces, operating in a secret universe into which the reader is given privileged admission, to save civilization from apocalypse. The line of production runs from early William le Queux and John Buchan to Ian Fleming and on to Tom Clancy in our day. Its formulaic alter ego offers a darker vision of intelligence agencies as microcosms of the corruption of power and of the triumph of amorality. In this alternative fictional world, spies are powerful agents of raison d'état, but have little or no redemptive function. They engage in dirty operations, dirty bureaucratic fights, dirty wars. Treason lurks in the corridors of power. Somerset Maugham, Graham Greene, and Eric Ambler were early craftsmen of this formula; their post-1945 successors came to the fore in opposition to Fleming's James Bond. The best of them, John le Carré, remains the master practitioner of the genre.[10]

The Canadian audience for spy fiction and film has rarely been treated to indigenous work in this genre. Instead, Canadian readers imbibe a non-mimetic treatment penned by British and American authors in which reference to (fictional) Canadian agencies is almost entirely absent. In the Canadian case, the legitimizing/de-legitimizing function of the popular culture of espionage serves mainly to sustain an illusion of Canadian innocence from the redemptive struggle or dark corruption of espionage. The illusion is aided by governmental secrecy, and by silence on other fronts, notably the absence of sustained journalistic investigation, and the paucity of serious literature on the subject of Canadian intelligence.[11]

The twentieth century intelligence revolution can be seen then as a product of both material and cultural factors, providing a variety of propulsive forces, but cumulatively sustaining the uneven, punctuated, but ultimately massive rise to power of intelligence services. One final thing needs to be said about this revolution. It has flourished from the beginning against a background of international tension and national insecurity. The massive transformation of power and of national sovereignty bequeathed by the nineteenth century, by the twin gods of the industrial revolution and nationalism, provided the initial fertile environment for the growth of fledgling intelligence services before 1914. At the close of the twentieth century, the lifeblood of intelligence services remains international instability and domestic turbulence. Only in an unimaginably peaceful world would the dynamic that has sustained the intelligence revolution begin to falter.

THE CANADIAN EXPERIENCE OF THE INTELLIGENCE REVOLUTION

A capsule history of the Canadian intelligence community suggests that Canada has ridden the intelligence revolution but adapted it to its own circumstances in its transformation from colony, to dependency, to sovereign state.[12] Canadian intelligence had its origins in the mid-nineteenth century, with the decision to establish a small secret service in the closing days of the American Civil War. While Gilbert McMicken's small band of 'detectives' had little success in stopping the illegal acts of Confederate and Union agents, they represented an institutional innovation that the government of John A. Macdonald quickly turned to when a new threat emerged to the Confederation in the late 1860s and 1870s. The Fenian Brotherhood, an Irish-American movement pledged to support the liberation of Ireland from British rule, took Canada as their target and spoke frequently of invasion and (national) hostage-taking. Armed incursions of bands of Fenian soldiers from the US actually occurred on three occasions; the

184

anxiety stirred in Ottawa was probably greater than any military threat the Fenians could mount, but the presence of a small intelligence service to engage in infiltration of the enemy (which they achieved in spectacular fashion) and provide warnings, was the government's first real taste of the potentialities of intelligence and was sufficient to give the intelligence branch of the Dominion police an institutional foothold and lease on life for the next forty years. One early Canadian prime minister proved to be fascinated by intelligence and adept at putting it to use – Sir John A. Macdonald. Macdonald also, alas, found it difficult to avoid the temptations posed by the existence of non-accountable secret service funds, a goodly portion of which he held on to even after he left office.

Once entering the mainstream of twentieth century history, Canadian institutions rode the forces of the accelerating intelligence revolution in such a way that a superficial inspection of their impact on Canada would suggest nothing unusual or distinctive at work. Canada mobilized an intelligence community to confront the challenges of World Wars I and II. It demobilized its intelligence community between the wars, and, as was common, turned what remained of its institutions inward in a fight against the perceived menace of bolshevism. World War II, again in a seeming typical fashion, brought an unprecedented level of intelligence activity and sophistication of resources into play in Canada. At the end of the war, a permanent intelligence community survived the transition to the quasi-peace of the Cold War. During the 1960s and 1970s, successive intelligence 'scandals' (principally the Munsinger affair in the 1960s and the revelations of RCMP Security Service illegalities in the late 1970s) when aired in a more contested political climate, in which an early Cold War consensus had begun to unravel, caused major public debates. These in turn, though safely channelled through government-appointed commissions of inquiry, led to significant institutional reforms – the most prominent being the creation of the new civilian Canadian Security Intelligence Service (CSIS) in 1984. The rise of terrorism as an international threat in the 1970s added a new target to the tasks of Canadian intelligence, but did not substantially alter the post-McDonald commission structures or modus operandi of the Canadian intelligence community, which was now required to operate within a well-defined legal framework, with propriety of operations as a significant factor, with an onus on civil liberties considerations, and under the eye of a set of appointed watchdogs (the Security Intelligence Review Committee and the Inspector-General of CSIS).[13]

Nor have the 1990s winds of change left Canadian intelligence untouched. Responding to new demands for openness and public accountability, CSIS has expanded slightly the range of information provided in its annual public reports, while the deputy clerk of the Privy Council Office, Ms Margaret Bloodworth, in her capacity as deputy minister for the Canadian Security Establishment, provided Parliament for the first time in May 1995 with a brief statement on the operational mandate, personnel and budget of Canada's signals intelligence (SIGINT) agency.

Even the future has arrived. In February 1992, acting at the request of the Solicitor-General, CSIS established a Director's Task Force to study the 'changing security intelligence environment', admittedly over the modest time frame of five years hence. The study was conducted purely as an internal affair, was classified at the Secret/Canadian Eyes Only level, and involved no consultation with outside (non-governmental) experts. The Breakspear report, as it is referred to, seems to have had little effect on the Service and is not regarded by members of CSIS to whom I have spoken as containing much of significance. Major sections of the report have been deleted in the version made available under the Access to Information Act (principally those identified as dealing with 'Need for Foreign Intelligence'). The Breakspear report, while largely arguing for the continuity of threats and a matched continuity of efforts (the no change model), did highlight new concerns about the shift to economic espionage activity and fears of nuclear proliferation, and made modest suggestions about increased Canadian defensive activity in these realms.[14]

On the face of it, this long history is one of unbroken conformity to the broad trends of the twentieth century intelligence revolution, always, of course, adjusted to Canada's national concerns and lesser power status. But probe beneath the surface a little and one comes up with some surprising features. It is an old Canadian theme – conformity masks significant departures from the norm. The first thing that one notices is the over-riding concern with domestic security intelligence over the past 130 years. This concern, and the concomitant investment of resources, has reflected a political assessment of national insecurity which stretches unbroken from the Confederate marauders and rag-tag paramilitary bands of the Fenians of the 1860s down to the present.

A related, and equally significant feature of Canadian intelligence has been the eschewing of a clandestine foreign intelligence gathering capability, and the attendant heavy reliance on first colonial masters and subsequently on unequal partnership in intelligence alliances for the bulk of Canada's foreign intelligence. This is particularly the case with respect to high-technology intelligence gathering, where Canada has made few efforts, despite a sophisticated R & D and industrial base, to develop any independent capabilities and must rely on its allies. The seeming exception to the rule is the Communications Security Establishment (CSE), though the available documentation suggests that CSE largely operates as a source of raw material for the assessment machinery and all-source collation institutions, again, of Canada's allies. CSE operates in this fashion to establish a Canadian quid pro quo for access to finished intelligence – a role imagined for the CSE's predecessor, the Communications Bureau of the National Research Council, in 1946, and based further back still in the lessons of the operations of the Examination Unit during World War II.

Canada is the only G-8 power not to have a foreign intelligence agency. The practice of sending Canadian agents beyond our borders, actively encouraged during the nineteenth century, simply faded away after World War I. At the same time, on the few occasions in recent years when the issue has been raised, no overwhelming case has been made for the establishment of such an agency.[15]

The Canadian fixity on security intelligence at home had three further effects which profoundly shaped the Canadian intelligence community for much of this century. One was the dominance of police forces in the intelligence community, and the attendant conceptualization of intelligence work as a form, perhaps exotic, of policing. The drawbacks of such practices and conceptualizations were apparent to the Mackenzie commission in the late 1960s and to the McDonald commission a decade later. But it was not until 1984 that institutional change finally began, and it took several years before CSIS could begin to wean itself from its RCMP Security Service past. A second, related effect of the police dominance of the intelligence effort in Canadian history was a dangerous decoupling of intelligence practice from political scrutiny and control. The practice began as early as the reign of Robert Borden, when Borden gave the task of security intelligence, and in particular the watch over supposed Red subversion, to a resurrected Royal Canadian Mounted Police force in 1918. Inherited, Victorian-era gentlemanly distaste for espionage fused in the Canadian case with a sense of the legal prudence of separating ministers of the Crown from close involvement with a form of policing. The harnessing of police forces to security intelligence work at home, matched with the comforting supply of foreign intelligence from Canada's great power allies, created an environment in which there seemed little need or desire for close political scrutiny. The result was political disengagement and policy drift that stretched over decades and ended in the highly public security intelligence scandals of the late 1970s. What was lost in this long process of political disengagement is incalculable – it represents a missing education and inheritance for senior politicians and officials in the potentialities and limits of intelligence. A third effect of the Canadian practice of security intelligence was the inevitable identification in the minds of the Canadian public of intelligence with the potential abuse of police powers: creating an unhealthy environment for debate in which both political authorities (disliking controversy) and the public (disliking policing) shy away from any penetrating appraisal of Canadian intelligence requirements.

Because the Canadian practice has been to embrace security intelligence, the police function, and eschew foreign intelligence gathering; and because of the way in which the Canadian government adopted a British model for the organization of its intelligence community based on wartime experience but not necessarily Canadian needs, the evolution of Canadian organizational structures has lacked coherence and precision. The current structures seem a curious hotchpotch of ministerial responsibilities and overlapping jurisdictions, without strong central control and without any clear sense of the relative significance to be attached to the various parts of the cycle of intelligence – comprising collection, assessment, and dissemination. The claim is often heard that it is a hotchpotch that works, but this is a claim difficult for outsiders to test. In any case, why a hotchpotch?

A capsule history of Canadian intelligence, utilized for didactic purposes, and in any case suffering from large gaps in available documentation, cannot claim to do justice to the issues or necessarily be a fair representation. But with these limits acknowledged, what conclusions can be drawn in this final, backward glance? Canada has clearly experienced its own intelligence revolution during the course of the twentieth century. It has been, just as clearly, a revolution selectively absorbed.

High-technology collection resources, whether directly obtained from Canadian agencies like CSE, or by proxy from Canada's allies, have transformed the kinds of information available to the Canadian government. But the Canadian concentration on security intelligence at home has served to blunt the dynamic impact of high technology, when low-technology resources still suffice to do the job. Canada now has global interests and even its security intelligence fixation warrants something of a global watch – especially in regards to issues of terrorism, the importation of homelands conflicts through immigration flows, and the shared responsibility to monitor nuclear weapons proliferation.

The Canadian intelligence community has expanded in size and scope dramatically from the handful of Dominion police agents of pre-1914 days to the current establishments of CSE and CSIS. The individual agencies that comprise the Canadian intelligence community have all engaged in burrowing towards the bureaucratic centre, though the success of bureaucratic repositioning has seemingly been blunted by an incoherent organizational structure and the tradition of political disengagement from the intelligence practice and product. There may be little visible Canadian content to the popular culture of espionage, but then this is a complaint that stretches across the entire breadth of popular culture; and in any case Canadian audiences have certainly imbibed strongly from British and American production and even associated its contents with a certain assumption of Canadian innocence. James Bond never came to Canada, and no Canadian kept watch for an overdue agent at Checkpoint Charlie with Alec Leamas. Canada has not been insulated from international crises by its geopolitical position or by any tradition of neutrality – quite the opposite. But Canada's geopolitical position has, at least in the past, afforded the luxury of allowing Canada to maintain a monocular intelligence system – with its single lens fixed on the security threat at home.

EPILOGUE: LOOKING TO THE FUTURE

In thinking about the future the past matters, maybe even determines outcomes. One of the most visible and decisive turning points in the history of Canadian intelligence came in the year 1945. As the wars in Europe and then in Asia moved to their conclusions, the Canadian Joint Intelligence Committee (CJIC) and the Chiefs of Staff took up the issue of the future of Canadian post-war intelligence. Both bodies enthusiastically embraced an expanded, all-source Canadian intelligence service with sufficient capabilities to allow Canada to sustain its security and independence in the new atomic age. A decisive break with past traditions was the key theme. But the vision of the CJIC and the COS was not to be. It was undercut by budgetary pressures, the indifference of then Prime Minister Mackenzie King, and the startling appearance of Soviet defector Igor Gouzenko on the scene. Yet the words of General Foulkes, the Chairman of the Canadian Chiefs of Staff, remain prescient. He argued that intelligence (and he was talking particularly about SIGINT) was 'a short road into the mind of others'. In the new information age, the Canadian intelligence community will need this mind-reading ability more than ever before. It is doubtful that the monocular system established by historical tradition will suffice to do the job for the twenty-first century. Yet where the political will might be found to alter the status quo of Canadian intelligence community practice remains very unclear.

NOTES

1. US, Commission on the Roles and Capabilities of the United States Intelligence Community, 1 March 1996 (Washington, DC: GPO, 1996).
2. US Congress, House of Representatives, Permanent Select Committee on Intelligence, *IC21: Intelligence Community on the Twenty-first Century* (Washington, DC: GPO, 1996).
3. Council on Foreign Relations, *Making Intelligence Smarter* (New York: Council on Foreign Relations, 1996); *In From the Cold: The Report of the Twentieth Century Fund Task Force on the Future of US Intelligence* (New York: Twentieth Century Fund Press, 1996).
4. Among such studies: R. Godson, E.R. May and G. Schmitt, eds., *US Intelligence at the Crossroads: Agenda for Reform* (London: Brassey's, 1995); and more recently Bruce D. Berkowitz and Allan E. Goodman, *Best Truth: Intelligence in the Information Age* (New Haven: Yale University Press, 2000); Craig Eisendrath, ed., *National Insecurity: US Intelligence after the Cold War* (Philadelphia: Temple University Press, 2000); Loch K. Johnson, Bombs, *Bugs, Drugs and Thugs: Intelligence and America's Quest for Security* (New York: New York University Press, 2000); and Gregory F. Treverton, *Reshaping National Intelligence for an Age of Information* (Cambridge: Cambridge University Press/RAND, 2001).
5. J.S. Nye Jr. and W.A. Owens, 'America's Information Edge', *Foreign Affairs*, 75:2 (March/April 1996), pp. 20–36.

6. For one effort to define the phenomenon, see W.K. Wark, 'The Intelligence Revolution and the Future', *Queen's Quarterly*, 100:2 (Summer 1993), pp. 273–87.

7. Michael Handel, 'The Politics of Intelligence', *Intelligence and National Security*, 2:4 (October 1987), pp. 5–46. The article was reprinted in Michael Handel, ed., *War, Strategy and Intelligence* (London: Frank Cass, 1989).

8. W. Laqueur, *A World of Secrets: The Uses and Limits of Intelligence* (New York: Basic Books, 1985), especially ch. 10.

9. Government of Canada, Commission of Inquiry Concerning Certain Activities of the Royal Canadian Mounted Police, *Second Report*, 1 (23 January 1981), p. 81.

10. See Wesley K. Wark, 'Introduction: Fictions of History', *Spy Fiction, Spy Films and Real Intelligence*, ed. Wesley K. Wark (London: Frank Cass, 1991), pp. 1–16.

11. The best book-length historical survey remains J. Granatstein and D. Stafford, *Spy Wars: Espionage and Canada from Gouzenko to Glasnost* (Toronto: Key Porter, 1990).

12. W.K. Wark, 'Security Intelligence in Canada 1864–1945: The History of a "National Insecurity State"', *Go Spy the Land: Military Intelligence in History*, eds. K. Neilson and B.J.C. McKercher (Westport, CT: Praeger, 1992).

13. For one account by a journalist of post-1984 developments in Canadian security intelligence, see R. Cleroux, *Official Secrets: The Story Behind the Canadian Security Intelligence Services* (Toronto: McGraw-Hill, Ryerson, 1990).

14. Canadian Security Intelligence Service, 'Report of the Director's Task Force', undated, classified secret, submitted to the Solicitor-General for Canada on 4 Nov. 1992. Copy made available under Access to Information Act.

15. The most recent examination of the issue comes from the pen of a former senior Canadian Security Intelligence Service officer, Alistair S. Hensler, 'Creating a Canadian Foreign Intelligence Service', *Canadian Foreign Policy* (Winter 1995), pp. 15–35. Hensler argues for a modest foreign intelligence gathering capability. See also J. Sallot, 'To Spy or Not To Spy', *The Globe and Mail*, 2 September 1996, A1, A5.

Index